CW00952673

Night Duel
Over Germany

Night Duel Over Germany

Bomber Command's Battle Over the Reich During WWII

Peter Jacobs

Pen & Sword
AVIATION

First published in Great Britain in 2017 by
Pen & Sword Aviation
an imprint of
Pen & Sword Books Ltd
47 Church Street
Barnsley
South Yorkshire
S70 2AS

ISBN 978 1 78346 337 4

Typeset in Ehrhardt by
Mac Style Ltd, Bridlington, East Yorkshire
Printed and bound in Malta by Gutenberg Press

Pen & Sword Books Ltd incorporates the imprints of Pen & Sword
Archaeology, Atlas, Aviation, Battleground, Discovery, Family
History, History, Maritime, Military, Naval, Politics, Railways, Select,
Transport, True Crime, and Fiction, Frontline Books, Leo Cooper,
Praetorian Press, Seaforth Publishing and Wharncliffe.

For a complete list of Pen & Sword titles please contact
PEN & SWORD BOOKS LIMITED
47 Church Street, Barnsley, South Yorkshire, S70 2AS, England
E-mail: enquiries@pen-and-sword.co.uk
Website: www.pen-and-sword.co.uk

Contents

Acknowledgements

Books like this could never be written without the help of so many people. Before thanking individuals for their contribution to this publication, I must pay tribute to all those members of Bomber Command who took the war to Nazi Germany during the Second World War. With courage and determination they went against fierce opposition, night after night, in the full knowledge that their chances of surviving a tour of operations were slim.

Amongst these gallant individuals I include the late Marshal of the Royal Air Force Sir Michael Beetham, then a young Lancaster pilot serving with 50 Squadron who went on to enjoy a highly successful post-war career in the RAF, and his crew colleagues, Les Bartlett and Reg Payne. Sadly, only Reg is still with us but I was privileged to work closely with Les when I wrote *Bomb Aimer Over Berlin* (2007) and also with Sir Michael while writing his biography *Stay The Distance: The Life and Times of Sir Michael Beetham* (2011). Reg, meanwhile, although well into his nineties, remains an active supporter of Bomber Command and its associations, in particular through his wonderful art work.

During many years of involvement with the 50 & 61 Squadrons Association, the last thirteen of which have been as its chairman, I have been privileged to meet many distinguished individuals. They include Bill Reid, who was awarded the Victoria Cross while serving with 61 Squadron, and Jimmy Flint who was awarded an impressive array of decorations and was uniquely recognized with two bravery awards, the Distinguished Flying Medal and the George Medal, for the same mission. Both Jimmy and Bill have left us now but my memories of them and their stories of courage will forever remain.

Those I have mentioned are, of course, just the tip of a huge iceberg. I could go on listing names, not just from 50 or 61, but from other squadrons as well. For example, when I wrote *The Lancaster Story* (1996) many veterans responded to my appeal for help. Amongst those who helped me then were John Chatterton, Frank Cornett, Bert Dowty, Eric Howell, Ron Irons, 'Buck' Rogers, Alan Rowe and Bill Spence. All had experiences and photos to share, many of which are included in this book.

During my long career in the RAF spanning nearly thirty-seven years I was fortunate to fly in many aircraft types, but I feel particularly proud that the last entry in my log book was Lancaster PA474 of the Battle of Britain Memorial Flight. It was the second time I had the privilege to fly in this historic aircraft and it gave me a chance to try and understand what it would have been like to have gone to war over Germany, and so I will be forever grateful to the Battle of Britain Memorial Flight at RAF Coningsby for allowing me two experiences that I will never forget.

As far as helping me with the book you see today, I must first of all thank my former RAF colleague Ken Delve, for it was through Ken that my true passion for Bomber Command began. Ken and I wrote *The Six-Year Offensive* in 1992. It was my first go at writing and I could never have imagined then that I would still be writing today. I must also thank the staff at The National Archives at Kew, who continue to maintain our national treasure, and thank Seb Cox and his staff at the Air Historical Branch (AHB) at RAF Northolt for their help over so many years, particularly Graham Day and Mary Hudson. I have also been privileged to have access to the library at the RAF College Cranwell, one of the finest libraries in the country, and so this gives me an opportunity to publicly thank Hazel Crozier, the Curator of College Hall, and Tim Pierce for their continued support.

As far as other sources of information are concerned, I would like to pay tribute to Martin Middlebrook and Chris Everitt for their excellent book *The Bomber Command War Diaries: An Operational Reference Book 1939–1945*. I have always considered their book to be the authoritative work when it comes to facts and figures about Bomber Command during the Second World War, and when it comes to squadrons and aircraft types I always use James J Halley's excellent book *Squadrons of the Royal Air Force and Commonwealth 1918–1988*, which I consider to be the best and most consistent record under one cover.

As for the illustrations in this book, many have been generously provided by individuals over the years or have come from the AHB but for those of the Luftwaffe I must thank another former RAF colleague, Chris Goss. I learnt much about the Luftwaffe when writing *Aces of the Luftwaffe: The Jagdflieger in the Second World War* (2014) but Chris, a well-known and respected author and historian, has become my first port of call when it comes to all matters relating to the Luftwaffe. I have also been fortunate to learn about the Luftwaffe from other established authors such as Mike Spick, Donald Caldwell and John Weal. I consider all these colleagues to be experts in their fields and so I am extremely grateful to them for their time and willingness to help me over the years.

There are many other authors, too, who help keep stories such as this alive. Amongst these I include Kenneth Ballantyne, a colleague of mine who is always happy to share his knowledge and views with me. But where I am unable to thank these writers personally, I have acknowledged their work throughout the book.

Finally, when writing about a large subject such as this it is always difficult to decide what to include and what to leave out, and so much is down to personal choice. In some areas I have been able to dwell while in others I have had to quickly move on, but I am keen to tell the story across the spectrum from both sides, from the strategic level of those in command to the individual stories of those who actually fought the battle. I believe it is important to understand the reason why a bomber crew was in a particular place at a particular time. Only the limited space prevents me from writing more. It only leaves me to thank the management and staff at Pen and Sword, in particular Laura Hirst for all her effort behind the scenes to turn my work into the publication you see today. Enjoy the book!

Peter Jacobs

Introduction

Bomber Command's offensive against Nazi Germany was one of Britain's major contributions of the Second World War. For almost six years its crews took the war to the Reich, demonstrating to the Nazi leader, Adolf Hitler, that the British were not prepared to give up, even when defeat followed defeat in theatres elsewhere. With the British public behind the offensive, every bomb that fell on German soil was seen as a justifiable reply for all those falling on the UK.

But Bomber Command had not been best prepared for the Second World War, a situation stemming back to the pre-war years. Despite having set and agreed doctrine many years before, in that the bomber was seen as a strategic weapon operating primarily independently of ground and naval forces, the doctrine of air power application had been switched more towards co-operation with the other services, and had become more of a tactical application rather than a strategic one.

Not until the mid-1930s had there been considered any need for an offensive bomber with the range and performance to attack targets in Germany. The formation of Bomber Command in 1936, under its first commander, Air Chief Marshal Sir John Steel, was a major step forward and it was not long before planning for war against Germany was underway. Gradually, the Air Staff started to believe in the concept of fewer but more capable bombers; a squadron of twelve light bombers, for example, could deliver 6,000 lb of bombs whereas a squadron of ten new heavier bombers could deliver 20,000 lb.

When the Second World War broke out in September 1939, Bomber Command had fifty-five squadrons across five operational groups, plus a sixth training group. Nos 1 and 2 Groups, both equipped with light bombers (the Fairey Battle and Bristol Blenheim), formed elements of the RAF's Advanced Air Striking Force (AASF) sent across the Channel to

France (although both groups would later re-emerge within the structure of Bomber Command), leaving three operational groups in England equipped with twin-engine medium bombers: No. 3 Group with Vickers Wellingtons, under the command of Air Vice-Marshal John Baldwin; No. 4 Group (Armstrong Whitworth Whitleys) led by Air Vice-Marshal Arthur Coningham; and No. 5 Group (Handley Page Hampdens) under its new Air Officer Commanding (AOC), Air Vice-Marshal Arthur Harris.

All three twin-engine medium bombers were an improvement on the previous generation of lumbering and ungainly biplane bombers they had replaced. The Hampdens of No. 5 Group equipped ten squadrons, mostly in Lincolnshire, all of which would be required to play an integral part in the full range of Bomber Command's operations during the months ahead, by day and by night. With a crew of four (pilot, observer/bomb aimer, radio operator/dorsal gunner, and ventral gunner), the Hampden was quite manoeuvrable for an aircraft of its class. When operating with a balanced load of 2,000 lb of bombs (907 kg) and maximum fuel, its operational range was 1,800 miles (2,900 km) but its performance – less than 250 mph (400 km/h) and below 20,000 feet (6,100 metres) – was inadequate to guarantee its protection, and its design had been overtaken by the developments in more modern and more capable fighter aircraft.

The Wellington, meanwhile, known affectionately to its crews as the Wimpy, was still a relatively new aircraft having entered operational service less than a year before. Bomber Command was still building up its squadrons but it was not long before ten squadrons were serving with No. 3 Group in East Anglia. With a crew of six (two pilots, an observer, a wireless operator and two air gunners), the Wellington IC was also limited in performance (similar to the Hampden) but it could carry a bomb load of 4,500 lb (2,040 kg) over 1,200 miles (1,930 km), and that range could be extended to more than 1,500 miles (2,400 km) by reducing the aircraft's bomb load to increase the amount of fuel.

The third of the medium bombers, the Whitley, was also relatively new in service but it would soon equip eight squadrons of No. 4 Group in Yorkshire. With a crew of five, it was a sturdy aircraft with few vices and was said to be a pleasure to fly. Unlike the Wellington and Hampden, the Whitley was the only aircraft of the three to be designed with night operations in mind.

The Mark IV was fitted with a revolutionary Nash and Thompson power-operated rear turret with four 0.303 inch machine guns to counter the new generation of enemy fighters. But even the latest variant, the Whitley V, could only reach a maximum speed of 220 mph (354 km/h) and an operational ceiling of 18,000 feet (5,500 metres), and it could also only cruise at 185 mph (300 km/h) when carrying a full bomb load of 7,000 lb (3,175 kg).

Meanwhile, in Germany rearmament had been continuing at pace. The Luftwaffe had officially come into existence in 1935 under the leadership of the First World War fighter ace Hermann Göring, and had been given the opportunity to test its capabilities during the Spanish Civil War when some 200 fighter pilots received their baptism of fire.

The Luftwaffe was expanding rapidly, in particular its fighter arm, the Jagdwaffe, with more than 600 single-engine Messerschmitt Bf 109s in service, with the 109E being the latest and most capable variant to have been introduced. With its top speed of more than 550 km/h (350 mph) and a rate of climb that took it above 6,000 metres (20,000 feet) in just eight minutes, it represented the cutting edge of technology.

The Luftwaffe's largest fighting unit was the Geschwader (wing), consisting of a hundred or more aircraft. Leading it was the Geschwaderkommodore who varied in rank from Major to Oberst (equivalent to squadron leader to group captain) depending on its size. The Geschwader was further broken down into three of four Gruppen (groups), each typically commanded at one rank lower than the Kommodore. A Gruppe usually consisted of three Staffeln (squadrons) with each commanded by a Hauptmann or Oberleutnant (flight lieutenant or flying officer).

However, despite its military strength the Luftwaffe's resources would be committed to a tactical conflict rather than a strategic one, and fragmentations within its hierarchy, even at the outbreak of war, would never go away. Furthermore, the Nazi leadership's initial failure to recognize there might one day be a need for an effective defensive system of the Reich would eventually come to haunt them.

From the opening day of the Second World War Bomber Command was involved in active operations. Its first recorded operational sortie of the war, flown on 3 September 1939, was a reconnaissance mission carried out by a lone Blenheim of 139 Squadron when its crew went looking for enemy warships off the north German port of Wilhelmshaven.

The following day a mixed force of fifteen Blenheims and fourteen Wellingtons crossed the North Sea to attack the German warships spotted in harbour at Wilhelmshaven and Brunsbüttel in the mouth of the Kiel Canal to mark the RAF's first raid of the war. But this opening raid simply highlighted the problems Bomber Command would face in the early months of the war. The Wellington crews struggled to find any ships in poor weather and although four crews reported attacking ships at Brunsbüttel, it appears that navigational problems led to some bombs falling on a Danish town more than 100 miles to the north instead. Furthermore, seven aircraft were lost during the raid, some falling to the defences of the enemy warships with at least two Wellingtons shot down by German fighters; these were the Jagdwaffe's first successes in the west.

With an overall loss rate of 24 per cent it had been a costly start to Bomber Command's war against Germany but the raid was important for two significant reasons. It had shown the Nazi leadership that Britain was willing to hit back and the air war had now opened up a second front, years before Europe could be regained. From now on the unpredictability of Bomber Command's attacks would make the front a gigantic one. The night war about to be fought over Germany would be one of the fiercest campaigns of the Second World War.

Chapter One

Only Owls and Fools Fly at Night

Searchlights try to pick us up, but that's useless, they can't get through the cloud. On and on we roar passing an occasional track marker put down by the Pathfinders. They quickly improve on that and follow up with 'REDS' cascading into 'GREENS' gradually descending into the clouds. These are the ones we bomb. Already I can see the first wave unloading their bombs. At the same time a line of fighter flares goes down, brilliant and bright, parallel to our track about 2 miles away, but don't panic, it's a decoy laid down by our Mosquito boys. Things are getting larger and clearer as we approach the target. Then the final turn in – this is it!

It was November 1943 and the words are taken from the diary of one Lancaster bomb aimer flying his first bombing mission. It was the opening phase of the Battle of Berlin and the night war over Germany was being fought equally hard on both sides.

Bomber Command had been forced into conducting its main operations at night after suffering heavy losses by day during the opening months of the Second World War. Even then, it had not been best equipped to conduct a lengthy campaign at night. Its medium bombers were found to be lacking in modern air warfare with navigation and bombing techniques having changed little since the 1920s.

The RAF's first night sorties of the Second World War were flown as early as the opening night, when ten Whitleys based at Linton-on-Ouse, seven from 58 Squadron and three from 51 Squadron, dropped leaflets over a dozen German cities, mostly in the industrial heartland of the Ruhr. With the packs of leaflets stacked inside the Whitley there was not much room left for the crew and the task of shoving the bundles down the flare chute proved quite tiring.

The dropping of leaflets, known as Nickelling, was hardly offensive and it would be a long time before bombs were dropped on German soil. Even though Britain was at war with Germany those early days were more about caution than aggression with the leaflets carrying a '*warning message from Great Britain*', informing those who read them that the war had been brought about by the policies of the Nazis and was not in the interest of the German people.

During the first month of the war more than 20 million leaflets were dropped. Nickelling would soon become a secondary activity but for now propaganda leaflets were all the crews of Bomber Command were allowed to drop. Even when Blenheim and Wellington crews were sent to attack German warships at Wilhelmshaven and Brunsbüttel for Bomber Command's opening raid of the war, the Operation Order included words of caution:

> *The greatest care is to be taken not to injure the civilian population. The intention is to destroy the German fleet. There is no alternative target.*

For the Whitley squadrons the Nickelling sorties went on, with the monotony of leaflet dropping only being broken during the occasional moonlit nights, when the crews were tasked with carrying out visual reconnaissance of specific areas of Germany. During one of these sorties on the night of 1/2 October 1939, a Whitley of 10 Squadron flew over Berlin. It was the first Bomber Command aircraft to do so.

As winter approached the weather made Nickelling sorties difficult and extremely uncomfortable for the crew. The temperature inside the aircraft fell to −20 degrees centigrade with the crew having to endure hours in freezing cold conditions with no heating and no way of alleviating the problem, other than bashing the extremities of the body to try and create some heat. The poor rear gunner, in particular, cramped in his rear turret and almost open to the elements, suffered most of all. George Dove, a gunner with 10 Squadron, later recalled:

> *The Whitley was ungainly but built like a tank, and never once let us down. I had great confidence in it. The trouble was that in the winter the tail turret was no place to be, no heating to speak of and no electric-heated clothing. I*

wonder how we were able to sit there for as long as nine or ten hours without moving. I was glad when I was finally able to move into the cockpit as first wireless operator, which we did after half a tour.

The Wellington crews, meanwhile, had been carrying out daylight sweeps of the North Sea in search of enemy shipping. The limitations of the Hampden had already become apparent and so it had been left largely to the Wimpy crews to carry out this task.

These missions had, so far, managed to avoid confrontation with enemy fighters but this run of luck came to an end on 14 December when a mixed force of forty-two bombers, the largest raid mounted so far, found an enemy convoy to the south-west of Heligoland. With the weather in the area poor, the crews were already down at low level beneath the cloud. But as they started their attacks several enemy fighters appeared and during the carnage that followed, five of the twelve Wellingtons were shot down.

RAF sources were reluctant to admit high losses to enemy fighters, choosing instead to state they were due to accurate flak from the warships, but just four days later there were further losses when twenty-four Wellingtons were sent to attack enemy warships docked at Wilhelmshaven. The outcome of the previous raid meant the crews were ordered to bomb from above 10,000 feet to avoid losses to enemy flak. In near-perfect conditions the bombers carried out their attacks but as they headed for home twelve Wellingtons were shot down by marauding German fighters.

It appears the Wellingtons had been detected by a *Freya* radar station located on a nearby island, after which it had been relatively easy for the German controllers to direct the Luftwaffe fighters on to the bombers, and so this engagement provides an early example of just how big a part technology would play in the air war ahead.

Developed by Gesellschaft für Elektroakustische und Mechanische Apparate (GEMA) for the detection of ships, *Freya* was the first operational early warning system introduced into service with the German Navy shortly before the war. It had a smaller antenna system compared with the British Chain Home equivalent, which enabled the detection of smaller targets, and with a range of nearly 40 miles (60 km) and a resolution of around 1.5 degrees in azimuth, it was more advanced than its British counterpart.

However, *Freya* had no true height-finding capability and with only eight units deployed there would be large gaps in coverage. Improvements would see the detection range double and an angular resolution of less than one degree. Furthermore, it would soon be paired with another system called *Würzburg*, a more accurate radar using a rotating dipole antenna and a pulsed radar, with a concentrated beam for gun-laying and the control of heavy anti-aircraft batteries. These would be deployed to Germany's industrial area of the Ruhr, the idea being that *Freya* would detect and track incoming aircraft while *Würzburg* would determine the exact range and height of the targets as they got closer.

The losses suffered by Bomber Command during December 1939 were not only disastrous for its squadrons involved but were also a major concern for the Air Staff. The Wellington was to be the RAF's single-most important bomber of the early war years, but with seventeen shot down in just two raids – half of those that had carried out their attacks – it provided unwelcome evidence that the aircraft, and the other medium bombers for that matter, would not be able to survive daylight operations over Germany against determined fighter opposition.

Not everyone was convinced and some even suggested that it had been poor formation-keeping that had allowed the enemy fighters to get between the bombers' zones of mutual defence. The reality was, however, that the German fighter pilots, the Jagdflieger, had found the close formations of bombers easy to spot and made shooting them down that much easier.

The first four months of war had seen little, if any, change in Bomber Command's tactics. For the Wellington crews operating by day the losses would average an unsustainable 13 per cent in the first six months of the war, whereas Whitley losses while Nickelling at night had been as low as 2 per cent over the same period.

While bombing at night offered much potential and had obvious advantages, the problems of navigation raised severe doubts as to whether targets could be found. In the absence of sophisticated systems, the primary method of navigation was still DR (dead or deduced reckoning), a technique relying on accurate flying and the ability to obtain positional information to update the navigational plot. By taking the wind into account it was possible to determine the aircraft's position over the ground. However, any calculation errors when travelling over long distances, no matter how small, could easily result in the bomber straying many miles away from its intended position and so making it impossible for the crew to find their target.

As far as bombing techniques were concerned, there were essentially two options; either to bomb from high altitude, with the obvious disadvantage of lacking accuracy, or to bomb from low level, which offered better accuracy but put the crew at greater risk from the enemy's ground defences. There was a third option too, and one that was better developed by the Luftwaffe, of dive-bombing yet this was seen by the RAF as a compromise.

While the training of RAF bomber crews focused on high-level bombing, other suggestions were put forward to help improve bombing techniques. These ideas included using flares to help illuminate targets at night, but without a trials and development unit these ideas were rarely taken much further. There was simply too much that needed doing and not enough resources to do it. In practical terms, Bomber Command was not equipped for the role that it had been assigned.

The early weeks of 1940 saw the Wellingtons and Hampdens join in with leaflet dropping, although this was more to give the crews valuable experience of operating at night rather than a desire to drop more leaflets. It was still the period of the so-called Phoney War and the bombing of mainland Germany remained prohibited. It was, more often than not, the weather that was the enemy.

The night of 19/20 March 1940 marked an early but important raid in the night war against Germany. German aircraft had dropped bombs on British soil two nights before while attacking naval shipping in Scapa Flow. One civilian was killed and several more injured, and so the British Government ordered Bomber Command to carry out a reprisal attack on a German seaplane base, but only where there was no risk to civilians.

The base chosen was Hörnum, on the southernmost tip of the island of Sylt and well away from civilian areas. With thirty Whitleys and twenty Hampdens taking part it was Bomber Command's largest raid so far. More than 20 tons of high explosives and a thousand incendiary bombs were dropped, although a post-raid reconnaissance could not be carried out until the following month and so it was not really possible to assess whether the raid had been a success.

It had now been more than six months since Britain's declaration of war, yet this raid marked the RAF's first real bombing operation of the war and was the first time aircraft of Bomber Command dropped bombs on a land target. But the Second World War entered a new phase in April 1940 when German forces invaded Denmark and Norway.

While Britain immediately declared its support for the two countries, nothing in reality could be done to help Denmark. Although Bomber Command did what it could to slow down the German advance on southern Norway, it took the loss of nine bombers attacking enemy shipping at Stavanger to bring daylight bombing missions to an end. Finally, Bomber Command turned its attention to operating at night.

A directive issued to Bomber Command's new chief, Sir Charles Portal, saw the first significant change in bombing policy, although it was more of a reaction to recent events rather than the creation of a long-term strategy. Two policies were put forward depending on which series of events transpired. As there had been no German invasion of the Low Countries at this stage, the directive called for general air action at night with the priorities given as: identifiable oil plants; identifiable electricity plants and coking plants; self-illuminating objectives vulnerable to air attack; and main German ports in the Baltic if specifically authorized. However, if the Germans were to invade the Low Countries then the entire plan changed, in which case the emphasis was:

> *To attack vital objectives in Germany, starting in the Ruhr, to cause the maximum dislocation to lines of communications of the German advance through the Low Countries.*

In this latter case the stated objectives were troop concentrations, communications in the Ruhr, especially marshalling yards, and oil plants in the Ruhr, but there was still no suggestion of a general bombing campaign.

That night, 13/14 April 1940, Bomber Command commenced its first minelaying operations of the war. Given the codename of Gardening, fifteen Hampdens laid mines in sea lanes off Denmark between the German ports and Norway.

The early Gardening sorties were carried out by Hampdens of No. 5 Group with anything up to six squadrons at a time allocated to the task and with each aircraft carrying a single 1,500 lb mine. Although the idea of dropping mines into the sea sounds simple enough, it called for skill and precision to ensure that the mine, known as the vegetable, was laid in exactly the right place, with locations for the mines given suitable agricultural names.

A typical Gardening sortie was that of a Hampden of 49 Squadron from Scampton on the night of 21/22 April, flown by a 24-year-old Canadian, Flying Officer Wilf Burnett. The crew report reads:

On 21 April we were detailed to carry out Gardening operations in 'Daffodil' area. We took off at 1930 hours and set course for coast, climbing at 135 mph to 5,000 feet. At 1952 hours we set course 083 degrees for Sylt. We proceeded uneventfully at 5,000 feet above 8/10 to 10/10 cloud until we saw Sylt through a break in the cloud at 2150 hours. We continued on the same course and at 2205 hours observed a green light on our port bow which we mistook for a sea navigation light. It was, however, the navigation lights of another aircraft which we identified as an enemy aircraft. We descended through cloud at 2230 hours and at the ETA [estimated time of arrival] determined our position to be south of the target so set North and fifteen minutes later recognized the target area. We ascertained our target and dropped 'Melon' according to plan at 2315 hours. We set course of 255 degrees Magnetic for base and began climbing through cloud to 6,000 feet. At 0030 hours we crossed the German coast at Yarding. At 0136 hours we obtained fix from Heston and altered course at 267 degrees for base. Coast crossed at 0250. We received several homing bearings from base and landed at 0310.

The Daffodil area referred to in the report was the major strait separating the large Danish island of Zealand from the southern Swedish province of Scania, through which German shipping between the Baltic Sea and Kattegat Channel could pass.

As the war entered its ninth month Bomber Command was still constrained by politics and there was only so much that its crews were allowed to do. It was a difficult period, like a boxer having to enter the ring with one hand tied behind his back. But in a matter of days, not only would the boxer have both hands free to fight, the gloves would be well and truly off.

On 10 May Germany launched its long-awaited offensive in the West. Even now, Bomber Command was politically restricted to targets west of the Rhine as stated in the latest directive to Portal:

> *It is preferable not to begin bombing ops in the Ruhr until we have definite news that the Germans have attacked targets … which would cause casualties to civilians.*

It was only after the Luftwaffe bombed Rotterdam on 15 May that Bomber Command was finally let off its leash. At last its crews were permitted to cross the Rhine to extend their bombing operations into the heartland of Nazi Germany.

That night, a mixed force of ninety-nine bombers (Wellingtons, Hampdens and Whitleys) attacked sixteen different oil and rail targets in the industrial Ruhr, while a dozen more (Wellingtons and Whitleys) attacked enemy lines of communications in Belgium. It was the first time Bomber Command dispatched more than a hundred aircraft in a single night.

At last the RAF's strategic bombing offensive was underway, but by the end of June France had fallen and Nazi control of the European coastline stretched from Norway to the border of Spain. Furthermore, Italy had joined the war to fight alongside her Axis partner. Britain now stood alone and was fighting for survival with the remaining need to maintain an offensive against enemy ports and shipping, spreading from Germany's capital warships at Kiel and Hamburg to invasion barges in the occupied Channel ports.

With the priority being enemy ports and shipping, it was only when the weather dictated otherwise or there was any spare capacity that attacks were carried out against other targets, such as the German aircraft and oil industries, or key lines of communications such as road, rail and canal links. One raid to fall into this latter category took place on the night of 12/13 August when eleven Hampdens, six from 49 Squadron and five from 83 Squadron, were tasked with attacking the Dortmund–Ems Canal, a heavily defended and vital waterway in Germany.

The attack was to be carried out at low level and would hit a point to the north of Münster where the canal crosses the River Ems by means of an old aqueduct. The aqueduct had been attacked before and so German defences had been reinforced with additional anti-aircraft guns. The plan involved four of the Hampdens carrying out diversionary attacks against other targets in the local area, while the rest attacked the aqueduct with special high-explosive canister bombs, each fitted with delayed fuses and dropped at two-minute intervals to avoid aircraft becoming caught up in the blast from the attack before.

It was around 8 p.m. when the Hampdens took off from Scampton. Led by Squadron Leader Jamie Pitcairn-Hill of 83 Squadron, they were due over the target around three hours later. All initially went to plan with the four diversionary Hampdens carrying out their attacks, but two of the seven heading for the aqueduct could not find their target and so bombed Texel Island instead.

The five remaining Hampdens arrived in the target area to find the conditions good and the moon reflecting enough off the canal to aid the run-in towards the target. Pitcairn-Hill ran in towards the aqueduct first. At just 100 feet he charged in but his Hampden had been spotted and immediately came under intense anti-aircraft fire from the well-positioned flak guns along both edges of the canal. Despite the wall of flak Pitcairn-Hill completed his attack before swiftly breaking away towards safety.

The second Hampden to attack was seen to receive a direct hit while running in towards the target and crashed in flames alongside the canal, killing all the crew. The third Hampden was also hit, many times, and burst into flames, although its crew managed to bale out to be taken as prisoners of war, while the fourth successfully bombed the target before heading for home; albeit on just one engine. It was then the turn of the fifth Hampden, 'EA-M' of 49 Squadron, to make its attack.

At the controls was 27-year-old Flight Lieutenant Rod Learoyd, an experienced pilot with more than twenty ops under his belt. Descending to 150 feet he began his run-in from 3 miles to the north of the aqueduct, but being the last to attack the defences were more than ready for him. As the Hampden thundered in towards the target it was twice hit by anti-aircraft fire, the shells passing through the starboard wing and the rounds from multiple machine gun emplacements raking the underside of the fuselage.

Even though he was barely able to see because of the blinding glare of searchlights and intense wall of flak, Learoyd pressed on to complete his attack before turning the Hampden hard away. It was a long way home and his attention now turned to the ruptured hydraulic system, the result of flak damage, as this would make landing difficult.

It was the early hours of the morning and still dark when the Hampden arrived back overhead Scampton, but with no hydraulics to lower the undercarriage and flaps Learoyd decided to circle the airfield and wait for first light rather than to attempt a crash-landing in the dark. Finally, when there was just enough light to make an emergency landing, he expertly touched the Hampden down. It was just before 5 a.m.

Post-raid intelligence showed the target had been destroyed. For his leadership of the raid, Jamie Pitcairn-Hill was awarded the Distinguished Service Order (DSO) but it had been Learoyd's attack against the heavily defended and well alerted target that had been the most hazardous of the operation. Just days later came the announcement that Rod Learoyd was to be awarded the Victoria Cross (VC) for having '*repeatedly shown the highest conception of his duty and complete indifference to personal danger in making attacks at the lowest altitude regardless of opposition*'.

It was the first VC to be awarded to a member of Bomber Command but it would not be the last!

Chapter Two

Defending the Reich

He enthused about flying in bright moonlight, about the stalking missions they flew along the roads of Flanders so as to spot the enemy's silhouette against the paler night sky overhead, how they then increased speed and commenced the attack from below....

The war was still only days old when 26-year-old Johannes 'Macky' Steinhoff, the son of a mill worker and former student of the classics and languages, was summoned to Berlin to attend a conference on night fighting. Now the Staffelkapitän of 10./JG 26, a Messerschmitt Bf 109D fighter unit based at Jever in north-west Germany, Steinhoff listened with the rest of the assembled audience to Göring reminiscing, boasting even, about his days over the Western Front more than twenty years earlier.

Steinhoff's recollection of Göring's diatribe that day comes from Mike Spick's book *Luftwaffe Fighter Aces*. Being a First World War fighter ace, Göring was undoubtedly an inspiration to those listening to his tales but the young Steinhoff was quick to point out that things were going to be different now. With no dedicated night fighter, the Luftwaffe was having to use a handful of its Staffeln operating as dual day and night fighter units to provide Germany's defence. There were no specialist aircraft or trained crews and so any aerial activity at night was conducted using existing aircraft and methods, and by making the best of whatever weather conditions prevailed at the time. The latest aircraft entering service flew at higher altitude and from such heights in the dark it was not easy to identify landmarks below. The long winter nights over north-west Germany were going to be quite different from those summer nights over Flanders many years ago.

To the new breed of night fighter pilots, men like Johannes Steinhoff, it was already evident that the Luftwaffe hierarchy had little or no grasp of what it was like to fly night fighter operations in 1939. Steinhoff was no young fool, far from it. He would go on to become one of the Luftwaffe's highest-scoring and finest fighter leaders of the Second World War, after which he would reach the rank of general and fulfil a distinguished career as one of Germany's senior post-war officers and military commanders within NATO. But even in those early days of hostilities Steinhoff could see that what was needed was better navigation aids for the night fighter and an accurate way of locating, and then tracking, the bombers; particularly if night operations were to be conducted in bad weather.

Göring's reaction was typical of the man. Not only did he leave Steinhoff in no doubt that his views were naïve and unwelcome, Göring did what he so often did when opinions differed from his own – nothing. While his influence and power could have done so much to shape the Luftwaffe's night war over Germany during the early years of the Second World War, nothing happened. While Britain moved forwards in the technological world, Germany stood still. Steinhoff, meanwhile, frustrated and unhappy at the lack of any development in the night fighter programme, transferred to day fighters.

This would not be the last altercation between Steinhoff and Göring, but the reality was that when Germany entered its offensive campaigns in the early months of the Second World War there was a strong feeling amongst the Nazi leadership that there was no need for any night air defence of the Reich. It was once said that it would never come to that!

Germany's only real defence policy during those early days was to rely on anti-aircraft flak batteries (flak taken from the German word *Fliegerabwehrkanonen*), supported by an extensive array of searchlights and all under the responsibility of the flak arm of the Luftwaffe. An area called Air Defence Zone West, an element of the German's Siegfried Line system, contained nearly 200 heavy batteries, usually with four or six guns per battery, and nearly fifty light batteries used for point-defence of important establishments and to counter attacks at low level. These lighter guns were only effective up to heights of 17,000 feet and had a range of less than 4 miles. Nonetheless, the high rate of fire, as high as 200 rounds per minute, would be enough to terrify bomber crews when first seen, particularly when used with tracer and when operating amongst the glare of searchlights.

The heavier guns were aimed using data fed into a predictor but if no data was available they would be used to create a box barrage. One type, the 88 mm, was capable of firing fifteen rounds per minute over a short range, typically only a mile, and up to a height of 32,000 feet, while the modified 88 offered an improved rate of fire of twenty rounds per minute up to 40,000 feet and out to 10 miles. There was also the heavier 105 mm gun capable of ten rounds per minute, a range of 10 miles and a maximum height of 37,000 feet, and the similarly capable 128 mm. In heavily built-up cities and industrial areas, such as Berlin and the industrial Ruhr, large flak towers with multiple gun emplacements were erected to give the anti-aircraft gunners a clear line of fire, all supported by hundreds of searchlights.

During those early months of the war the Luftwaffe had just one designated night fighter unit, IV.(N)/JG 2 under the command of Hauptmann Albert Blumensaat. Equipped with Bf 109Ds the Gruppe was assigned defensive duties of Berlin but the RAF's initial reluctance to bomb land targets saw it moved away and dispersed around the north German seaboard instead.

By the time Germany launched its offensive into France and the Low Countries, Blumensaat's Gruppe had been redeployed inland and had already scored the Luftwaffe's first night success of the war. This had taken place during the night of 20/21 April 1940 when Oberfeldwebel (equivalent to a flight sergeant) Willi Schmale brought down a Fairey Battle of the AASF to the north-east of Stuttgart. Then, just five nights later the Gruppe scored its second success when Oberfeldwebel Hermann Förster shot down a Hampden off the southern tip of Sylt; it was Bomber Command's first aircraft lost to a Luftwaffe fighter at night.

It took the end of the Phoney War and an increased number of RAF attacks against targets in Germany for the Nazi leadership to change their stance and finally admit the need to create a night defensive force. Apart from having to bolster Germany's ground defences it was already apparent that the Luftwaffe lacked a dedicated night fighter. No matter how good a day fighter the 109 was proving to be, it had not been born with night fighting in mind. It had no effective navigational aid and even when the position of enemy bombers was reported, it was near-impossible for the night fighter pilot, the Nachtjagdflieger, to find them in the dark.

The idea of adopting traditional day fighter tactics at night had brought little success but the 109's counterpart, the twin-engine Messerschmitt Bf 110 Zerstörer (destroyer), was a different aircraft altogether and offered much potential as a night fighter. With a crew of two it had been designed as a long-range escort fighter but had proved vulnerable during day combat when up against the RAF's more capable fighters. Nonetheless, the 110 would be more than adequate for the night fighter role. With a top speed approaching 550 km/h (350 mph) it was fast enough to chase down the RAF bombers and its service ceiling of 11,500 metres (35,000 feet) was well above that of any Bomber Command aircraft. The 110 was also heavily armed with a battery of two 20 mm (0.787 inch) cannons plus four 7.9 mm (0.312 inch) machine guns mounted in the nose. Although its size and weight meant it was far less manoeuvrable and slower to accelerate than the 109, these limitations would not be so crucial in a night war.

The Luftwaffe's first dedicated night fighter wing, Nachtjagdgeschwader 1 (NJG 1), formed in the summer of 1940 from elements of two Zerstörergeschwader under the command of 29-year-old Major Wolfgang Falck.

The son of a priest, Wolf Falck had been amongst the first to fly the 110 before the outbreak of war and had claimed three successes during the opening days of hostilities over Poland. His fourth victim was claimed to the south-west of Heligoland during the 18 December mauling of RAF Wellingtons attacking German warships at Wilhelmshaven and by the end of the campaign in Denmark he had taken his personal score to seven.

It was while he was based in Denmark as a Gruppenkommandeur that Falck had written a tactical appraisal on how to intercept enemy aircraft at night. He had then been invited to another of Göring's top-level conferences about night fighting, this time in Holland, and during one of Göring's lengthy rants the audience was told how the increasing number of night attacks by the RAF had become annoying and an embarrassment. This, Göring said, was the reason why he was forming a new night fighting organization called the Nachtjagd and he then announced that Falck was to be Kommodore of the first night fighter wing.

The news came as a shock to Falck. He was then a rather lowly Hauptmann and one of the most junior officers at the conference but for all his failings elsewhere, Göring at least had confidence in his junior officers. Falck's promotion and appointment was one of a number that saw young but very capable Luftwaffe pilots suddenly propelled into commanding front-line combat units.

Falck's appointment turned out to be an inspired one and he quickly became an early influencer of Germany's night war. However, setting up a new night fighter unit was never going to be easy. There was no template to follow. A new training programme was required and with no aircraft designed with night fighting in mind, Falck had to make do with whatever resources he could pull together. His unit initially consisted of standard Bf 110s and apart from painting the aircraft in an all-black scheme they did not differ at all from the daytime fighters that they had once been. Modifications were required and amongst the first to be carried out were the fitting of flame dampers to the engine exhausts and changes made to the aircraft's cockpit lighting.

With the development of a dedicated night fighter now at least underway, what was also needed was the creation of a sophisticated and capable defence system on the ground. Germany's first and rather primitive system involved listening posts and searchlights for detection, the idea being that the Bf 110s would get airborne once a raid was detected and then patrol to the rear so that they did not interfere with the detection methods being used. Then, once an enemy bomber had been caught in the searchlights, the night fighter would strike.

It was a tactic known as *Helle Nachtjagd* (bright night fighting) but the night fighter had to strike quick because of the limited depth of the searchlight belt, and also because of the amount of time the searchlight operators could be expected to maintain contact with an enemy bomber: a few minutes at best.

NJG 1's first success using this tactic occurred on 20/21 July 1940 when 29-year-old Oberleutnant Werner Streib shot down a Whitley to claim the Nachtjagd's first official night success of the war. But Streib's success that night had been more by chance than anything else. He had seen the silhouette of an aircraft and had initially believed it to be another Bf 110. It was only when he closed on the aircraft and almost reached its wingtip that he realized it was an enemy bomber. Quickly positioning for an attack, it took Streib just two bursts of fire before the Whitley was on its way to earth.

Streib added to his score the following night, the same night that another Nachtjagdflieger, Walter Ehle, scored his first night success to add to his three by day. Ehle would go on to become the Luftwaffe's longest serving Gruppenkommandeur, leading II./NJG 1 from October 1940 until his death more than three years later, by which time he had been credited with thirty-eight aircraft shot down.

The Nachtjagd's early successes during the summer of 1940 were encouraging and might have easily misled the Luftwaffe's hierarchy into feeling more optimistic than perhaps should have been the case. Falck knew that to create a truly effective night fighter force required the support and co-operation of many facets: ground radar units, anti-aircraft flak batteries, searchlights and, of course, the night fighters. Furthermore, a recent increase in the number of night raids against Germany had also reinforced the Luftwaffe's lack of training for its ground-based personnel serving with the defensive units.

In short, Germany's defensive system was ineffective. It would take time for the Nazi leadership to realize that the hub of Germany's war machine, the industrial heartland of the Ruhr, was not getting the protection it needed. For now the war went on but Germany's failure to recognize that it was likely to become a long one meant that strategic decisions were often delayed and resulted in resources being committed too late.

Despite his own personal drive and enthusiasm for the task he had been given, Falck knew that it would take someone beyond his rank to create the night fighter force that Germany needed. That man, above all others, was Josef Kammhuber, a Luftwaffe career officer in his forties with the rank of Oberst who Göring entrusted with the setting up of the first Nachtjagddivision (night fighter division). Kammhuber would pioneer the development of Germany's night war and set up the first truly successful night fighter defence system.

The system he put in place soon became known to the RAF bomber crews as the Kammhuber Line. It consisted of a series of control sectors, equipped with radars and searchlights, with overlapping coverage and layered three deep, stretching from Denmark to the middle of France. Each sector was approximately 20 miles (32 km) long (north-south) and 12.5 miles (20 km) wide (east-west), while a second defensive belt of radars, guns and searchlights protected Berlin.

RAF bombers had to cross the Kammhuber Line at some point but *Helle Nachtjagd* would only ever have limited success. Using searchlights to illuminate a bomber was fine but searchlights were mostly located in and around the target area, and any amount of cloud reduced their effectiveness. It was also difficult for the Nachtjagdflieger to spot an illuminated bomber from above, and so they soon learned to position themselves beneath the bombers so that they could look up to see if a bomber was caught in the beam. This, again, had its problems as it meant the night fighter pilots were often dazzled by the beam and there were also occasions when they came under attack from overly eager flak batteries below.

Even when everything was in favour of the Nachtjagdflieger the RAF bombers could only be attacked when overhead the target. And that was too late. The answer was to move some of the searchlights away from the target areas to form a protective belt, which helped, but poor weather often meant that cloud made the searchlights completely ineffective. And so the next idea was to introduce the use of a *Freya* radar to provide a form of close control, with information provided to the night fighter by a Jägerleitoffizier using radio until the enemy bomber was seen; a tactic known as *Dunkel Nachtjagd* (dark night fighting).

Based on this idea night radar intercept areas called *Dunkelnachtjagdräume* were set up, but while the Nachtjagd's latest tactics were all well and good, there remained a lack of urgency amongst the Nazi leadership to develop a better and more suitable defensive system. With the war seemingly going well for Germany, some still felt it unnecessary. Britain, after all, was very much on the defensive and still faced a very real threat of invasion.

Chapter Three

Taking the Offensive to Germany

When the British air force drops two or three or four thousand kilograms of bombs, then we will in one night drop 150, 230, 300 or 400 thousand kilograms – we will raise their cities to the ground.

So enraged was Hitler after a string of raids against the Nazi capital that he delivered this promise at a Berlin rally in early September 1940. The normal pattern of targets for Bomber Command had suddenly changed when German bombs fell on London on 24 August. Britain's Prime Minister, Winston Churchill, demanded an immediate retaliatory raid on Berlin and the following night the first bombs were dropped on the Nazi capital. Despite all that had been said earlier by the Nazi leadership, bombs had fallen on Berlin.

The RAF had made its point, but while bombing Berlin had demonstrated an ability to hit back, Britain would remain under the threat of invasion for some time.

Bomber Command continued to chip away at targets in Germany as part of its long-term strategy whenever the opportunity arose and on the night of 23/24 September concentrated its main effort against one target for the first time. The target was again Berlin and involved 129 aircraft (a mix of Hampdens, Wellingtons and Whitleys) and for three hours several different targets were attacked, including rail yards, power stations, aircraft factories and gas works; one aircraft of each type was lost during the raid.

The crews of Bomber Command were now settling into a routine, although for many there had been little or no rest in recent months. The cycle began during the morning with the selection of targets for that night. These were then passed down to the respective groups and the AOC then tasked his stations, which, in turn, handed the task to the squadron commanders. The squadron commander then worked with his own staff to determine the route to the target and timings, with any associated adjustments being made to fuel and bomb loads. Meanwhile, the ground crew prepared the right number of aircraft required for the op that night, with those airframes usually undergoing a night-flying test before being bombed-up for the raid.

The first each crew knew of the target was when they entered the main briefing room. While the exact format of the briefing varied from squadron to squadron, the overall procedure was much the same. The brief included details of the target, its importance, associated defences and the suggested route to the target, as well as any relevant signals and intelligence information, until every last detail had been covered. The crews then went off to finish their planning.

Although a route had been suggested, at that stage of the war it was generally left to each crew to decide the exact detail of the route they would take to the target. The observer was given a simplified target map, showing key navigation features such as rivers and lakes, and, if available, a target photo. With the planning complete the crew were left to get whatever rest they could and grab something to eat. They would then pick up their flying kit, escape pack (the contents of which varied but typically contained items such as a silk map, mini-compass and currency) and rations (such as biscuits, chocolate and fruit) with a thermos flask containing a hot drink.

After climbing aboard the aircraft, each crew member ran through his pre-flight checks, with the wireless operator checking the radio with the watch office. Finally, the engines were started and once happy the crew made their way to the holding point at the runway to await a green light, giving them clearance to go.

Once airborne the crew rarely saw another aircraft. The observer would be busy working his navigation plot, supported by any information provided by the wireless operator, while the gunners were busy scanning the night sky. Crew discipline was tight. It had to be. Then, having arrived in the target area, the observer gave directions to the pilot in short-sharp bursts until bombs were gone.

Once back at base the crew attended debriefing with the Intelligence Officer, followed by breakfast. They would then go off to get whatever sleep they could before it was time to get up again to check if they were on the ops board again that night. If so, the cycle started again.

By the end of October 1940 the threat of invasion was over, for the time being at least, and so Bomber Command could now get its major night offensive against Germany under way. With Portal elevated to Chief of the Air Staff, Sir Richard Peirse was appointed as the new head of Bomber Command.

Peirse was immediately issued with a new and lengthy directive. There were two primary targets – oil and aircraft manufacture – but there remained other targets as well:

> ... *regular concentrated attacks should be made on objectives in large towns and centres of industry, with the primary aim of causing very heavy material destruction which will demonstrate to the enemy the power and severity of air bombardment and the hardship and dislocation which will result from it.*

As if this did not spread Peirse's resources thinly enough, he was also to ensure that his command continued to attack targets in Italy, submarine targets on the Atlantic coastline of France, enemy-occupied ports and airfields, and to continue laying mines.

To conduct such a broad bombing campaign during the coming winter months would be hard. Poor weather was becoming a problem, not only over continental Europe but also back in eastern England when fog at Bomber Command's bases often provided the biggest hazard of all.

If Peirse was to manage his limited resources efficiently through such a broad campaign it would require a reliable and effective way of assessing the accuracy of his bombers. But this was an area not without its problems. During the first six months of the war Bomber Command had only acquired around 150 usable night photographs that gave sufficient ground detail to determine whether the bombers were actually attacking the right place.

Night photography was far from easy and it was a procedure not liked by the crews. The camera started operating when the bomb–release tit was pressed and it continued to run until the calculated moment of bomb impact. This typically required the bomber staying on the attack heading for another thirty seconds after bomb release with light being provided by a photoflash and from any ambient source, such as searchlights, flak or fires on the ground. However, any evasive manoeuvring while the camera was running resulted in the photograph being unusable.

Another problem was the lack of cameras. Even after being at war for more than a year a squadron was lucky if it had a handful of cameras, and some of those were likely to be broken or unusable. But Peirse knew that good photographs would provide him with evidence of success, or not, from which strategies, tactics and techniques could be modified and then employed.

After a brief lull in bomber activity, the night war over Germany stepped up a gear when Bomber Command launched Operation *Abigail Rachel*, an attack against Mannheim, on the night of 16/17 December. It was a raid in response to recent Luftwaffe attacks on English cities and the attack against Mannheim was intended to be the first time an attacking force exceeded 200 bombers.

In the end a mixed force of 134 bombers went to Mannheim; bad weather forecast at a number of airfields had reduced the number taking part. Most of the crews arrived over the target to find it clear of cloud but the largest of the fires, caused by incendiaries dropped from the leading Wellingtons, were not in the centre of the city and so the subsequent bombing was scattered.

Although the raid was not a success, *Abigail Rachel* had seen the largest attacking force sent to a single target to date. It might not have been the 200 bombers that had been hoped but the War Cabinet's order to mount such a large-scale operation had shown the intent. It had also shown the Nazi leadership that Britain was far from a defeated nation. The night war over Germany that was to follow would prove to be one of the fiercest air campaigns of the Second World War.

Chapter Four

The Nachtjagd Hits Back

I was well positioned at the correct altitude of 3,300 metres … and directed on to the enemy by means of continual corrections. Suddenly I saw an aircraft in the moonlight, about 100 metres above and to the left; on moving closer I made it out to be a Vickers Wellington. Slowly I closed in from behind, and aimed a burst of 5–6 seconds' duration at the fuselage and wing root. The right motor caught fire immediately, and I pulled my machine up. For a while the Englishman flew on, losing height rapidly. The fire died away but then I saw him spin towards the ground, and burst into flames on crashing.

The Wellington was an aircraft belonging to 311 Squadron, a Czech squadron based at East Wretham in Norfolk, and flown by Pilot Officer Bohumil Landa. It was the only Wellington lost over Germany on the night of 16/17 October 1940, having been shot down by a Dornier Do 17Z-10 of 4./NJG 1. The successful Nachtjagdflieger was 29-year-old Oberleutnant Ludwig Becker and the words are taken from part of his combat report included in Mike Spick's book *Luftwaffe Fighter Aces*.

Becker was another of the Nachtjagd's early pioneers and his success that night was the Luftwaffe's first attributed to a form of close control from the ground, but he had been fortunate to find conditions completely in his favour. Having been directed on to the Wellington he was able to see its shape silhouetted in the bright moonlight as he closed in from astern. Unfortunately for Landa and his crew they had been in the wrong place at the wrong time.

At that stage of the war the Nachtjagd was equipped almost entirely with Bf 110s – mostly based in Holland, Belgium and north-west Germany – but the fact that Becker was flying a Do 17 that night shows how the Luftwaffe was converting other aircraft to the night fighter role. The Z-10 *Kauz* II (screech owl) had been developed from the Z-7 *Kauz* I, itself a development of the fast Do 17 twin-engine light-bomber used during the early years of the war. Three solid-nosed Z-7 prototypes had been converted from existing airframes and from these prototypes came the Z-10.

With a crew of three the Z-10 was armed with two 20 mm MG FF cannons and four 7.92 mm machine guns mounted in the nose above a *Spanner Anlage* short-range infra-red detection system. It was a fast aircraft for its class and could exceed 400 km/h (250 mph) at 5,000 metres (16,000 feet). However, less than a dozen of these sub-variants are believed to have been in existence as the infra-red system proved ineffective, although the Z-10 would lead to the later night fighter variant, the Dornier Do 215B-5 *Kauz* III.

Ludwig Becker thus paved the way during the early night war against Bomber Command, his success that night showing the German defensive system was moving forward. Werner Streib, meanwhile, who had claimed the Nachtjagd's first official night success of the war, was given command of I./ NJG 1 based at Venlo in Holland, from where his unit could more easily hassle known RAF bomber routes into the industrial Ruhr. Streib now had eight successes to his name and was awarded the *Ritterkreuz des Eisernen Kreuzes* (Knight's Cross of the Iron Cross) just days after Wolf Falck had become one of the Luftwaffe's earliest recipients for his leadership of NJG 1.

With Falck's vision, Kammhuber's organization and the skill and courage of men like Becker and Streib, the Nachtjagd was finding its way. At that stage of the war Bomber Command was sending its aircraft to the target in relatively low numbers and not in any specific formation. The idea was to stretch the German defences as much as possible but this tactic simply played into the Nachtjagd's hands. A highly effective form of close control, known as *Himmelbett* (canopy/four-poster bed), had now been set up using *Freya* and *Würzburg* radars, with designated intercept areas allocated a primary and back-up night fighter. Although limitations in technology meant the *Himmelbett* tactic could only deal with one or two bombers at a time, this was not a problem with so few bombers coming through and made it easier to achieve success.

British intelligence soon discovered the existence of the Kammhuber Line and how it operated, and started to look at ways of countering its success. As it turned out, a simple change in tactics soon rendered the Line ineffective.

Bomber Command sent its aircraft through the area in a single stream, the so-called 'bomber stream', on a narrow front to overwhelm the German defences within that sector.

Although the Kammhuber Line had been countered, its network of radars and plotting stations would continue to prove their worth and while the night war over Europe went on, the Luftwaffe sought other ways of hitting the RAF bombers.

One idea was to fly intruder missions over the bomber bases in eastern England. It was not an entirely new idea and had been put forward for discussion before, but it would require an aircraft with the range and endurance to loiter over the North Sea and eastern England, and to then have the firepower to strike the RAF bombers over their own territory. The Bf 110 was unsuitable for this role and so it was to a Junkers Ju 88 unit based in Norway that the Luftwaffe first turned to carry out this new role.

With a crew of four, the twin-engine Ju 88C was another aircraft to have been designed as a fighter-bomber, but it was as a night fighter that it would excel and this would soon become its main role. Although it was less manoeuvrable than the Bf 110, its size and performance made the Ju 88 well suited for night fighting. The first modified sub-variant was the Ju 88C-2, initially with a crew of three and then four, armed with one 20 mm MG FF cannon and three 7.92 mm machine guns placed in a new metal nose.

Re-designated 4./NJG 1, the Ju 88s left Norway to join up with another C-2 unit, 6./NJG 1, and the Do 17Z-10s of 5./NJG 1 to become I./NJG 2 based at Gilze en Rijen in Holland. Under the command of Major Karl-Heinrich Heyse this new unit, called a *Fernnachtjagd Gruppe* (far night group), was tasked with carrying out long-range night intruder missions over eastern England.

Heyse flew the Luftwaffe's first mission in this new role but was lost over the North Sea in late November after his Ju 88C encountered a Hampden. He was replaced by Karl Hülshoff who would successfully lead the unit for the next year, during which more than a hundred claims were made against aircraft of Bomber Command.

Although RAF losses do not seem to tally exactly with this overall figure there were, nonetheless, several successful intruder pilots: Feldwebel (equivalent to a sergeant) Wilhelm Beier who was credited with shooting down fourteen aircraft in this role; Leutnant Hans Hahn who was the Luftwaffe's first intruder pilot to be awarded the Knight's Cross for his twelve successes; Oberfeldwebel Alfons Köster with eleven; and Feldwebel Heinz Strüning who was credited with nine successes during his sixty-six intruder missions over England.

The intruder tactics varied. Heinz Sommer, for example, who was credited with shooting down ten RAF aircraft in this role, had the audacity to find a bomber airfield and then loiter overhead before making his attack once a bomber had committed to land. In Mike Spick's book *Luftwaffe Fighter Aces* Sommer recalls his experiences while patrolling over East Anglia during the early hours of 30 April 1941:

> *I saw an English aircraft fire recognition signals and flew towards it where I found an airfield, illuminated and very active. I joined the airfield's circuit at between 200 and 300 metres [altitude] at 0015 hours, and after several circuits an aircraft came within range. I closed to between 100 and 150 metres and fired. After a short burst the aircraft exploded in the air and fell to the ground. At 0020 hours I saw another aircraft landing with its lights on, which I attacked from behind and above at roughly 80 metres. The aircraft crashed after my burst of fire and caught fire hitting the ground. In the light of the flames from the two wrecks, I could see fifteen to twenty aircraft parked on the airfield. I dropped my bombs on these….*

As techniques became more advanced, radio signals were intercepted to pin-point Bomber Command airfields so that the intruders could be scrambled from their base to intercept bombers as they returned home. But despite the successes, these missions never really impacted on Bomber Command's night war on Germany and came to an end just a year after the first success. They had also proved costly for the Luftwaffe. Hans Hahn, for example, lost his life over Lincolnshire when his aircraft collided with what would have been his thirteenth victim. Furthermore, Hitler did not favour the idea, preferring instead for the German people to see the wrecks of RAF bombers shot down over Germany. This, he felt, would avoid the public becoming doubtful about the Luftwaffe's claimed success.

When Hitler turned on Russia in June 1941, much of the Luftwaffe departed for the Eastern Front but its night fighter force, then consisting of more than 130 twin-engine aircraft based mostly in Holland, remained largely intact.

With the change in Bomber Command's tactics and advances in technology the *Himmelbett* system was modified using two of the more accurate *Würzburg* tracking radars; one locked on to the night fighter while the other was used to track the enemy bomber. However, the absence of an air-mounted Identification Friend or Foe (IFF) still meant that only one fighter at a time could be controlled from the ground.

Combined night fighter zones called *Kombinierte Nachtjagdgebiete* were set up around priority areas and supported by anti-aircraft flak batteries, but the system still had its weaknesses. The night fighter crews remained swamped with more targets than they could possibly handle and the bomber stream tactic meant that as few as one-in-six night fighters ended up intercepting the raids. Furthermore, the two plots obtained from the two separate *Würzburg* radars were not displayed on a single scope and with information coming from two separate sources, the controller was left to provide the night fighter crew with the best information he could; range errors of several hundred metres could easily occur.

Kammhuber had been sceptical about the performance and capability of radar but technology was now advancing at pace and it was not long before the *Freya* and *Würzburg* radars were able to work in conjunction with the FuG 25a *Erstling* (FuG being short for *Funk-Gerät*, translated as 'wireless equipment'), an IFF system installed in Luftwaffe fighters from early 1941. The system worked by the fighter's transceiver receiving impulses from the *Freya* or *Würzburg* system, activated from the ground station by switching the pulse repetition frequency. The fighter's on-board encrypted device would then reply by sending a pre-defined Morse code signal, and by using this method of IFF, Luftwaffe fighters could be identified as friendly at a range of up to 100 km (60 miles).

These were major steps forward for the defence of the Reich but the greatest challenge in Germany's night war remained how to find the enemy bombers from the air, and not just from the ground. One German report concluded that from nearly 3,500 night fighter sorties flown, less than 7 per cent reported interceptions and only one-third of these turned into an attack. Or put another way, only 2 per cent of the Luftwaffe's night sorties being flown ended up with an attack against a bomber.

In this extremely specialist field Germany was lagging well behind the British and it would be nearly another year before operational radar sets were widely installed into German night fighters. One of the earliest developments was the FuG 202 *Lichtenstein* B/C radar. Developed by the German radio company Telefunken, the FuG 202 operated in the low UHF band. Its design, and that of the follow-on FuG 212 *Lichtenstein* C-1, required a complex *Matratze* (Mattress) arrangement of antennas, consisting of thirty-two dipole elements, mounted in four groups of eight and each at the forward end of four forward-projecting masts. With a maximum range of just over 4 km (2.5 miles) for a bomber-sized aircraft, the target was displayed to the night fighter's operator on a cathode ray tube; the left display showing a target aircraft as a bump, the centre display giving range and elevation, and the right displaying the target's azimuth.

The *Lichtenstein* series would be the most widely used airborne radars installed into the Luftwaffe's night fighters during the war, but unsurprisingly the rather unusual arrangement at the front of a fighter was not particularly favoured by the crews. Its installation increased drag on the aircraft and so reduced its top speed by around 20 mph.

It would take some time for those crews who still favoured the old method of being directed on to the bomber stream from the ground to realize the benefits of radar. There was a further problem, too. In those early days the radar's narrow search cone meant that any evasive manoeuvring by a bomber would result in the night fighter crew losing contact. As far as airborne radar was concerned, these were early days for the Nachtjagd and while some of the Luftwaffe's leadership needed persuading, including Göring, others were more taken by the potential offered by airborne radar and so the FuG 202 was introduced to night fighters on a trial basis during the summer of 1941.

The first success attributed to *Lichtenstein* was claimed on the night of 8/9 August. Unsurprisingly, the successful pilot that night was Ludwig Becker flying a Do 215B-5. He had taken off from his base at Leeuwarden in Holland with his regular *Bordfunker* (radar operator) Feldwebel Josef Staub.

After climbing to their patrol height and position, Staub soon obtained a radar contact just over a mile away and directed Becker onto the target. The bomber was manoeuvring and Staub lost contact a couple of times but he remained patient and soon regained contact once more, allowing Becker to close in on their intended prey. Once in range he opened fire.

During the next six weeks Becker would add five more RAF bombers to his total. He was again leading the way and his tactics were soon being introduced across the Nachtjagd. The normal procedure when using *Lichtenstein*-equipped night fighters was to scramble the experienced crews first because of the limited capacity of the control system. This would give these crews ample time to get into the main bomber stream.

Becker's preferred technique was to climb to a height above where the main bomber force would be, and using any information available from the ground he would then loiter in the area looking for a return from his own airborne radar. Once a contact had been established, he would descend just below the unsuspecting bomber, while taking care to keep outside the visual scan of its gunners, so that he could then look up and silhouette the enemy bomber against the night sky. Then, using any ambient light to his advantage, he would edge his aircraft closer to his intended victim until he was just a matter of yards away and little more than a hundred feet below. He would then pitch up slightly and open fire, aiming at a point where the bomber would fly through his burst of cannon shells and machine gun rounds.

By attacking from below it reduced the chances of the night fighter being spotted by the bomber's rear gunner but on very dark nights, and when in and out of cloud, it was all but impossible to see the target. Besides, it was a risky manoeuvre from the attacker's point of view if the bomber was intercepted on its way to the target when it was still laden with bombs.

The Nachtjagd was now expanding with two more night fighter wings formed during 1941. NJG 3, led by Major Johann Schalk and equipped with a mix of Ju 88Cs and Bf 110C/Fs, formed in northern Germany to provide protection for the ports and naval installations while NJG 4, a similarly equipped unit under the command of Major Rudolf Stoltenhoff, was formed to counter Bomber Command's nightly raids over Germany.

By the end of the year the Nachtjagd had claimed more than 400 RAF bombers; nearly 60 per cent of Bomber Command's losses at night. Amongst the high scorers was 23-year-old Oberleutnant Helmut Lent, a holder of the Knight' Cross and Kommandeur of the newly-formed II./NJG 2 based at Leeuwarden near the Dutch coast. It was a Gruppe operating a mix of types including the Bf 110C/F, Ju 88C, Do 17Z, Do 215B and the Do 217J (the final Dornier variant, although it was overweight and its performance was poor).

Lent had recently claimed his twentieth night success, a Wellington on the night of 7/8 November, to earn him a mention in the coveted *Wehrmachtbericht*; a daily information bulletin issued by the Oberkommando der Wehrmacht (OKW being the High Command of the German Armed Forces). To be personally mentioned in the *Wehrmachtbericht* was one of the highest honours and earned an entry in the individual's service record book. The entry for 20 November 1941 simply read: "*Oberleutnant Lent errang seinen 20 Nachtjagdsieg*", translated as "*Oberleutnant Lent achieved his twentieth nocturnal air victory.*"

The Wellington shot down by Lent that night was one belonging to 75 (New Zealand) Squadron flown by 27-year-old Flight Sergeant John Black. It was part of a mixed force of 169 aircraft attacking Berlin and the encounter took place at 1.21 am while the bomber was on its way home from the target. The Wellington came down at Soarremoarre in Holland, about a mile (2 km) to the north-east of Nes, with the loss of all six of the crew, but it was not until eleven years later that the remains of the airmen were found and recovered from the crash site. They are now buried at Bergen-op-Zoom in the Dutch Province of Noord-Brabant and a small monument now stands where the Wellington had crashed.

Black's aircraft was one of ten Wellingtons lost that night. With nine Whitleys and two Stirlings also failing to return, the overall loss rate for the raid was above 12 per cent. These losses show just how hard Bomber Command's campaign at night had become and it was to be the last raid against Berlin for more than a year. Whereas some bomber crews were fortunate to reach their target and make it home unscathed, and without ever seeing a night fighter, for Black and his crew they had been extremely unfortunate to have been found by such an experienced night fighter pilot as Helmut Lent. Such was the night war over Germany.

Chapter Five

Enter the Heavyweights

Good wishes to 35 Squadron and the heavyweights on the opening of their Halifax operations tonight. I hope the full weight of the squadron's blows will soon be felt further afield.

T he message to 35 Squadron was from Air Vice-Marshal Arthur Coningham, the AOC of No. 4 Group, and arrived ahead of the operational debut of the Handley Page Halifax. Its entry into the night war during March 1941 had come just a month after that of the Short Stirling, the first of Bomber Command's new four-engine heavies to enter service.

At 87 feet (26.5 metres) long and with a wingspan of 99 feet (30.2 metres), the Stirling was a big aircraft. Its four Bristol Hercules radial engines gave a top speed of 280 mph (450 km/h) and a service ceiling of 16,500 feet (5,000 m), and enabled a bomb load of 14,000 lb (6,350 kg) to be carried over a range of 600 miles (960 km).

The Stirling flew its first operational sortie on the night of 10/11 February 1941 when three aircraft belonging to 7 Squadron at Oakington joined forty other bombers to attack fuel storage tanks near Rotterdam. Each of the Stirlings carried a bomb load of sixteen 500 lb bombs and all three aircraft returned safely.

With a crew of seven, the Stirling's capability was a vast improvement on that of the squadron's Hampdens they had replaced but the design of the Stirling's bomb bay, with a neat system of cells, would ultimately limit its capability as the largest single bomb it could carry was 4,000 lb (1,815 kg).

Just two weeks after the introduction of the Stirling, the second of the RAF's new bombers, the twin-engine Avro Manchester, went into action for the first time when six aircraft of 207 Squadron from Waddington joined more than fifty other bombers to attack German warships in the French

Atlantic port of Brest. Then, on the night of 10/11 March, it was the turn of the Halifax to make its operational debut.

The Halifax had initially been designed to the same specification as the Manchester but was fitted with four Rolls-Royce Merlin engines instead of the two Vultures that powered the Manchester due to the Vultures likely to be in short supply. The Halifax was a bit shorter than the Stirling but had a slightly greater wingspan. Its performance, in terms of speed and payload, and its crew composition were similar to the Stirling, although the Halifax did benefit from a higher service ceiling of up to 24,000 feet (7,300 metres) and would prove to be a more sturdy and reliable aircraft.

The target for the first Halifax raid that night was the French port of Le Havre. 35 Squadron was based at Linton-on-Ouse and it was around 7 p.m. when the first Halifax, 'TL-B', flown by the squadron commander, Wing Commander R W P Collings, took off and set course for Le Havre. Collings later reported:

The weather was excellent to the French coast where 8/10 cloud was encountered. Le Havre was located first by searchlights and flak, and then seen through a good break in the cloud, the dock area being clearly visible. A level attack was delivered from 13,000 feet in one stick of twelve 500lb SAP; the bombs were seen to burst along the edge of the main docks. Only slight heavy flak and scattered searchlights were encountered. Landed base 2309.

The operational debut of the Halifax had coincided with Bomber Command's main effort being diverted away from its strategic bombing campaign against Germany to help Britain's desperate fight during the Battle of the Atlantic. During February and March 1941, some 850,000 tons of Allied merchant shipping had been sunk in the Atlantic and the situation had become so desperate that Churchill decreed that the defeat of the Nazi menace at sea was all that mattered.

Although Bomber Command's main effort during the second quarter of 1941 was in support of the Battle of the Atlantic, its bombers took any opportunity to attack German towns and cities where enemy ports were situated. While one part of the attacking force would be given the port as the target, the rest of the bombers would bomb elsewhere; and when attacks against maritime-related targets were not possible, there were always other targets in Germany to bomb.

This kept up the pressure on the German defences and so raids were carried out against a number of key cities, including Cologne, Münster, Dortmund, Osnabrück, Wilhelmshaven, Hannover, Duisburg and Düsseldorf. It was during one of these raids that a Hampden pilot serving with 49 Squadron at Scampton, 28-year-old Sergeant Jimmy Flint, was uniquely decorated with two gallantry awards for separate acts of bravery during the same mission.

Flint and his all-sergeant crew were part of a force of thirty-nine Hampdens sent to attack Osnabrück on the night of 5/6 July. Having crossed the Dutch coast at 10,000 feet they were spotted by searchlights and then attacked by an enemy night fighter. Flint eventually managed to shake off the night fighter and the searchlights before disappearing into the darkness of the night, but the Hampden had been badly damaged during the attack.

With no thought of turning back, Flint pressed on but having arrived over the target the Hampden was again coned by searchlights. Flint held the aircraft steady for long enough for the bombs to be released and then immediately headed for low level. For a while everything settled down and the crew were looking forward to getting back to base but when they were over the North Sea, and just 50 miles from the English coast, the Hampden was attacked yet again.

This time they had been spotted by two night fighters. Three times they attacked, setting the Hampden's port engine on fire. With his crew wounded and with no way of communicating with them, Flint took the aircraft down as low as he dared where he continued on one engine just feet above the waves. He later recalled what happened next:

Having finally shaken off the night fighters, we were approaching the Norfolk coast but I was struggling to maintain height. I thought there was no way we could gain enough height to clear the coastline and so I decided to ditch into the sea just before we reached the shore.

Flint had successfully ditched the Hampden just 800 yards from the shore. Three of the crew, including Flint, were able to get out of the aircraft but the dinghy had been shot up and it was then that they realized the navigator was still inside. Despite the obvious danger, Flint went back into the sinking aircraft where he found his badly wounded comrade. Flint continues:

> *I remember the aircraft was filling up with water and sinking but I managed to haul the navigator out of the escape hatch. But without a dinghy I had to support him as I swam towards the shore.*

Fifty yards from the beach a soldier appeared and helped drag the wounded airman to the shore. Flint then realized that his air gunner had not made it to safety and refused to leave the beach until all efforts to find his missing colleague had been exhausted. Sadly, the navigator would also die after succumbing to his wounds.

Jimmy Flint was awarded an immediate Distinguished Flying Medal (DFM) for his courage and determination to press on during the raid and when his gallant efforts to save his colleague became known he was also awarded the George Medal (GM). One newspaper ran the headline '*One Night, Two Medals*', while the citation for his GM concluded:

> *This airman displayed great gallantry, fortitude and disregard of personal safety in his efforts to save his helpless navigator.*

Bomber Command's renewed offensive against Germany began two nights later, on 7/8 July with raids against four targets. More than a hundred Wellingtons went to Cologne while nearly fifty more went to Münster and a mixed force of more than fifty Whitleys and Wellingtons went to Osnabrück, and forty Hampdens went to Mönchengladbach.

One of No. 3 Group's Wellingtons taking part in the raid against Münster was from 75 (New Zealand) Squadron. Although the squadron was made up mostly with men from New Zealand, the Wellington was being flown by a Canadian, Squadron Leader Reuben Widdowson. It was one of ten squadron aircraft taking part in the raid and alongside him was his young co-pilot from New Zealand, Sergeant Jimmy Ward, who had just celebrated his twenty-second birthday.

Being summer, darkness did not occur until late and so it was just after 11 p.m. when the Wellington got airborne. The transit to Münster passed without incident and having dropped their bombs, Widdowson turned for home. It was a clear night and not at all what the crew would have wanted for their return.

As the Wellington approached the Dutch coast at 13,000 feet it was attacked by a night fighter, believed to be a Bf 110. A hail of cannon shells and incendiary bullets ripped through the bomber's belly from below. A fire then broke out in the starboard engine and, fed by fuel, it quickly spread to threaten the entire wing. The crew in the rear of the aircraft forced a hole through the fabric of the mid-fuselage adjacent to the burning engine. Ward then attempted to reduce the fire with a hand-held extinguisher, but the aircraft's slipstream prevented the mixture from having any effect. Then, as the crew were preparing to abandon the aircraft, Ward decided to make one final attempt to smother the fire using an engine cover found inside the aircraft.

With a rope from the aircraft's dinghy tied to him, Ward removed the cover of the astrodome above and having donned his parachute he climbed through the narrow hole. Widdowson had reduced the aircraft's speed as much as possible but the slipstream nearly swept Ward away. Slowly the gallant co-pilot made his way down towards the wing, making use of existing holes in the Wellington's fabric and tearing holes where there were none to help, until he reached a position just behind the engine. Struggling to hang on, he tried his best to smother the fire by pushing the engine cover into a hole in the wing to cover the leaking pipe that was feeding the fire. Somehow, he managed to do so but as soon as he withdrew his hand the cover blew away. Tired as he was, Ward managed to get back inside the aircraft with the help of his crew. The fire was still burning but eventually it blew itself out. Quite remarkably, the Wellington made it back to the safety of the English countryside and landed at Newmarket.

Jimmy Ward had displayed tremendous courage in helping save the bomber despite the great risk of losing his own life. The squadron commander, Wing Commander Cyril Kay, wasted no time in recommending the young co-pilot for the highest possible recognition and soon after came the announcement that Ward was to receive the Victoria Cross. Sadly, though, Jimmy Ward was killed just weeks later when his Wellington was hit by flak during a raid on Hamburg.

Britain had now been at war for nearly two years but despite such individual acts of courage and sacrifice Bomber Command was still not having the impact that many had hoped, or believed, it would have. Churchill turned to his leading scientific advisor, Frederick Lindemann, The Lord Cherwell, to initiate a study into Bomber Command's night offensive to determine the accuracy of the raids.

The period under scrutiny was June and July 1941 and involved an assessment of raids against twenty-eight different targets carried out on forty-eight nights. The task of analysing more than 4,000 bombing photographs, and then comparing them with the crews' claims, was given to David Bensusan-Butt, a 27-year-old civil servant and assistant of Cherwell.

The Butt Report that followed came as a shock to many of the most ardent supporters of the bomber offensive. In fact, the report did not make pleasant reading for Bomber Command at all and failed to impress either the Air Ministry or the War Cabinet. From the evidence provided it worked out that only one in three bombers managed to get within 5 miles of the correct aiming point, and when assessing those targets in the Ruhr the figures were of even more concern; only one in ten bombers got within 10 miles of the target.

Statistics, of course, do not tell the full story and senior RAF commanders were quick to argue that Butt's findings did not take into account other important factors, such as the effect of bombs landing elsewhere or just how much the countless number of air raid warnings across Germany had disrupted the Nazi war effort; before, during or after every raid. Besides, it was only a small sample of bombing raids.

The RAF responded by commissioning another report. Delivered in September by the Directorate of Bombing Operations, it enabled Portal to argue that a bomber force of 4,000 aircraft could destroy the forty-three German towns and cities listed as having a population greater than 100,000, and so win the war in six months. Not everyone, including Churchill, was convinced but the Air Staff responded by saying that even if a determined strategic bombing campaign failed to knock Germany out of the war, it would at least weaken the enemy sufficiently to allow the Allies back into Europe.

The arguments against a strategic bombing campaign from those outside the Air Staff would never really go away but for now the RAF won its case. Although there was no denying the basic conclusions of the Butt Report, Bomber Command had expended a great deal of effort against targets in Germany during the summer of 1941 and might even have been reasonably pleased with its effort to date. Furthermore, new technology was in the pipeline that would help with the long-standing problem of navigation, including a new radio navigation system called Gee, which would allow bombers to carry out an attack even when the target was not visible, for example at night or when the target was covered by cloud; a technique known as blind-bombing.

Gee, or to give its technical term TR.1355, had been developed by the Telecommunications Research Establishment (TRE) at Swanage and was first trialled operationally on the night of 11/12 August when fitted to two Wellingtons of 115 Squadron and used during a raid against Mönchengladbach.

The concept of Gee was fairly simple and relied on the bomber receiving signals from a series of ground stations. The ground component comprised three stations; a Master (A) and two slaves (B and C) set along a 200-mile baseline with each slave being locked to the master. The time difference for signals A/B and B/C to reach the bomber was measured and displayed on a cathode ray tube in the aircraft, giving the airborne operator two position lines, known as the Gee co-ordinates. By using a special chart he could then plot the intersection of the lines and obtain a fix of the aircraft's position above the ground.

The idea had initially been developed as a short-range blind landing system to improve safety while operating at night but it soon developed into a long-range navigation aid. Its accuracy, in theory, was anything between half a mile and 5 miles but over a distance of 350 miles, for example, the aircraft's position over the ground could be determined to within a mile; far better than any other navigation aid available at the time and accurate enough to use against large fixed targets such as German cities.

The system was not yet ready to go into full production and so 115 Squadron had been given the responsibility of carrying out the operational trials. The first use of Gee during the Mönchengladbach raid was followed up with more trials the next night, this time on a raid against Hannover.

As far as the system was concerned these early flights proved successful, with the navigators not encountering any problems with obtaining Gee fixes for most of their route, but on the second night of trials one of the Gee-equipped Wellingtons failed to return.

At that early stage there was no way of destroying the Gee set on board and the initial concern was that it had fallen into enemy hands. Operational testing was immediately suspended and a disinformation campaign began to try and cover up the fact that a new system was in existence, although there was never any evidence to suggest that the set had fallen into enemy hands.

Although the trials were over after only limited testing, Gee had shown its worth and went into production, although it would be some months before enough sets had been produced to equip the Main Force.

The technological world was moving on and new bombers brought into service but Peirse was becoming increasingly concerned that his bomber force was showing no obvious signs of expanding in size. Although new squadrons were being formed, others were being transferred elsewhere; mostly to the Middle East or Coastal Command. Of his fifty-six front-line squadrons available, just one-quarter were equipped with new heavy bombers. While this was an improvement on the start of the year, there was still a long way to go.

As Portal continued to push the War Cabinet for more resources, the Wellingtons, Whitleys and Hampdens remained, for now, the mainstays of Bomber Command. Although there were some slack periods because of unfavourable weather, Bomber Command's new campaign in the early autumn of 1941 saw targets spread throughout the Ruhr. The tonnage of bombs being dropped was now greater than at any time in the war but in the four months commencing in July more than 400 bombers had been lost at night; a figure equivalent to nearly the entire strength of Bomber Command.

Bomber Command was now analysing its performance, and its losses, far more closely than ever before. The findings of the Butt Report had led to a new Bomber Command Operational Research Section (ORS), under the leadership of Dr Basil Dickins, to study four main areas: bomber losses; the success of bomber operations; the vulnerability of bombers; and radar and radio problems. A fifth area of interest, the study of daylight operations, would be added later.

Most members of the ORS, of which there were more than fifty, mainly scientists and technicians, were based at High Wycombe, with the rest being detached among the bomber groups. The ORS looked at all aspects of operations with impartial scrutiny. Many of its reports were to be quite hard-hitting and its *Bomber Command Quarterly Review* provided a better understanding of what the command was achieving. It was, quite frankly, long overdue.

As 1941 drew to a close, a new directive outlined the War Cabinet's view that it was *'vital to conserve our resources in order to build a strong force to be available by the spring of next year'*. It also instructed Peirse to bear this principle in mind when planning future operations and that the command should not carry out attacks if the weather was unsuitable. It was a directive that caused concerns within Bomber Command's hierarchy, not least by Peirse who may well have felt that his tactical judgement was being brought into question; which it probably was.

Although few bombs were finding their intended targets, new technology was on the way and more trials continued. During one minor raid against Brest on the night of 7/8 December, involving Stirlings from 7 and 15 Squadrons, a new navigation aid was given an operational trial. This was Oboe, based on radio transponder technology and the most accurate of the electronic aids to enter service.

Oboe had also been developed by the TRE and enabled aircraft fitted with the device to carry out blind-bombing of a target. It consisted of two ground stations – the 'Cat', a tracking station sending a dot-dash signal, and the 'Mouse', another station sending a release signal. The system worked by the bomber flying to its target along an arc of a circle using a start point ten minutes from the target. With Oboe switched on the bomber crew received a series of dot-dashes from an operator at the Cat ground station, indicating if the bomber was on track (indicated by a steady tone) or if it was to one side of the intended track or the other (indicated by a series of dots or dashes). If an aircraft was well off track then a Morse letter was received by the crew; the letter would depend on just how far off-track the bomber was. The operator at the Mouse ground station, meanwhile, sent signals indicating the time to go until the release point, at which a bomb release signal was sent to indicate to the crew to drop their bombs. At that point the aircraft transmitter would cut out, indicating to the ground stations the point and time of weapon release.

The approach path to the target was just 35 yards wide (32 metres), allowing for greater accuracy over the target than Gee, but the limitation of Oboe was that it took ten minutes to carry out the procedure, during which only one aircraft could use the system. The solution to this would be to develop a wider range of frequencies or build more ground stations but, even then, its range was limited because it relied on line-of-sight to work. This was of particular concern as for targets in the Ruhr bombers would have to fly at around 25,000 feet to be able to use Oboe. As none of the Main Force bombers in service at the time were capable of this, it meant that it would be another year before the system could be used operationally.

There is no doubt that 1941 had been a year of struggle for Bomber Command and, at times, a frustrating one, but there was hope for the future. New technology was on its way, as was a new aircraft that would shape Bomber Command's strategic offensive for the rest of the war.

Chapter Six

A Turning Point

In the last night the enemy dropped bombs with weak forces in the northwest German coastal region. There was some damage to houses. Four of the attacking British bombers were shot down. Here Oberleutnant Becker achieved his ninth, tenth and eleventh night fighter victory.

The words are a translation from the *Wehrmachtbericht* dated Wednesday 21 January 1942 and refer to Ludwig Becker's achievements the night before, after intercepting a small-scale raid by Wellingtons and Hampdens against Emden, a town and seaport in north-west Germany.

It was not long before Becker earned his second mention in the *Wehrmachtbericht* for taking his total to sixteen. The entry for Thursday 26 March is translated as follows:

The enemy dropped explosive and incendiary bombs on several places in West Germany during last night. The civilian population suffered killed and wounded casualties. Single disruptive flights of enemy aircraft led to the southern territory of the Reich. Night fighters and anti-aircraft artillery shot down eight of the attacking bombers. Here Oberleutnant Becker achieved his 15th and 16th night fighter victories.

Becker's latest successes had come during a raid against Essen when, according to Bomber Command's figures, nine of its attacking force of more than 250 aircraft were lost; one more than the eight claimed in the entry. As Staffelkapitän of 12./NJG 1 Becker would soon earn his third and then fourth *Wehrmachtbericht* entries after taking his total to twenty-five night successes, for which he was awarded the Knight's Cross.

The Nachtjagd was now enjoying success on a regular basis but 1942 was to prove a turning point for Bomber Command. In early January, Sir Richard Peirse left his post amidst increasing losses to be replaced the following month by a man who was to inspire and lead Bomber Command for the rest of the war – Air Marshal Arthur Travers Harris, a former group commander and deputy to Portal. The change was welcomed amongst the squadrons as it came at a time when the command's fortunes and spirits were at a low ebb.

Harris had become increasingly concerned about the way the strategic bombing offensive was being conducted but he could now ensure it was run his own way. This meant his resources would neither be misused nor bled away. He also appreciated the great strain under which the crews were operating. As an AOC during the early months of the war he had tried to introduce a policy where every crew received two nights rest between operations. While this, in reality, proved hard to sustain, his thinking was to stand him in good stead as the command's new head.

Harris' strong views would result in many heated discussions, arguments even, at the higher level. There would, of course, be errors along the way but many of these would only be proved much later with the benefit of hindsight. Harris later said:

The bomber force of which I assumed command on 23 February 1942, although at that time very small, was a potentially decisive weapon. It was, indeed, the only means at the disposal of the Allies for striking at Germany itself and, as such, stood out as the central part in Allied offensive strategy.

Harris hit the ground running. Only a week before he took up his appointment a new directive had been issued to Bomber Command by the Air Staff stating that the primary objective was to break the morale of the German people and, in particular, of the industrial workers. To achieve this, the Air Staff had provided a list of suitable major towns and cities, with Essen being the priority.

One of the directive's central themes was the advent of Gee, the suggestion being that this specialist equipment would permit the concentration of effort to an extent that had not been seen before. This, it was suggested, would enable bombing results of a '*much more effective nature*'.

It had been six months since the first operational trials of Gee but the equipment was still not available in sufficient numbers to equip all the front line squadrons. The first of 60,000 mass-produced sets were due to arrive in May and these were to be fitted to all the new four-engine bombers coming off the production lines as well as the Wellington III. In the meantime, a separate order for 300 sets, made in quicker time, had been delivered to allow some use of Gee, although exactly how best to employ it was a subject that taxed many of the most experienced personnel within Bomber Command.

The creation of a specialist Pathfinder force was still some way off but until Gee could be made available in all the command's aircraft, the tactical solution to its use became known as the Shaker technique. The idea was to have three waves of bombers, with the first two waves consisting of Gee-equipped aircraft. The first wave would be the 'Illuminators'. Made up of experienced crews, their task was to drop triple flares from a time designated as 'zero hour' to illuminate the target. The so-called 'Target Markers' would follow close behind as the second wave. They would drop a maximum load of incendiaries from two minutes after zero hour. The final wave, consisting of the majority of the raiding force and known as 'Followers', would then drop their load of mainly high-explosive bombs from fifteen minutes after zero hour onwards.

Gee was used operationally for the first time on the night of 8/9 March during a raid against Essen. A mixed force of over 200 aircraft took part, more than half of which were Wellingtons, including the Gee-equipped Wellingtons of 115 Squadron; the same squadron that had carried out the trials several months before. After the raid crews reported that '*targets were found and bombed as never before*' but the facts did not match the enthusiasm of the crews.

Despite great expectation the raid went down as a disappointment. The weather was generally fine and Gee clearly helped the bombers find the right area, but industrial haze over the target prevented accurate bombing. Post-raid reconnaissance photos showed that the main target, the Krupps factories, Germany's vital engineering and armaments conglomerate, had not been hit, although one-third of the raiding force had reached the target area; a considerable improvement on figures before.

A raid against Cologne five nights later proved far more successful. It was a smaller raid than Essen but the Cologne raid can be considered the first successful use of Gee. The attack was almost text-book in its execution with 135 aircraft of six different types taking part. The leading Gee-equipped aircraft were able to locate the target and drop flares and incendiaries to locate the target, after which far more accurate bombing results were achieved. Only one bomber, a Manchester, was lost.

This latest raid on Cologne was assessed to be five times more accurate than the previous raid on the city earlier in the year and convinced planners to draw up a list of sixty or so targets all within the range of Gee.

The first Gee chain provided cover over much of France and the Low Countries but as far as targets in Germany were concerned, the practicalities of its accuracy at range generally limited its use to the Ruhr. Nonetheless, the industrial Ruhr was always a high priority and Gee was an immediate success with the bomber crews; not so much for blind-bombing but more as a navigation aid, for which it had been designed, particularly when finding their way home. It was quick and easy to use, and so dependent were the crews on it that the normal procedure if the set did not work was to abort the mission. As far as accuracy was concerned, the operational height of the bombers when operating over the Ruhr enabled accuracies within a mile, and even when operating as far east as Heligoland the system was accurate to within 5 miles. With favourable conditions a maximum range of 400 miles was possible but, more typically, signal strength would start to reduce beyond 150 miles.

The increasing use of Gee inevitably led to a set falling into enemy hands and within five months the Germans had learned how to jam the transmissions. This was first noticed in August 1942 and led to British scientists creating an anti-jamming device, which worked. Gee became Bomber Command's most widely installed piece of airborne equipment of the war, with the possible exception of IFF, and proved to be a highly successful navigation aid with three chains eventually set up to provide full coverage of the UK. Statistics later showed that after the introduction of Gee the number of aircraft lost over the sea reduced and the number of aircraft successfully recovering to their home base increased, with losses amongst Gee-equipped aircraft being around a third of those not fitted.

The introduction of Gee had been timely for Harris but one of his first priorities was the expansion of Bomber Command. While he was fortunate to some degree that much of the ground work had already been put in place, the production of heavy bombers was taking time to have an effect at the front line. On the day he took over command his operational strength was less than 400 bombers, of which fewer than seventy were four-engine heavies. Harris later summed up the overall situation at the time as:

> *Lack of suitable aircraft in sufficient numbers, absence of efficient navigation aids and deficiency of trained crews.*

Harris would set about putting each area of concern right but the current rate of heavy bomber production was not sufficient for the re-equipment of squadrons to their full operational establishment. Harris was, however, boosted by the arrival into operational service of the Avro Lancaster, the last of the four-engine heavy bombers to enter service.

The Lancaster had grown out of the failed twin-engine Manchester and was of similar size to the Halifax, but one of the Lancaster's most notable features was its bomb carrying capacity. Its unobstructed bomb bay, 33 feet (10 metres) in length, meant that it was capable of carrying a maximum bomb load of 14,000 lb (6,350 kg). Furthermore, the Lancaster could carry a mixed load of bombs of various sizes and incendiaries. Its performance was also better than the other heavies. As far as its top speed was concerned, it was capable of more than 280 mph (455 km/h) at medium altitude and depending on its load the operational ceiling could exceed 24,500 feet; higher than the other bombers.

Like any new aircraft the Lancaster took a bit of getting used to. One pilot later described starting the aircraft as:

> *A four-handed job until one is used to it, and the pilot and flight engineer work together. The engineer has control of the main fuel cocks, booster pump, booster coil switch, and starter buttons, while the pilot operates engine master cocks, magneto switches and throttles. Invariably one of the engines will refuse to start, so one works on the principle that one starts the remaining engines, thereby providing the stubborn unit with what one hopes is a good example.*

The position of the flight engineer, to replace the second pilot, had come about following a shortage of pilots and the complexities of the larger four-engine heavies. Other advances in technology and the introduction of more specialized equipment had also seen the tasks of navigation and bomb-aiming split, with the addition to the crew of an air bombardier, or bomb aimer as he was more commonly known. And so the standard crew of seven for the Lancaster comprised: pilot, flight engineer, navigator, bomb aimer, wireless operator, mid-upper gunner and rear gunner.

The Lancaster's first operational sorties were minelaying off the Heligoland approaches and flown by four aircraft of 44 Squadron on the night of 3/4 March 1942. Led by 25-year-old Squadron Leader John Nettleton, each aircraft dropped four mines from 600 feet with all four aircraft returning safely to Waddington.

A week later, on the night of 10/11 March, two of the squadron's aircraft took part in the Lancaster's first bombing mission of the war. The target was Essen but only half of the mixed force of 126 aircraft claimed to have bombed due to the amount of cloud. Flying Officer Ball was flying the first Lancaster to arrive over the target. It was 9.48 pm and the crew's report reads:

Height 18,000 feet, bombs 14 SBCs each 90 × 4lb dropped in area believed to be south-east of 'blitz' area. 16 bundles of Nickels G.1 dropped over target area. At this height not worried much by searchlights and flak activities, but on leaving target area, flak very accurate both for height and direction.

On the night of 13/14 March it was Cologne's turn to be on the end of a raid led by Gee-equipped aircraft. This night marks the first successful attack during a series of Gee-led raids, with half of the bombs dropped by the Main Force falling within 5 miles of the aiming point. The raid was later assessed to have been five times more effective than the average of previous raids, with many factories hit in the industrial areas of the city and seriously disrupting production.

Two raids on Essen followed and one against the coastal town of Lübeck in northern Germany. This latter raid, which took place on the night of 28/29 March, differed from other raids because it tested the theory of using incendiaries to destroy a town.

Everything seemed to favour the raiding force of 234 aircraft (mostly Wellingtons but also included Hampdens, Stirlings and Manchesters). The weather was good and the defences light. More than 80 per cent of the crews claimed to have bombed the target, the outcome being that nearly two-thirds of the town's buildings were destroyed. But the raid caused heavy casualties amongst the civilian population with a reported figure of more than 300 killed and hundreds more injured. It was the heaviest German death toll suffered in a single raid so far. Nonetheless, the British press were quick to report the success:

Over 200 aircraft of Bomber Command tonight launched a shattering raid on the Baltic port of Lübeck, a shipbuilding and industrial centre. Hundreds of tons of incendiaries and high explosive were dropped, and about half of the built-up area has been destroyed by fire. The RAF has begun a round-the-clock offensive against German arms factories.

The headlines and reports were welcomed in Britain, particularly by those living in cities that had been so heavily targeted during the Luftwaffe's bombing campaign earlier in the war. Good news was rare at that stage of the war. There was grim news coming from the desert in North Africa and also from the Far East where Britain had suffered a humiliating defeat with the surrender of Singapore. In Europe the Germans had pushed the Russians back towards Moscow and the U-boats were winning the Battle of the Atlantic. The United States, meanwhile, was still licking its wounds suffered at Pearl Harbour. And so it went on. Lübeck was, indeed, some welcome news for a change and was seen by many as justifiable revenge against the Nazi bombing of British cities.

But in Germany the Lübeck raid had shocked the public and infuriated the Nazi leadership. Joseph Goebbels, the Reich Minister of Propaganda, was furious, branding the attack as the English *Terrorangriff* (*terror raid*) and was keen to instigate 'retaliatory measures' to the point where the Luftwaffe was directed to make a series of reprisal raids on English cultural towns.

These were the so-called Baedeker Raids (the name Baedeker coming from the 1937 book *Baedeker's Great Britain*) with the targets being of cultural or historical importance rather than being of any military value.

However, such comments were seen by the watching world as an admission of guilt by the Germans that they were deliberately targeting cultural and historic places of interest, something the Nazi leadership was keen to avoid for propaganda reasons. Although Goebbels would take steps to ensure that comments such as these did not happen again, there followed a series of Luftwaffe raids against cultural cities – including Exeter, Bath, Norwich, York and Canterbury – in a period later known as the Baedeker Blitz.

The Lübeck raid brought to an end the first quarter of 1942 and shows just how much of an impact Bomber Command's offensive was beginning to have on Germany. More resources were put in place to combat the night raids as the number of anti-aircraft guns doubled to nearly 4,500 heavy guns and 7,500 medium and light guns, all supported by over 3,000 searchlight units. The Kammhuber Line was deepened and elements of the system, including early warning and ground control, improved.

Amongst the night fighter units, personal scores had started to mount. Helmut Lent, for example, had taken his number of night successes to twenty-three. Not far behind him was one of his young pilots, Oberleutnant Egmont Prinz zur Lippe-Weissenfeld, a 23-year-old Austrian of royal descent and the Kapitän of the 5th Staffel of NJG 2. After shooting down four aircraft in a single night on 26/27 March, taking his total to twenty-one (all at night), Prinz zur Lippe-Weissenfeld was awarded the Knight's Cross. He was now one of the Luftwaffe's leading night fighter aces, earning him his third mention in the *Wehrmachtbericht* on 27 March, the same day that another night fighter ace and holder of the Knight's Cross, Oberfeldwebel Paul Gildner of 3./NJG 1, was recognized for shooting down his twenty-eighth aircraft.

These were impressive scores and came at a time when Harris was about to unleash the new Lancaster into the combat arena in ever-increasing numbers. But before he did so he wanted to show that he now had a bomber that was capable of hitting anywhere in Nazi Germany of his choosing and at any time. On 17 April a low-level daylight attack against a diesel engine factory at Augsburg in southern Bavaria, deep in the heart of Nazi Germany, was carried out by twelve Lancasters; six from 44 Squadron at Waddington and six from 97 at Woodhall Spa. The raid caused significant damage to the factory, holding up diesel engine production for several weeks, but only five aircraft returned. The leader of the 44 section, Squadron Leader John Nettleton, was awarded the Victoria Cross, although his was the only aircraft of the squadron to survive the raid.

The value (or not) of the Augsburg raid has been debated ever since but it did make a point. It was a huge propaganda success with national papers reporting headlines such as '*War's Most Daring Raid*', '*Amazing Day Raid by the RAF*' and '*Augsburg Success – Our New Bombers Used – Diesel Works Damaged*'. The survivors of the raid suddenly found themselves propelled into the public spotlight and the subjects of newsreels and newspaper reports.

Bomber Command was now building up its Lancaster force. LAC Eric Howell, a flight mechanic (engines) who had just completed his training and was posted to 44 Squadron at Waddington, later recalled the servicing pattern for the Lancaster during those early days:

The vast majority of the time there were only two engine mechanics and one airframe mechanic (rigger) on duty to service one Lancaster over a 24-hour period in the dispersal area; two on night duty for operations and the third who would be off-duty from about 5.30 pm until 8 am the following morning. After take-off [for a night op], one member would then be off duty until 8 am and the remaining member would wait for the return of the aircraft. When the aircraft returned from its sortie, he would marshal the aircraft to the pan stand. He would collect any 'snags' from the pilot and flight engineer and then refuel the aircraft to a minimum load (about 1,200 gallons) and check the engine oil for excessive use. He would then be off duty until around 1 pm the following day. This cycle of duty would be repeated every three days as long as there were operations or training flights. Other tradesmen (armourers, electricians, radar and wireless technicians etc) were constantly in and out of the flight dispersal areas and when on operations there was usually one electrician and instrument basher on duty with the ground crew.

The vast effort of the ground personnel often goes unrecognized except, of course, by the bomber crews who have always paid tribute to the men and women left back at base while they flew deep into enemy territory. Any losses were felt by all those at the bomber stations involved. Howell goes on to explain:

> *The most distressful time of all was the all night duty. After the pre-flight ground test, the aircrew would debark from the Lancaster for about half an hour to smoke and talk to try and relieve the tensions. After months and years of seeing the aircrew off on operations, the ground crew had a feeling for the emotions of the aircrew even though there was an effort on their part to conceal their feelings. When the time came to re-board the aircraft for take-off it was all business again and the ground crew could finally retire to the safety and warmth of their billets. To depict the loneliness and apprehension of one of those ground crew waiting in the black of night for his aircraft to return from operations, I can offer the following. Thirteen of my Lancasters failed to return from operations over enemy territory. I was not on duty every time this happened, as there were three of us sharing the duties, but the loss was always felt by us all. We would get a hollow feeling in our stomachs and wonder if we had ever missed something in our inspections, which always made us all the more determined to be more diligent.*

Harris was now issued with a new directive, focusing on attacking Germany's industrial war machine to help ease pressure on the Eastern Front. Top-level thinking had also been influenced by a memorandum sent to Churchill by Lord Cherwell. Known as the Dehousing Paper, Cherwell's work had followed on from the Butt Report and was delivered at a time of mounting criticism from within the War Cabinet about the RAF bomber offensive.

The paper helped fuel the government's debate about how to best use Britain's scarce resources against Germany. The paper argued that from an analysis of the reaction of the British population to the Luftwaffe's blitz against England, the demolition of people's houses was the most effective way to affect their morale and even more effective than killing their relatives. The paper also went on to suggest that the most effective use of Bomber Command's aircraft would be to destroy about 30 per cent of the houses in Germany's fifty-eight largest towns and cities because it would break the morale of the German people.

There were other options on the table as well, involving the other services, but the Cabinet chose the strategic bombing campaign. Not everyone agreed and amongst those to challenge the decision was Sir Henry Tizzard, a renowned leader in technological and scientific advances. Tizzard was quick to point out that the new navigation aids required to get the bombers accurately to their targets would not be ready for at least another year and so it remained unlikely that anything more than 25 per cent of bombs dropped would land on the intended target.

There clearly remained doubters about the value of a bombing campaign but Bomber Command could now at least get on with its offensive. With a new commander in Harris, a new piece of technology in Gee, a new tactic in Shaker and a new aircraft in the Lancaster, 1942 was already looking like it could be a decisive year.

Chapter Seven

One Thousand Bombers

The bombing strength of the RAF is increasing rapidly, and I have no doubt that, if the best use is made of it, the effect on German war production and effort will be very heavy over a period of twelve to eighteen months, and such as to have a real effect on the war position.

T he words are taken from a report delivered by Mr Justice Singleton, a High Court Judge, asked by the British Cabinet to look into competing points of view about the RAF's bombing offensive. In his report, delivered in May 1942, he concluded that providing Russia could hold on in the East, Germany would be unlikely to withstand a period of a year to eighteen months of continuous and intensified bombing, which would affect her war production and power of resistance, including morale.

Combined with the earlier Dehousing Paper this view delighted the RAF's leadership, but although Singleton's report had come as music to Harris's ears, he still had a hard fight on his hands. The report had raised concerns about Gee not yet having a significant effect on bombing results and had also suggested that a trained target-finding force would greatly increase the efficiency of the bombing. It also went on to say that until greater accuracy could be assured, Bomber Command should stick to easily found targets.

One way to silence those who doubted the value of a strategic bombing campaign was to carry out a demonstration of the devastating power of a large bomber force, and so to prove his point Harris ordered an all-out effort. It was the start of a series of three so-called 'Thousand Bomber Raids', with the first taking place on the night of 30/31 May 1942 against Cologne.

The order to prepare as many aircraft as possible for that night arrived at Bomber Command's airfields across eastern England soon after midday. It would take a monumental effort, not only by Harris's own command but from elsewhere.

From his front-line strength of between 600 and 700 bombers, Harris would normally expect in the region of 400 to be available for operations on any one night but he also knew there were many more aircraft and crews out there in his operational training units (OTUs). Since his arrival the Bomber Command training system had been re-organized, with the formation of Nos 91 and 92 (OTU) Groups, the latest of a number of changes reflecting the availability of resources and the requirements of the front line. In the end, one-third of the force made available that night would come from his own training units.

Harris had also appealed to his fellow Cs-in-C of Coastal Command and Flying Training Command. Only by scraping together every aircraft and crew would it be possible to mount a raid involving a thousand aircraft. As things were to turn out, and despite the willingness of Coastal Command's C-in-C, Sir Philip Joubert de la Ferté, the Admiralty refused the request for Coastal Command aircraft to take part. There was a further problem too. The lack of specialist equipment fitted in aircraft of Training Command meant that only four Wellingtons could be made available for the raid.

Nonetheless, never before had Bomber Command planned such a large raid and deciding on the best tactics to employ gave the planners their biggest challenge so far. The general feeling was that the best way of putting so many aircraft over one target was to opt for the bomber stream, with all the bombers flying the same route and at the same speed. This would avoid confliction and reduce the chance of a collision between bombers, particularly when over the target. To reduce the chances of collision even further, crews were given a height over the target from which to bomb.

It would effectively be one long conveyor belt, stretching over several miles, with Gee helping crews navigate more accurately along the specified route. As the squadrons prepared, Harris sent out a message to all his crews taking part in the raid:

The force of which you form a part tonight is at least twice the size and has more than four times the carrying capacity of the largest air force ever before concentrated on one objective. You have an opportunity, therefore, to strike a blow at the enemy which will resound, not only throughout Germany, but throughout the world. In your hands lie the means of destroying a major part of the resources by which the enemy's war effort is maintained. It depends, however, upon each individual crew whether full concentration is achieved. Press home your attack to your precise objective with the utmost determination and resolution in the foreknowledge that, if you individually succeed, the most shattering and devastating blow will have been delivered against the very vitals of the enemy. Let him have it – right on the chin.

Harris's squadrons did not let him down and an impressive air armada of 1,047 aircraft was assembled for the raid. In *The Bomber Command War Diaries* by Martin Middlebrook and Chris Everitt, this total figure is broken down as follows: No. 1 Group – 156 Wellingtons; No. 3 Group – 134 Wellingtons and 88 Stirlings; No. 4 Group – 131 Halifaxes, 9 Wellingtons and 7 Whitleys; No. 5 Group – 73 Lancasters, 46 Manchesters and 34 Hampdens; No. 91 Group (OTU) – 236 Wellingtons and 21 Whitleys; No. 92 Group (OTU) – 63 Wellingtons and 45 Hampdens; and Flying Training Command – 4 Wellingtons. These figures add up to a total attacking force of: 602 Wellingtons, 131 Halifaxes, 88 Stirlings, 79 Hampdens, 73 Lancasters, 46 Manchesters and 28 Whitleys.

There are so many individual stories to tell from this historic raid, far too many to be told here, but one aircraft taking part was a Manchester of 50 Squadron flown by 20-year-old Flying Officer Leslie Manser. Having taken off from his base at Skellingthorpe near Lincoln just after 11 p.m., Manser set course for Cologne but with a full bomb load and overheating engines he was unable to get the Manchester above 7,000 feet.

Had it not have been an all-out effort, Manser's aircraft, L7301 'VN-D', known to the crews as 'D-Dog', would probably not have been on the order of battle that night, and being perilously low he would have been fully justified in turning back. But Manser decided to press on, hoping that by being well below the Main Force they would be able to sneak under the searchlight and flak defences. It worked. The Manchester reached the target without further problem and having released their bombs, Manser turned for home.

No sooner had the Manchester started its long journey home it was hit by flak. With searchlights and more anti-aircraft fire threatening, Manser put the aircraft into a dive and took it down to 1,000 feet. Away from further danger the crew assessed the damage. The Manchester had been peppered by shrapnel from the burst of flak and part of the bomb bay had been torn away. The fuselage was full of smoke and one of the gunners had been wounded.

Manser was finding the aircraft increasingly difficult to control but he managed to get it back up to 2,000 feet but then the port engine caught fire. The second pilot, Sergeant Les Baveystock, quickly operated the fire extinguisher but nothing seemed to happen. The crew watched anxiously in the hope the flames would go out, which they eventually did, but the bomber was now losing height. Flying on just one engine Manser was unable to maintain enough height to make it home and so he ordered his crew to bale out, but when handed his own parachute he waved it away, insisting that the others should jump while he held the aircraft steady long enough for them all to get out. As the crew drifted down on their parachutes they watched in horror as the Manchester hit the ground and burst into flames, still with their gallant young captain on board.

All but one of the surviving crew members evaded capture through the hands of the Belgian resistance. Having been brought together the five evaders were passed down the Comet escape line, through France and across the Pyrenees, and eventually made it back to England via Gibraltar. It was then that the full story of the young pilot's bravery was told, after which it was officially announced that Leslie Manser was to be posthumously awarded the Victoria Cross. The citation appeared in the Third Supplement to the *London Gazette* on Friday 23 October 1942 and concludes:

> *In pressing home his attack in the face of strong opposition, in striving, against heavy odds, to bring back his aircraft and crew, and, finally, when in extreme peril, thinking only of the safety of his comrades, Flying Officer Manser displayed determination and valour of the highest order.*

In a letter to Manser's family, Harris wrote '*no Victoria Cross has been more gallantly earned*'.

As for the overall result of the Cologne raid that night, just under 900 aircraft bombed the target, dropping 1,500 tons of bombs, although damage was less than had been hoped. However, a number of industrial and administrative areas had been hit and the defences had been overwhelmed by the strength of the force. The attack also had a devastating effect on the city's population, with an estimated one-quarter of the civilian inhabitants fleeing the city in the immediate aftermath of the raid.

With so many bombers taking part it was inevitable that losses would be high. And they were. The forty-one aircraft lost on the raid, mostly Wellingtons, far exceeded the command's previous highest loss in a single raid. Cologne's defences were good but in percentage terms the losses on this first Thousand Bomber raid were less than 4 per cent of the attacking force, and reinforced the belief that saturating the enemy defences was the way forward.

The British press were quick to jump on the story, stating '*RAF chiefs claim to have destroyed more than 200 factories in last night's raid on Cologne*' and that '*the scale of the attack was over four times bigger than the largest raid on London*'. The raid also did much to silence many doubters of Bomber Command and seemingly persuaded the government to allocate Harris more priority for aircraft, as well as approving the development of vital navigation aids that would ensure the accurate delivery of bombs on target.

From the Luftwaffe hierarchy's point of view, the Cologne raid was seen as a one-off. It was felt the RAF had yet to make its mark in other raids against Germany, and the United States had yet to enter the fray in any considerable numbers. The raid had also come at a time when the defence of the Reich was still considered a low priority and to the Nachtjagdflieger the large attacking force had simply presented a target-rich environment. The raid had seen NJG 1 claim its 600th night victim of the war, with Hauptmann Werner Streib being credited with two successes that night, earning him an entry in the *Wehrmachtbericht*. The entry for Sunday 31 May 1942 translates as follows:

A night fighter unit under the leadership of Generalleutnant Kammhuber achieved hereby their 600th aerial victory at night, Hauptmann Streib achieved his 25th and 26th and Oberleutnant Knacke his 20th nocturnal aerial victory.

The other pilot specifically mentioned in the entry, Oberleutnant Reinhold Knacke, was another combat veteran despite being just twenty-three years of age. He had flown Bf 110s during the campaign in France two years earlier and was now serving with 3./NJG 1. Knacke would soon receive the Knight's Cross and would continue to score freely throughout the year, including the night of 16/17 September when he set a remarkable record for that time of shooting down five aircraft in one night.

The day following the Cologne raid marked the operational debut of the RAF's de Havilland Mosquito IV twin-engine light-bomber. With a crew of two, the versatile and highly acclaimed Mosquito was capable of 380 mph (610 km/h) and could carry a bomb load up to 4,000 lb (1,815 kg). Speed was its defence and its performance was excellent anywhere from low level up to its operational ceiling of nearly 29,000 feet (8,800 metres). Five aircraft of 105 Squadron, operating as singles, flew reconnaissance missions over Cologne. The first took off as early as 4 a.m. and the last at 5.10 p.m., although the crews arrived overhead the city to find the weather too bad to take meaningful photos; and so three of the aircraft bombed instead. The day was only marred by the loss of one Mosquito, believed to have been hit by flak and then come down in the North Sea; Pilot Officer Bill Kennard and his navigator, Pilot Officer Eric Johnson, were both killed.

Just two nights after the Cologne raid, on 1/2 June, the Thousand Bomber force was called upon once more. This time the target was Essen, a target that had always had its problems for Bomber Command. Coming so soon after the previous all-out effort the total number of aircraft fell short of the thousand that had been hoped and in the end 956 aircraft of all types took part.

The tactics employed for this second large raid were similar to those of the first. The weather forecast was favourable but as things turned out conditions over the target were poorer than expected with low cloud and haze, making it difficult for the crews to locate their aiming points, despite the extensive use of flares to illuminate the target. Bombing was scattered and results were poor. In fact, bombing was so scattered that bombs had fallen across a number of smaller towns in the surrounding area. Thirty-one aircraft were lost.

Again, the training units had been involved and inevitably there were losses amongst the OTU crews as best summed up by Flight Lieutenant John Price, then an instructor with 10 OTU based at Abingdon. In *Raiders of the Reich* by Martin W Bowman and Theo Boiten, Price recalls his feelings that night, an excerpt of which is given below:

As an instructor, I had been ordered to go, but as there were not enough instructors to fill the aircraft, pupil pilots were called upon, ditto navigators and air gunners. I was besieged by my pupils, pleading with me to let them go. I knew that half of them would not come back, but I chose my dozen or so, then prayed for their safety. None came back – eighteen-year-old boys!

The disappointment of this second all-out effort was immediately apparent and another raid was ordered against Essen the following night. After all that had gone on the night before, the follow-up raid involved a much smaller force (less than 200 aircraft) and resulted in no better success than the night before. Bombing was again scattered with no significant damage caused. A further fourteen aircraft were lost.

Essen was attacked three more times in the next two weeks. Also targeted heavily during mid-June was Emden, the seaport of the Ruhr, with four raids in just two weeks. Bremen, another industrial city in north-west Germany with a major port, was also attacked and it was to be Bremen that Harris turned his attention for the third, and what would be the last, of his Thousand Bomber raids.

The Bremen raid took place on the night of 25/26 June. This time 1,067 aircraft took part, twenty more than the Cologne raid, although this figure was only achieved after the intervention of the Prime Minister. Included in the large force were more than a hundred aircraft from Coastal Command (Wellingtons and Lockheed Hudsons) and five from Army Co-Operation Command. From Bomber Command came every available aircraft, ten different types in all, including Bostons and Mosquitos.

Most of the Main Force were given the city centre as the aiming point, although those of No. 5 Group were given the Focke-Wulf aircraft factory as their target while the crews of Coastal Command were to bomb the Deschimag shipyards. Meanwhile, intruder missions by more than fifty aircraft of No. 2 Group were flown against night fighter airfields to distract and spread the enemy's defences.

The increased distance to Bremen, 100 miles further than either Cologne or Essen, meant the total time spent over the target was reduced to just over an hour. The crews arrived to find that cloud covered much of the area. Nonetheless, the lead bombers, helped by the accuracy of Gee, were able to drop flares with some precision, causing fires for the following waves of aircraft to bomb. At least two-thirds of the attacking force claimed to have bombed their targets with damage caused to a number of industrial plants and factories, including the Focke-Wulf factory. There was further widespread damage across Bremen, with thousands of houses either destroyed or damaged, mostly in the southern and eastern parts of the town.

In the aftermath of the raid both sides were quick to claim success. The British press reported that a thousand bombers had taken part in the raid while German reports stated less than a hundred. The Germans were also quick to report a large number of bombers shot down.

The actual losses suffered by Bomber Command that night were forty-eight aircraft. The heaviest casualties, percentage wise, were suffered by the OTUs, particularly No. 91 (OTU) Group, which lost twenty-three of its 198 Whitleys and Wellingtons taking part (11.6 per cent). Five of Coastal Command's aircraft were also lost.

Amongst those losses were two claimed by Helmut Lent, now a Hauptmann and the Kommandeur of II./NJG 2 based at Leeuwarden in Holland. He was scrambled during the early hours to intercept the bombers as they headed for home. Flying a Bf 110 he shot down a Wellington at 2.37 a.m. to the north-west of Enkhuisen in Holland and twenty minutes later a Whitley crossing the coast over Noordwijk; both aircraft were from training units.

It rounded off a good month for Lent. He had earlier been told of his award of the Oak Leaves to his Knight's Cross and these latest successes made it five during the week and forty-seven overall. His Gruppe was also doing remarkably with more than sixty RAF bombers shot down that month alone.

Most of the Nachtjagd's successes were being claimed by hardened veterans like Lent, while others newer to night fighting were left to pick up whatever scraps they could but from this latter cadre of young men would come some of the Luftwaffe's finest Nachtjagdflieger of the war. These include 24-year-old Oberleutnant Werner Hoffmann, the Kapitän of 5./NJG 3, and another Bf 110 pilot, 22-year-old Oberleutnant Georg Hermann Greiner of 4./NJG 2, both of whom scored the first of their eventual fifty successes during the Bremen raid.

In the case of Hoffmann, he had been one of the last to be scrambled after being held on the ground at Schleswig while those with more experience had taken off to meet the main bomber stream. However, the northerly route home from Bremen took the RAF bombers towards Germany's most northern state of Schleswig-Holstein and it was around 2 a.m. when Hoffmann climbed away from his base.

Suddenly the voice of the Jägerleitoffizier burst into life. Hoffmann was vectored onto a Hudson, an aircraft belonging to Coastal Command. As he closed on his target, he and his *Bordfunker*, Oberfeldwebel Kohler, could make out the shape of the small American-built twin-engine light-bomber but it was not at all what they had expected to see. Then, having closed unobserved from astern, Hoffmann positioned the 110 and after a short but deadly burst, the Hudson was on its way to earth, its starboard wing lighting up the night sky before it crashed near the small town of Heide.

Loitering over Schleswig-Holstein and waiting for his next instruction, Hoffmann was eventually vectored onto another bomber, a Whitley belonging to one of the RAF's training units, which he also attacked from the stern. The Whitley, flown by Sergeant Makarewicz, went into a rapid dive. Hoffmann followed it down but he could not finish it off. However, he had damaged it enough to convince the Whitley crew not to risk the long return transit across the North Sea. Makarewicz put the stricken bomber down on a beach to the north of Büsum where the crew were taken as prisoners of war. Both of Hoffmann's victims had come down within a few miles of each other and less than 50 miles from his home base.

Georg Hermann Greiner, too, with his *Bordfunker*, Feldwebel Rolf Kissing, had been one of the last night fighters to get airborne that night. Daylight was already starting to break and as they climbed through heavy cloud, knowing that the main raid was over, there was little for the crew to be optimistic about. But then the voice of the Jägerleitoffizier changed everything. Vectored onto one of the straggling bombers they broke through cloud to find the sky clear above. It was already approaching 6 a.m. and the sun was already above the horizon over north-west Holland, and with the benefit of daylight Greiner could make out a Wellington in the distance. Expecting the bomber to escape into the safety of the cloud, Greiner opened fire. As he had expected, the Wellington did disappear into cloud and his belief that he had hit the bomber was later confirmed after it crashed into the ground.

Bremen was the focus of Bomber Command's attention on three more occasions in the following week, although all three raids were much smaller efforts. It was never going to be possible to keep assembled such a large force of aircraft. The OTUs, for example, needed to return to their training task and other participants, such as those from Coastal Command, could no longer be diverted from their own commitments.

Of the three Thousand Bomber raids it could be argued that only the first, the one against Cologne, was truly successful. They had, however, been the first serious attempt to stream a main bomber force and to saturate and overwhelm the enemy's defences to reduce overall losses.

Harris had hoped the results of these large raids would prove to his doubters that the power of the bombing offensive was enormous, just as long as he was given the resources needed to sustain it. But some felt differently. They believed these raids achieved little other than the 'wholesale bombing of civilians' and so brought into question the whole concept of large-scale bombing of towns and cities.

The discussions, arguments even, continued but Harris remained undaunted by the opposition and continued to put his case forward whenever the opportunity arose. In a letter to Churchill, written during June while the Thousand Bomber raids were taking place, Harris summarized his thoughts and his anger:

> *An extraordinary lack of sense of proportion affects outside appreciation of the meaning, extent and results of Bomber Command's operations. What shouts of victory would arise if a Commando wrecked the entire Renault factory in a night, with a loss of seven men! What credible assumptions of an early end to the war would follow upon the destruction of one-third of Cologne in an hour and a half by some swift-moving mechanized force which with but 200 casualties withdrew and was ready to repeat the operation twenty-four hours later! What acclaim would greet the virtual destruction of Rostock and the Heinkel main and subsidiary factories by a Naval bombardment! All this and far more has been achieved by Bomber Command; yet there are many who still avert their gaze, pass on the other*

side, and question whether the thirty squadrons of night bombers make any
worthwhile contribution to the war.

The letter succeeded in silencing the wolves at Bomber Command's door, for the time being at least. While it had been Bremen at the forefront of Bomber Command's focus during early July 1942, a similar campaign was aimed at Duisburg later in the month. The shorter nights had now restricted Bomber Command to attacking coastal targets and the Ruhr. This brief campaign against the industrial city of Duisburg on the western edge of the Ruhr, with four raids in less than two weeks, fared little better than the earlier campaign against Bremen.

Flying as aircrew with Bomber Command was voluntary but there never seemed to be a shortage of volunteers. By mid-1942 the command had settled into a rhythm where an individual's tour of duty was thirty operations, after which he would be rested from ops with his next tour typically being an instructor. A second operational tour, if there was to be one, would then consist of twenty ops, after which the individual would no longer be required to fly any further operations, unless he chose to do so.

There were, of course, variations to this general rule but if not enough crews survived their first operational tour then the instructor pool would not be big enough to train the new crews coming through. Of particular concern was the loss of junior officers. This would impact downstream as it meant those individuals would not be able to return to the squadrons as flight commanders or squadron commanders at some point in the future.

A crucial planning figure for squadron manpower was the casualty rate at that particular stage of the war, and this had now become a problem. With the overall loss rate exceeding the critical planning figure of 4 per cent, there were doubts as to whether Bomber Command was sustainable as a force.

In addition to its manpower there was much for Bomber Command to rectify, not least bombing accuracy, or rather the general lack of it. Essentially, there were two main ways to take this forward if accuracy was to be improved; one was to develop new equipment to aid blind-bombing and the other was to create a target-finding force. Both ideas had been under discussion for a year or more, with the creation of a specialist target-finding force having received special mention in the recent Singleton Report.

It was also time for the ORS to analyse the performance of the heavy bombers since entering service. It was too early to assess the Lancaster but the Manchester, for example, was fairing particularly badly. As well as its recurring problem of overheating engines, it was far more vulnerable to flak damage than any of the other types. This was partly attributed to the design of its fuel tanks. The Manchester had two main tanks and two smaller tanks, whereas the Stirling, for example, had fourteen fuel tanks, meaning the Manchester suffered critical levels of damage more easily.

With more Lancasters now available, the Manchester was withdrawn from operations to become a training platform for crews destined for the Lancaster. The ORS had also been critical of the Halifax, which over the past year had suffered a loss rate exceeding 5 per cent. The conclusion was that many losses were due to enemy night fighters, perhaps because of the unsatisfactory design of the exhaust shrouds on its engines, which made the aircraft easier to pick up visually in the dark than other types.

An examination of bomber losses showed that from nearly 5,000 sorties evaluated, German night fighters had achieved an interception rate of more than 8 per cent, of which one-in-four interceptions turned into full attacks, leading the ORS to conclude:

Losses have reached a very high level, since they have occurred mostly under conditions of heavy cloud and in the absence of searchlight co-operation it seems likely that effective GCI (ground control intercept) must be responsible. The proportion of attacks from below which result in serious damage emphasises the need for more protection from that direction.

Analysis also showed that losses amongst inexperienced Halifax crews during their first couple of sorties was higher than the average, whereas losses suffered amongst experienced crews with twenty or more ops was well below the average. However, the same could not be said of Lancaster crews. In the air war over Germany, where luck clearly played its part, it was difficult to draw conclusions.

Chapter Eight

Pathfinders

The need for a RAF specialist target-finding force was generally agreed by all parties.

The statement sums up the general view within Bomber Command during the summer of 1942, but the manner of its inception and composition caused heated debate. Options on the table included ideas such as forming a new and special force, made up of six squadrons with new equipment and with aircraft manned by the best crews from across the command, to each group having its own specialist squadron.

Opinions were divided with a case for and against the various options put forward, but the reality was that for every successful night raid by Bomber Command there were probably two or three failures. Furthermore, the German defences were now getting stronger and Bomber Command was being forced more and more to use nights when there was no moon at all rather than the preferred method of bombing under moonlit conditions. The Germans were also learning how to jam Gee.

The excitement, euphoria and expectations following the first Thousand Bomber raid against Cologne seemed well and truly in the past. Morale, something which generally remained high amongst the bomber crews throughout the war, had for the first time started to dip following a run of poor results and losses. The Halifax force, in particular, had suffered more than the other types and its overall loss rate was now running at more than 6 per cent. With such high losses the Halifax was removed from operations for a month to give the squadrons of No. 4 Group time to recover.

There was clearly a need to do something new. For some time Bomber Command's groups had been using their own experienced crews to lead raids, with some aspects of target-marking already tested under the Shaker technique, and so Harris favoured an extension of this idea rather than the creation of, as he saw it, an elite and separate force. His main argument, and one that was supported by his group commanders, was that the creation of a new force would mean the groups losing their best squadrons or crews, with an adverse effect on the group as a whole.

Feelings at the Air Ministry differed. The Deputy Director of Bomber Operations, Group Captain Sidney Bufton, for one, had long argued for a specialist target-finding or target-marking force. Having commanded two bomber squadrons, one of them being the first to be equipped with the Halifax, Bufton was a specialist. Long before his arrival at the Air Ministry he had advocated the need to utilize the skill of the more experienced crews to locate and mark the target for the benefit of the main bombing force.

It was now Bufton's opportunity to get his ideas put into practice, although the idea of using a specialist unit for marking targets for bombers to attack was not new; the Luftwaffe had first used the idea during the Blitz on London in 1940. The discussions and arguments continued. In fact, they turned out to be some of the most heated of the war. With such a disagreement between the Air Staff and one of his most senior commanders, Portal had no option but to intervene. The pressure was mounting on Harris as a result of his command's poor results thus far and, in the end, Portal supported his own staff. Harris was forced to concede defeat.

Harris was directed to form a new and specialist target-marking force to be called the Path Finder Force (PFF), more simply known as the Pathfinders. It was initially made up of four standard bomber squadrons, one from each of Bomber Command's heavy bomber groups: 7 Squadron (Stirlings) from No. 3 Group; 156 Squadron (Wellingtons) of No. 1 Group; 35 Squadron (Halifaxes) of No. 4 Group; and 83 Squadron (Lancasters) of No. 5 Group.

Although he had been forced to concede defeat in having to form the Pathfinders, Harris dug his heels in when it came to the decision over who should lead it. The Air Staff had their own ideas, with the highly decorated night fighting expert Group Captain Basil Embry the preferred candidate, but Harris was determined to win this particular battle and, in the end, he got his way.

The man Harris chose to lead the Pathfinders was 31-year-old Donald Bennett, a talented, energetic and pioneering Australian aviator and former squadron commander. Bennett was promoted to the rank of group captain and in August 1942 the PFF was formed, its squadrons lodged on four adjacent airfields of No. 3 Group in Huntingdonshire and Cambridgeshire: at Oakington (7 Squadron); Graveley (35 Squadron); Wyton (83 Squadron), which was also the headquarters of the PFF; and Warboys (156 Squadron).

The only squadron already in place was 7 Squadron at Oakington and so during the following days the three other squadrons moved into their new bases. Within a week the Pathfinders were ready to commence operations. There was also welcome news from elsewhere as the formation of the PFF had coincided with the first American heavy bomber raid of the war. With the Americans bombing by day and Bomber Command at night, a combined strategic bombing offensive was under way.

Having the four Pathfinder squadrons so close to each other would give the crews the chance to get together to develop target-marking techniques but such was the urgency to get the Pathfinders operational, there was no time to do so before they were airborne for the first time. On the night of 18/19 August 1942, thirty-one Pathfinders (a mix from each of the squadrons) were amongst a force of 118 aircraft that attacked the north German town of Flensburg.

Being a coastal town on an inlet of the Baltic it should have been reasonably easy to locate but the target-marking, and the raid for that matter, proved a disappointing failure. It was not at all what had been expected from this first Pathfinder mission; the combination of bad weather over the target area and different winds to those forecast being the reasons why. Although half of the Pathfinder crews claimed to have marked the target, and most of the Main Force claimed to have bombed the right place, the town was not hit at all.

It appears the force had drifted slightly northwards where part of Denmark's coastline looks very similar to the area of the intended target. Reports of scattered bombing across the extreme south of Denmark, particularly on the Danish towns of Sønderborg and Aabenraa, merely confirm the failure of the raid. The raid also witnessed the first loss of a Pathfinder aircraft on operations; a Halifax of 35 Squadron, although the crew survived to become prisoners of war.

While the failure of this first raid provided an opportunity for those who doubted the need for a new specialist target-marking force to voice their concerns, no adverse comments came. Whatever some opponents of the idea, including Harris, must have felt inside, criticism would have served no purpose.

It was an early setback but the redoubtable Bennett remained undaunted and he would go on to work tirelessly to build the PFF into a highly efficient and technical force, although his crews had to wait nearly a week before they had another opportunity to prove their worth. This time the target was Frankfurt with a raiding force of 226 aircraft taking part, but again the weather did not help and the Pathfinder crews struggled to identify the target through the broken cloud. Although some bombs fell on the city, bombing was scattered and sixteen aircraft were lost (7.1 per cent).

Amongst the losses were five aircraft from the PFF with 7 Squadron suffering most. Of its eleven Stirlings taking part in the raid, two had to turn back due to engine problems, one returned badly damaged and two failed to return. One of those lost was flown by the squadron commander, 32-year-old Wing Commander John Shewell, while the other was that of a Canadian, Flight Sergeant Bill Shumsky. It was another bad night.

Three nights later the Pathfinders were back in action again. The target was Kassel with just over 300 aircraft taking part. Weather conditions were more favourable than before with little cloud over the city and so the Pathfinders successfully marked the aiming points for the Main Force. Bombing was scattered but amongst the buildings severely damaged were three factories belonging to the Henschel aircraft manufacturing company. Sadly, though, losses had again been high with thirty-one aircraft failing to return; just over 10 per cent of the attacking force.

There was to be no rest and the next night, 28/29 August, more than 150 aircraft went to Nuremberg. The Pathfinders were now carrying a new target illuminator in the shape of a modified 250 lb bomb casing packed with an inflammable mix of benzol, rubber and phosphorous, instead of the flares used previously. The main advantages of the new illuminator was that it did not drift with the wind and the incendiary burned bright for some time, causing a distinctive red fire on the ground.

From the bombing photographs taken it was evident that marking had been good. Although some bombing was scattered it was a good attack overall and marked the first real success for the Pathfinders, but it had again been a costly night with twenty-three aircraft lost; more than 14 per cent of the attacking force. This time it was the Wellington crews that suffered most with fourteen of the forty-one aircraft taking part in the raid failing to return; an alarming 34 per cent!

By the end of August the Pathfinders had flown 175 sorties and lost sixteen aircraft. These losses of more than 9 per cent would, sadly, be typical for the PFF as casualties amongst its crews were to remain higher than the average across Bomber Command. Being the first over enemy territory they would often feel the full weight of the German defences, particularly if the bombers had been tracked and the target had been anticipated before they arrived.

The early days of Pathfinding were always going to be difficult and the following month started no better with a disappointing raid against Saarbrücken. This time the Pathfinders marked what they thought was the city, although it later became apparent that it was the town of Saarlouis, a small and militarily insignificant town, also on the River Saar but more than 10 miles to the north-west. More than 200 aircraft bombed, causing devastation to Saarlouis but no bombs fell on Saarbrücken.

The following night the target was Karlsruhe, the second largest city in south-west Germany. The attacking force of 200 aircraft included the Halifaxes of No. 4 Group's that had now returned to operations. Target-marking was good and the raid a success with damage to several residential and industrial buildings.

The Pathfinders had been operational for just two weeks but things were happening at pace. Each raid was analysed and whenever possible new ideas and improvements introduced. It was already clear that good target-marking resulted in a successful raid. The opposite was also true but things had to be tried and lessons learned if the Pathfinders were to progress.

Just forty-eight hours after the Karlsruhe raid, more than 250 aircraft returned to the industrial coastal city of Bremen. It was the night of 4/5 September and an important one for the Pathfinders as it provided the opportunity to try a new technique of illuminating, marking and backing-up.

This was achieved by splitting the Pathfinders into three groups. The first group, the illuminators, dropped white flares along the direction of attack to light up the target area. This enabled the aircraft following on to see the markers from distance and so refine their final attack heading. This was the second group, the so-called visual markers, responsible for identifying the aiming point and then visually marking the target using coloured flares. It was then the turn of the third group, the backers-up, to drop incendiaries on the coloured flares. This started fires at the aiming point, which would burn longer than the flares, making them easier for the Main Force crews to see.

With clear weather the Pathfinder plan worked well. Heavy and accurate bombing followed, causing severe damage to industrial buildings, oil storage depots and shipyards. Compared with recent raids the losses were relatively light with twelve aircraft lost, although this was still above the critical 4 per cent.

The success of the illuminating, marking and backing-up concept meant this technique would form the basis for future Pathfinder operations, with accuracy improved as better methods came along. One improvement was the introduction of 'Pink Pansies', converted 4,000 lb bomb casings packed full of inflammables, which marked the target by causing a notable and distinctive coloured fire on the ground. These were first used during a raid against Düsseldorf on the night of 10/11 September and resulted in severe damage to many industrial factories, causing production across some areas to come to a halt.

One report from a 7 Squadron Pathfinder crew that had taken part in the Düsseldorf raid that night shows the extent of determination and courage being displayed by the crews of Bomber Command. Nine of the squadron's aircraft took part in the raid but one Stirling, flown by Flying Officer John Trench, ran into severe difficulties over the target area. Having repeatedly been hit by flak, the Stirling was left in a critical state. The starboard fuel tank was holed and oil pipes severed, the port inner airscrew and reduction gear had been sheared but, worst still, the port outer engine had fallen out!

Aided by his wireless operator, Sergeant Ivor Edwards, Trench kept the aircraft on an even keel for long enough to complete the attack before finally turning the crippled bomber towards home. With the aircraft desperately losing height, all removable objects were discarded overboard until Trench was able to sustain a steady height just 150 feet above the ground; even the parachutes were slung overboard.

Eventually, the Stirling reached the English coast at which point the starboard inner engine cut out. A crash-landing was inevitable. Using all his skill Trench managed to bring the stricken bomber down near Weeley in Essex, just inland from Clacton-on-Sea, but as they hit the ground the aircraft burst into flames. Trench and Edwards were both knocked unconscious but the navigator, 22-year-old Pilot Officer Crofton Selman, managed to drag them both out of the wreckage. However, the rear gunner, Pilot Officer Glendenning, was still inside his turret. Without hesitation Sergeants Fred Thorpe and Henry Mallott dashed back inside the burning wreckage in an attempt to reach their trapped colleague but the fuel tanks blew up, killing them both. It was then that Flight Lieutenant Jenner, the seventh member of the crew, rushed in to the inferno and succeeded in dragging the badly burned Glendenning to safety.

It is hardly surprising that such courage and fortitude in the face of extremely harassing circumstances was rewarded; and deservedly so. Trench was awarded an immediate DSO, Selman the Distinguished Flying Cross (DFC) and Edwards the DFM, while Thorpe and Mallott were both posthumously awarded a Mention in Despatches. Sadly, both John Trench and Crofton Selman would be killed six months later while serving with the squadron.

With more experience the Pathfinders gained proficiency but there were always new problems to overcome. One was that the flares and incendiaries dropped by the Pathfinders would often go out long before a raid was complete. Another problem was something known as 'creep-back'. This usually occurred over heavily defended targets or if night fighters were known to be in the vicinity, when over-hasty or nervous crews released their bomb loads too early in order to turn for home as quickly as possible. It only took a handful of bombers in the first wave to release their bombs a second or two early for the fires to creep back along the direction of attack. It was also difficult for crews to estimate the range to the target on their final run-in to bomb, particularly when the whole area was a blazing mass. This could result in crews bombing the fires on the ground instead of the specified aiming point. In large-scale raids, when hundreds of bombers were involved, the problem simply got worse and it was not unusual for a tail of up to 8 miles long to form from the aiming point back along the line of approach.

The defenders also found a way of countering the illumination of a target by starting a decoy fire. This idea was first used in October 1942 during raids against Kiel and Cologne. In the case of Kiel it is estimated that a large decoy fire drew at least half of the 250 raiders away from the major port and out into the open countryside, while during the Cologne raid a decoy incendiary device was set alight. This succeeded in drawing the attention of the Main Force away from the intended target with few bombs falling on Cologne.

The battle of the decoys would continue for the rest of the war as the defenders did all they could to convince the Main Force crews to bomb the middle of nowhere. Although decoy fires and flares were not exactly like the real thing they certainly duped many crews into bombing the wrong area, particularly in the heat of battle. Once bombs had fallen on a decoy site then it did not take long for those fires to take on the appearance of the genuine target.

As 1942 drew towards a close the combination of poor weather over Germany and the need for a bombing campaign against Italy meant that raids over the Nazi homeland were limited. There were only two major efforts against German cities in November (Hamburg and Stuttgart) and two during December (Mannheim and Duisburg); none of which brought much success.

The Pathfinders were finally given group status in January 1943 when No. 8 (Pathfinder) Group was formed. Bennett was promoted to the rank of air commodore but he was still one rank junior to the other group commanders, although this would later be rectified when Bennett became the youngest air vice-marshal in the RAF at the age of thirty-three.

Other changes saw 156 Squadron exchange its Wellingtons for Lancasters, while a fifth squadron, 109 Squadron, was allocated to the new group with its Mosquitos moving into Wyton as a specialist Oboe marking squadron. The squadron had carried out its first operational trial with Oboe on the night of 20/21 December when six Mosquitos attacked a power station at the small Dutch town of Lutterade close to the German border. The first Oboe-assisted bombs were dropped by the squadron's commanding officer, Wing Commander Harry Bufton (the brother of Sidney Bufton), and his Australian navigator, Flight Lieutenant Edward Ifould. Two other Mosquitos also dropped but the equipment in the other three aircraft was not working correctly, and so they bombed elsewhere.

All the Mosquitos returned safely from this first Oboe raid, but the post-raid assessment was made difficult because the town had been bombed recently, making it all but impossible to determine the results of the Oboe attack. Another trial raid took place on the last night of 1942 when two of the squadron's Mosquitos were sent to Düsseldorf to mark the target for eight Pathfinder Lancasters. Although only one Mosquito was able to use Oboe to its full effect, bombing appears to have been a success with a number of industrial factories hit.

The Mosquito's performance made it an ideal aircraft to get the best out of Oboe. Its speed meant the time spent over the target was reduced and its operational ceiling of 30,000 feet plus was well above any other aircraft in Bomber Command. Because Oboe worked on line-of-sight, it could be used at far greater range than if fitted to any other type of aircraft, and certainly brought into range all of the industrial Ruhr.

The future for Oboe looked promising, although most of Germany would remain beyond its operational range until the latter half of 1944 when the Allies could operate from airfields in north-west Europe. Furthermore, its limiting factor of only being able to be used by six aircraft per hour was never going to be suitable for large numbers of Pathfinders to mark a target, but it could be used for the primary marking of a raid while non-Oboe Pathfinders followed up.

The technological war had stepped up to another level, but the limitations of Gee and Oboe meant that what was needed most was an on-board system that was completely independent of ground stations; not only to aid navigation but also to permit blind-bombing in all weather, by day or by night.

Among many ideas under consideration was an airborne radar system, the principle of which had already been proved by ASV (air-to-surface vessel, used to detect ships at sea), and other airborne intercept (AI) devices. Trials using an AI set fitted to a Blenheim had proved the concept of ground mapping and so all that was needed was a development of the idea to improve the definition of ground features. Further trials were conducted using a Halifax with a rotating scanner to give all-round mapping and a display for the operator, with the magnetron being used instead of the klystron to produce previously unobtainable power levels and so increase the range. The result of these trials was a device called H2S, the first airborne ground-scanning radar system.

H2S allowed the operator to map the ground below by identifying notable navigation features such as coastlines, towns, lakes and rivers. From these known features, general navigation was relatively easy, although using H2S as a bombing aid would be far more difficult. Using predictions and overlays would help the operator analyse what was being displayed but it would take practice and experience to become good.

Bennett had first seen H2S in the summer of 1942 and was instantly impressed by its potential for the Pathfinders, although there were still many problems to overcome. One was how to stabilize the picture for the operator when the aircraft was in a turn, while another was how to discriminate between important navigational features on the ground from the general clutter being displayed. Nonetheless, the first H2S sets were delivered to 7 and 35 Squadrons at the end of 1942 and within a month were used operationally for the first time. Although the images were then rather crude, they would improve over time to give better definition for the operator.

There were also improvements to target-marking techniques on the horizon as pyrotechnic companies worked hard to develop a new target-marker for the PFF. The result was the purpose-built Target Indicator (TI), a 250 lb bomb casing filled with pyrotechnic candles. Using a barometric fuse they were designed to fall to the ground in a mass of bright colours with red, yellow and green being the standard variants.

It was not long before three main methods of target-marking were developed, with each method named after a place in Bennett's New Zealand. Newhaven was the name given to visually marking the target on the ground while Parramatta was a blind-marking technique. The third method was a sky-marking tactic called Wanganui and in the case where sky marking was carried out by Oboe-equipped Mosquitos it was called Musical Wanganui.

The first main use of TIs was against Berlin on the night of 16/17 January 1943 but the raid turned out to be a disappointment. Berlin was well beyond the range of Gee and Oboe, and it was just too soon for H2S. Navigation along the long route was not helped by areas of dense cloud and Berlin was covered in haze, resulting in scattered bombing.

H2S was, in fact, almost ready and was first used two weeks later against Hamburg. With Hamburg being at the point where the Elbe estuary meets the North Sea, the new device enabled the lead Pathfinders to quickly find the target.

It would not be long before every Pathfinder aircraft was fitted with H2S and within a year there were enough sets to equip the whole of Bomber Command's Main Force. It was a superb technical achievement and turned out to be an excellent radar, with a long life extending way beyond the years of the Second World War. However, the initial belief that H2S could not be jammed did not prove to be the case, and it did not take the Germans long to learn how to listen out for its transmissions, after which the night fighters could home-in.

Further technological advancements also enabled Bomber Command to implement its first radio counter-measures (RCM) to counter the German's own devices. One was *Mandrel*, designed to jam the long-range early warning *Freya* radar, and another was *Tinsel*, a microphone fitted in the bomber's engine bay to blot out the German night fighter communications. In this case the wireless operator would search for the night fighter control frequency and then switch on the transmitter to broadcast the noise of the engine over the frequency in use. Neither of these early devices would cause major problems to the Germans but they were, nonetheless, a nuisance.

In the space of just a couple of months Bomber Command had introduced Oboe, H2S, TIs and RCM. Not only were they individually a significant step forward, collectively they were a massive stride. When an assessment was carried out to determine the effectiveness of the PFF during its first nine months of operations, two distinct phases were identified. The first was from its formation until the end of 1942, when there had been little improvement on the pre-PFF days, but since then, i.e. the second phase, it was estimated that these latest introductions had produced bombing results three-times better than before.

The PFF was fast becoming a highly effective force with volunteers to fill its ranks coming from across the entire spectrum of Bomber Command. There was usually the reward of being given the next rank and more pay. These were great incentives, as was the chance to wear the coveted Pathfinder badge.

A Pathfinder tour was generally forty-five ops rather than the thirty required on the Main Force squadrons. Training varied throughout the course of the war but was typically two weeks at Warboys, with Bennett usually there to welcome the volunteers at the start; such was his keenness to instill on them what it meant to be part of his group.

The Pathfinders learned to adapt their tactics as the war went on. The early principle of illuminating, marking and backing-up was sound but as navigation equipment improved, and with experience over time, techniques became more sophisticated and complex, although the focus always remained on making the bombing as accurate as possible.

Anything that could be done to help the Main Force crews was done. For example, illuminating flares were dropped along the route to aid navigation and to keep the force compact, and with better TIs the aiming point could be emphasized just before they arrived over the target. When large numbers of bombers were involved in a raid, Pathfinders known as 'Supporters' were spread amongst the main stream so that the target could be re-marked after the TIs and incendiaries dropped by the earlier markers had started to fade.

The ratio of Pathfinders to Main Force bombers varied from raid to raid, depending on the target's location and the resources available, but could be anything from as few as 1:15 to as high as 1:3. By 1944 bombing accuracy had improved so much that the majority of the Main Force crews were bombing within 3 miles of the TIs. This accuracy was further improved by the introduction of a Master Bomber. His task was to circle above the target to direct and co-ordinate the attack by broadcasting instructions to the Pathfinders and Main Force. This would also help prevent crews being diverted away from the main target by decoy fires or fake TIs.

Despite the reservations of some, including Harris, the creation of an elite unit within Bomber Command had not had the adverse effect that many had feared. No. 8 Group would go on to fly more than 50,000 operational sorties against nearly 3,500 targets at a huge cost of more than 3,700 lives. There was, of course, a healthy rivalry between all the groups, particularly between the crews of No. 5 Group and the Pathfinder crews of No. 8 Group, but as the PFF continued to grow in size and capability, the future for Bomber Command looked promising.

Chapter Nine

Duel at Night

The rear gunner was on his first operational sortie. Just before reaching the target area special signals gave warning of an approaching aircraft. This proved to be a Focke-Wulf FW 190, which came in to attack but made off without firing when the rear gunner opened fire at 600 yards. Twelve minutes later, after leaving the target, another FW 190 was sighted 500 yards away on the starboard quarter. The rear gunner at once opened fire while the Halifax turned in the direction of attack. The third fighter, encountered twenty minutes later, was most determined. This was a Ju 88 and was first sighted about 1,000 yards away on the port quarter. It passed astern the Halifax and came in on the starboard quarter. The Halifax turned to starboard, at 400 yards both rear and mid-upper gunners fired at the same time as the Halifax corkscrewed. The rear gunner gave the orders for evasive action and remained throughout complete master of the situation. The Halifax returned to base without damage of any kind.

These words are taken from a combat report describing an encounter between a Halifax of 51 Squadron and a number of German night fighters. The special signals mentioned in the report refers to *Monica*, an active system designed to provide the bomber crew with a warning of attack through a series of pips that could be heard on the aircraft's intercom.

Monica was a good idea but as there was no IFF, any aircraft to the rear of the bomber would be detected, and so when flying in a bomber stream the system was known to produce a series of rather annoying pips. To some it even became a nuisance and so the system was modified to produce a visual signal rather than an audio one, although the problem of producing too many signals in large bomber streams never went away.

There is no doubt that *Monica* will have saved many lives, although aircraft in large formations remained at risk of a collision when a bomber suddenly took evasive action. The Germans also learned how to take advantage of the system and the development of the FuG 227 *Flensburg* system, a passive homing device, enabled night fighters to home onto the transmissions of the *Monica* tail-warning device. It was only after the capture of a Ju 88G night fighter fitted with *Flensburg* that British intelligence officers were able to work out how the system worked and this ultimately led to the withdrawal of *Monica* from the Main Force bombers, although it was retained by specialist RCM squadrons.

While *Monica* might not have been as successful as originally hoped, its concept was sound and led to better devices. One was *Fishpond* (originally called *Mousetrap*), an improved version of *Monica* and one that used H2S scanner pulses. The *Fishpond* console was located at the wireless operator's desk and displayed any returned signal between the bomber and the ground, such as another aircraft. But because all returns were displayed the wireless operator had to observe the display closely. He had to determine which of the returns were moving faster than the others, suggesting an enemy night fighter closing in rather than being a return from another bomber in the main stream.

Fishpond could also be used to reduce the risk of mid-air collisions between bombers but for the system to be really effective it relied on the skill and expertise of the operator. Furthermore, because the H2S scanner tilted towards the ground (it was, after all, a ground mapping radar) it meant that only returns detected beneath the bomber were displayed. When flying high this was not so much of a problem but it did become a consideration for the crew when flying lower. There was a further problem, too. German night fighters fitted with FuG 350 *Naxos*, another passive homing device, could home in on the H2S or *Fishpond* transmissions.

The electronic war being fought in the night sky above Europe was a fascinating one but no matter what equipment was fitted on board the bomber its gunners had to maintain a constant vigil. They could not afford to put their lives solely in the hands of an electronic warning device and so they still searched the night sky without daring to relax for even a moment.

Amongst the many operational analyses carried out for Harris was the use of the bomber's guns for self-defence. Statistics showed that it was the rear turret that was mostly in action. For example, in the three months leading up to February 1943, nearly 90 per cent of enemy night fighters engaged had been by rear gunners.

There were many reasons for this. Success for the Nachtjagdflieger was normally the result of teamwork involving the controller on the ground and his own crew. It is certainly easier to carry out a night intercept from the stern. The geometry is easier to manage, as is the fighter's rate of closure. Also, there is little or no deflection when attacking from line astern, whereas firing at a crossing target, or one that is manoeuvring for that matter, needs good judgement to determine the amount of lead required. There was also a good chance of getting in to an attacking position unseen. The closer the night fighter could get the more likely it was to shoot the bomber down. Firing at excessive range meant the rounds fired were subject to the effects of ballistics, such as gravity drop, but if the attacker was to get too close then there was the bomber's defensive armament to take into account.

Shooting down a bomber was far from easy, particularly at night, but for the bomber crew their best form of defence was to avoid confrontation in the first place. Cloud and darkness became their friend. Aircraft performance was also important. Even when a night fighter did find them it still had to manoeuvre into a position from where it could carry out its attack, and so aircraft designers were always keen to improve the bomber's performance without impacting on its overall effectiveness.

For the bomber's gunners, their hydraulically powered turrets meant they could traverse quickly and accurately towards the threat. Enclosed power-operated turrets had been developed during the late 1930s by two engineers, Archibald Frazer-Nash and Grattan Thompson. With four belt-fed 0.303 inch Browning machine guns, which became the standard defensive armament for RAF bombers, the resulting design was the FN4 tail turret. With a rate of fire of 80 rounds per second, it was the most heavily armed turret in service with any air force at that time and was fitted to the Whitley, Wellington, Manchester and early models of the Stirling.

As the war progressed, comments by squadron gunnery leaders led to the FN4 being redesigned to become the FN20 and this became the tail turret most commonly featured on Bomber Command's aircraft. Its modifications included the fitting of an armoured shield to provide the gunner with protection from his front and a clear-vision panel to aid sighting, but the biggest improvement was how the ammunition was supplied. Instead of having ammunition boxes in the turret, large boxes were fitted to the sides of the rear fuselage with the ammunition being fed from the boxes along tracks to the base of the turret.

The rear gunner was known as the 'tail-end Charlie'. From inside his turret he could see no other part of the aircraft unless he traversed to one side. His field of fire was 94 degrees to either beam, 60 degrees in elevation and 45 degrees in depression. It was a lonely existence and he suffered from the cold more than the rest of his crew. In the book *Another Dawn Another Dusk* by Kenneth Ballantyne, Warrant Officer Trevor Bowyer, who flew two operational tours as a rear gunner and was awarded the DFC, describes what it was like to fly as tail-end Charlie in a Lancaster:

> *It is difficult to describe just how cold it got in the aircraft, but especially in the rear turret, which was not really part of the fuselage, but stuck outside it at the end. I was dressed in my thick long johns, a thick vest, a shirt, a sleeveless jersey, a scarf, a thick polo neck jersey, battledress, my Taylor flying suit, which would be heated once I was in the aircraft and plugged it in with my Sidcot suit over the top, heated slippers, fur-lined boots down which I tucked a commando knife and a torch, helmet and goggles. On my hands I wore silk gloves, then a pair of chamois gloves, then fingerless woolen mittens and finally a pair of thick outer leather gauntlets, which plugged into the heated suit. They didn't always work but they were good when they did.*

In the case of having to abandon the aircraft the rear gunner would first have to clip on his chest-type parachute, which was stored on quick-release hooks just outside the turret. He then traversed the turret to the beam stop to allow him to escape; this was done by powering the turret if the hydraulics were still in operation or otherwise manually. He then pulled the pin from his seat harness and fell backwards out of the open double doors. It was a lengthy procedure and in the dark and extremely cold conditions, with the aircraft out of control and under severe gravity forces, it sometimes proved impossible. Yet, tail-end Charlies did survive; in some cases where the rest of his crew perished.

The front turret for most Bomber Command aircraft was the FN5, a compact turret armed with twin Brownings. When fitted in the nose of the Lancaster (as the FN5A), it provided a field of fire of 190 degrees traversal, 60 degrees in elevation and 45 degrees in depression. The Lancaster's mid-upper turret, the FN50, was a development of the FN5 and replaced the FN7 upper turret fitted to the Manchester and Stirling. The FN50 was also fitted with twin Brownings and had an excellent view, with a field of fire of a full 360 degrees traversal, 20 degrees in elevation and 2 degrees in depression. Access to the turret was from the top of the bomb bay on to a step, and up into the turret in a standing position. The gunner then clipped the seat under him.

When a bomber came under attack the method taught to try and throw off the attacker was a manoeuvre called the corkscrew. It consisted of a series of steep diving and climbing turns in alternate directions to make it difficult for the attacker to bring his guns to bear. The manoeuvre required strength on the part of the bomber pilot and when the controls were reversed at the top and bottom parts of the manoeuvre, to change the direction of travel, there were vital seconds when the bomber was extremely vulnerable.

The initial steep dive and turn meant the attacking night fighter did not always have the speed to follow, but this so often depended on the skill of the bomber pilot. An experienced night fighter pilot soon learned to break away and hold off until he anticipated the bomber's change of direction or until it had stopped manoeuvring altogether. Once the bomber had resumed its course the night fighter could attack again. It was, of course, not as easy as it might sound. The manoeuvre was all but impossible to follow on an AI radar display and any amount of cloud for the bomber to hide, or simply the darkness of the night, would often mean the attacker would never see his intended prey again.

Operating conditions were little better for the night fighter crews than they were for the RAF bomber crews, particularly in bad weather. It would take several minutes to climb through seemingly endless layers of cloud, causing the aircraft to buffet and bounce around in the turbulent air, before the night fighter could reach an altitude that would put it above the main bomber stream. It was bitterly cold operating at such heights, even taking into account the electrically heated flying suits worn by the crew. Ideally, they would intercept a bomber on its way to the target rather than on its way home. Not only did this prevent bombs falling on the intended target but when laden with its bomb load and enough fuel to get home the bomber was heavy and cumbersome to handle.

The strain on the Nachtjagd's crews was starting to tell. Not only were they defending the Reich at night but they were being increasingly called upon to fend off the American raids by day. It was during one of these daylight raids, on 26 February 1943, that an early pioneer of night air combat fell. Ludwig Becker was flying a Bf 110G with his usual *Funker*, Josef Staub, when they intercepted a formation of American B-17s over the North Sea. Exactly what happened is unclear but their 110 came down off the Dutch island of Schiermonnikoog.

Becker was posthumously awarded the Oak Leaves to his Knight's Cross for shooting down forty-six aircraft, all at night. Given his expertise as a night fighter pilot, Becker's death by day can be considered a waste. Furthermore, he was killed just two days after the loss of Paul Gildner, another leading night fighter pilot at the time, whose Bf 110G-4 suffered an engine failure and then a fire near Gilze en Rijen. Although his crew colleague managed to escape, Gildner died in the crash. With forty-six night successes to add to his two by day, he was another to be posthumously awarded the Oak Leaves.

If these losses were not bad enough, they had come just three weeks after the death of Hauptmann Reinhold Knacke, the 24-year-old Kapitän of 3./NJG 1, who was another to be posthumously awarded the Oak Leaves for shooting down forty-four aircraft, all at night. Knacke had been flying a Bf 110F-4 (the first 110 sub-variant specifically produced as a night fighter) and was shot down while attacking a Halifax during a raid against Hamburg. Although his *Bordfunker*, Unteroffizier (a junior non-commissioned officer) Kurt Bundrock, managed to bale out of the burning aircraft, Knacke's body was later found in the wreckage near Achterveld in Holland.

With its own casualties also continuing to mount, Bomber Command searched for ways to reduce its losses. One idea under consideration was to improve aircraft performance by reducing the overall weight of the bomber. One piece of analysis looked at the use of gun turrets and ammunition, and from crew reports it became evident that the average number of rounds fired by an air gunner during an engagement was 235, while the maximum was 1,000; and this from a total of 6,000 rounds available for a Lancaster rear gunner, 4,800 rounds for the Stirling and 3,000 for the Halifax.

From this information it was apparent that much of the ammunition carried on sorties was not required or, at least, not being used. The ORS went as far to suggest that a limit of 3,000 rounds be imposed; thus saving weight with an associated improvement in aircraft performance. It was even suggested that consideration might be given to the removal of the front and mid-upper turrets, again to save weight and improve bomber performance, which some analysts felt would far outweigh the loss of firepower.

This last suggestion was a step too far, as was a proposed reduction in ammunition; certainly as far as the bomber crews were concerned. Most felt that the small increase in aircraft performance that might be achieved was not worth sacrificing what little defence they had.

The ORS had also raised concerns about the 0.303 inch machine guns with which the RAF bombers were equipped. Although they proved reliable and gave a high rate of fire, their effectiveness had come into question. Thoughts about fitting heavier-calibre weapons were, for now, put to one side, as was the addition of more armour to increase protection for the crew. These ideas would merely add weight to the aircraft rather than reduce it. It was a difficult balance to strike. The RAF's Official History of the Bomber Offensive would later state:

> *The heavy and medium bombers possessed neither the armament nor the performance seriously to damage the German Night Fighter force in the air. The best their gunners could do with their small calibre weapons was to provide some deterrent to the less skilled or more unwary among the German pilots.*

As the war progressed more improvements would be made to RAF bombers. These included lighter turrets, improved heating systems, electro ammunition feed, gyroscopic gunsights and, as proposed earlier, the heavier-calibre 0.5 inch Browning machine gun. There would even be radar tracking, known as Airborne Gun Laying in Turrets (AGLT), which enabled the rear gunner to engage an attacker even if he could not see it. This was achieved by fitting an antenna to the lower section of the tail turret. Called *Village Inn*, it was first fitted to aircraft of 101 Squadron, a specialist squadron of No. 1 Group based at Ludford Magna, and worked with an early IFF system to prevent the shooting down of friendly aircraft. Two infra-red lamps were fitted into the nose domes of Lancasters and the AGLT-equipped aircraft were fitted with infra-red detectors to detect the emissions.

Modifications such as these would have to wait, and so the RAF's bomber crews were left to take the war to Nazi Germany night after night in the knowledge that they were going up against a powerful adversary. At that stage of the war they knew there was little that could be done about it. The best chance they had of escaping a horrific death at the hands of the night fighter – caused by the mix of fuel, bombs and oxygen – was speed and manoeuvrability. However, the fact remained that not only were their aircraft not as fast as the night fighters defending the Reich, they were also out-manoeuvred and out-gunned.

Chapter Ten

The Ruhr

Your primary object will be the progressive destruction and dislocation of the German military, industrial and economic system, and the undermining of the morale of the German people to a point where their capacity for armed resistance is fatally weakened.

Today, the state of North Rhine-Westphalia, formed after the Second World War as a merger of the northern Rhineland and Westphalia, both formerly parts of Prussia, is the most populous in Germany and the fourth largest by area. Four of Germany's ten biggest cities – Cologne, Dortmund, Düsseldorf and Essen - are located within the state, as is the biggest metropolitan area of the European continent, the Rhine-Ruhr, with a population in excess of 10 million. The majority live in the Ruhr region (the Ruhr valley), the largest urban agglomeration in Germany and consisting of several large industrial cities bordered by the rivers Ruhr to the south, Rhine to the west, and Lippe to the north. As well as the state's four largest cities, the region also includes Bochum, Bottrop, Duisburg, Gelsenkirchen, Oberhausen and Wuppertal; all of which have grown into a vast industrial landscape.

During the Second World War about two-thirds of Germany's hard coal and coking coke came from the Ruhr area. With this as a basis, combined with the fact that the Ruhr was a hub of communications routes (road, rail and water), it was an obvious location for heavy industry. It was also a compact region with the main industrial belt stretching no more than 30 miles from east to west, and containing many key industrial cities and towns.

Of these, Essen, with its huge Krupps arms and engineering factories, was probably the most important, with the surrounding areas containing numerous foundries and engineering works, coal mines and coking plants. Dortmund also contained a variety of engineering works while Bochum, situated between Dortmund and Essen, was a centre for the coal and coke industry. It was also surrounded by the usual associated industries of petroleum and chemicals, including the manufacturing of explosives, as well as the principal high-grade steel works producing heavy armament such as gun barrels, armour plate and aircraft components. Duisburg, meanwhile, occupied a key position at the junction of the Rhine and Ruhr rivers, and had the largest inland port in Europe. And so it went on.

For Bomber Command, improvements in technology and the development of better tactics and target-marking techniques were now starting to bear fruit. For the first time in the war there were significant signs of improvements in navigation and bombing accuracy, while an increased tonnage of bombs was now being delivered on target. By concentrating resources and prioritizing effort it was estimated that by the end of 1943 the combined Anglo-American bombing force could deliver 50,000 tons of bombs every month, rising to 90,000 tons by 1944 when a total of 6,000 heavy bombers would be available.

Staff papers floating around the RAF's hierarchy suggested such a force *'could shatter the industrial and economic structure of Germany to a point where an Anglo-American force of reasonable strength could enter the Continent from the West'* and included comments such as *'Germany is in no condition to withstand an onslaught of this nature, her strength has passed its peak and is diminishing'*. One paper went on to say:

> *It is difficult to estimate the moral consequences of a scale of bombardment which would far transcend anything within human experience. But I have no doubt that against a background of growing casualties, increasing privations and dying hopes it would be profound indeed.*

Bomber Command had entered 1943 with sixty squadrons, of which more than half were heavies. Things were looking up and the year ahead would finally see the command deliver the long promised destructive power, and with previously unheard of accuracy. Indeed, the positive signs were already there. For example, the *Bomber Command Quarterly Review* analysed the effect of the bombing campaign upon the Ruhr during 1942 and reported:

Throughout 1942 our blows became increasingly severe. The German High Command could do nothing but apportion a still greater number of much-needed guns and, above all, fighter aircraft, to the defence of their western front.

Harris would later describe 1942 as the 'preliminary phase', during which techniques had been developed and technology had moved forward, while he saw 1943 as a new start and was keen to return to the heavy poundings of German towns and cities.

But Harris was still unable to get his own way and for millions of civilians in towns and cities across Germany the opening weeks of 1943 were the quietest of the war. Harris had been issued with a revised directive stating that future policy was: to render material assistance to the Russians; to prepare for the re-conquest of Europe; and to soften up north-west Europe by the bombing of the German industrial and economic system, submarine construction, sources of air power, and morale of the German people. He had also been instructed to renew an offensive against the U-boat bases on the Atlantic coastline of France.

To Harris it must have seemed like he was being told to cover everything but he was given some latitude as the latest directive had gone on to state that these attacks were not to prejudice concentrated raids on Berlin or on other important objectives in Germany.

This more broad instruction suited him. It meant that he did not have to become tied down to using his resources against what he might have considered to be unprofitable or unsuitable targets. And so a raid against Berlin on the night of 16/17 January 1943 was significant for more than one reason. Not only was it the first time that Bomber Command had been back to the Nazi capital for well over a year, but it was also the first time that a large attacking force of more than 200 aircraft had been made up totally of four-engine heavy bombers.

Heavy bombers were now rolling off the production lines in great numbers. By February Bomber Command could boast sixty-three operational squadrons, including nine Wellington and Halifax squadrons of the newly formed No. 6 (Canadian) Group based in North Yorkshire and Durham, plus the training units of Nos 91, 92 and 93 Groups. Harris now had available to him a notional strength of a thousand aircraft, some two-thirds of which were heavies, with nearly half being Lancasters.

For the first time the combined effort of the Main Force squadrons had delivered 1,000 tons of bombs on target in a single raid. It would not be long before the monthly total exceeded 20,000 tons, three times what had been possible just a year before, and by the time Bomber Command went to Cologne on the night of 26/27 February it was able to send well over 400 aircraft. However, because of all the other tasks, this latest raid was only the fifth against the Nazi homeland that month.

Fortunately for Harris things were about to change, the origins of which stem from the meeting of Allied leaders at Casablanca earlier in the year. Included in the long and complicated agenda was the prosecution of the combined Anglo-American bombing offensive against Germany, the outcome of which was a broad statement behind the Combined Bomber offensive for 1943, as stated at the top of the chapter:

> *Your primary object will be the progressive destruction and dislocation of the German military, industrial and economic system, and the undermining of the morale of the German people to a point where their capacity for armed resistance is fatally weakened.*

The directive issued by the Combined Chiefs of Staff went on to detail five main areas to attack: submarine construction yards; aircraft industry; transportation; oil plants; and 'others in the war industry'. None of this was new, of course, but again the broadness of the directive suited Harris.

It was a clear call to the advocates of strategic bombing to prove their case. Harris had now assembled a team of group commanders that, in the main, would see Bomber Command through to the end of the war. At the beginning of March he launched a sustained attack on Germany, with its opening phase aimed at flattening the vital factories in the industrial heartland of the Ruhr. It was the start of what would later become known as the Battle of the Ruhr, and for Harris it marked the start of his command's all-out effort that he would later call his 'main offensive'.

The opening raid on the night of 5/6 March was against the elusive target of Essen. Led by Oboe-equipped Pathfinders, it involved 442 aircraft.

The bombing lasted for forty minutes and was carried out in three waves – Halifaxes in front, Wellingtons and Stirlings behind, and lastly the Lancasters. One of the main targets, the Krupps works, received several hits with further damage being caused to the surrounding areas and towards the city centre.

During the coming weeks two-thirds of Bomber Command's effort would be against the Ruhr, although there were raids against other targets in Germany as well. This prevented the target area becoming too predictable and so three nights later the Main Force went to Nuremberg, a city well beyond the Ruhr. It was also beyond the range of Oboe and so a combination of H2S and visual marking techniques had to be used.

In terms of numbers, the raid was not as big as Essen but it still involved 335 aircraft. Although Nuremberg was clear of cloud, haze made visual identification difficult and so bombing was spread over a wide area, with more than half the bombs falling outside the city.

One Stirling mid-upper gunner serving with 7 Squadron, 21-year-old Sergeant Derek Spanton, had an unusual tale to tell after the raid. His aircraft was on its way back to Oakington, when over the English coast he realized he was the only member of the crew left on board. It is possible the Stirling was short of fuel but it had continued flying on its automatic pilot. Spanton had clearly not heard the order to abandon the aircraft and finally baled out over Kent before the aircraft came down in the Thames Estuary. His colleagues, however, were less fortunate. They may have believed they were overland at the time they had all baled out but were instead over the sea. They are remembered on the Runnymede Memorial for the missing. Sadly, Derek Spanton would also lose his life with another crew just five months later.

Following raids against Munich and Stuttgart, Bomber Command returned to the Ruhr on the night of 12/13 March. Again, the target was Essen and it was another big effort with more than 450 aircraft taking part. The use of Oboe ensured marking was good and the raid was a success. The Krupps works were again the focus of attention with the post-raid assessment reporting that considerably more damage, as much as 30 per cent more, had been achieved on this raid than the week before.

But not all raids were successful and the next, in late March against the city of Duisburg, was one that was not. A similar force to the size sent to Essen earlier in the month took part but it was a cloudy night over the Ruhr. The Pathfinding Mosquitos experienced technical difficulties with Oboe, which all added to the bombing being scattered.

Bomber Command's next two major efforts were against Berlin before it returned to Essen for a third time on the night of 3/4 April. Although the overall force was smaller than the two previous raids in March, it was the first time more than 200 Lancasters took part in a raid. The weather forecast suggested conditions might not be good enough for ground-marking and so a secondary plan was also put together for sky-marking. As things were to turn out, both methods were used because of the varying conditions over Essen. This, however, caused some confusion amongst the Main Force crews, although bombing overall was accurate and resulted in widespread damage to the city.

The following week the Main Force returned to Duisburg to put right the disappointment of the previous attempt. But again the crews arrived over the city to find it covered by cloud. The result of the bombing, as before, was scattered. Then, at the end of the month, a third raid against Duisburg took place with 561 aircraft taking part. It was the biggest raid against the Ruhr so far but despite the weight of numbers the raid was another disappointment with most bombs falling outside the city.

By the middle of May there had been four more heavy raids against the Ruhr: a fourth to Essen; one to Dortmund, the biggest raid of the campaign so far with nearly 600 aircraft taking part; a fourth to Duisburg, with this raid at last proving a success; and one to Bochum, which only achieved limited success due to decoy fires. This latest raid against Bochum, carried out on the night of 13/14 May, was the last for ten days as there was a temporary lull in operations over the Ruhr because a specialist raid, codenamed Operation *Chastise*, was about to take place.

Because of the importance of the industrial Ruhr to the Nazi war machine, the dams in the Ruhr valley had been studied in great detail. Although the Ruhr did not rely totally on water from the dams for the generation of electricity, it was estimated that it consumed around 25 per cent of Germany's water and so any breach of the dams would impact on hydroelectricity generation, as well as causing mass destruction in the area through severe flooding.

The story of the daring low-level attack against the Ruhr dams by Lancasters of 617 Squadron, the legendary Dam Busters, which was carried out on the night of 16/17 May 1943, has been well documented over the years. It has rightly earned the crews that took part their own special place in the history of air warfare. With two of the primary dams breached, one on the Möhne and the other on the Eder, which resulted in widespread devastation across the area, *Chastise* was understandably considered a success. The press were quick to report:

> *Tonight walls of water swept down the Ruhr and Eder valleys in Germany, destroying everything before them, after the RAF had attacked and breached two dams. The raids, by specially fitted Lancaster bombers using new 'bouncing' bombs, were planned to cripple Germany's vital industrial heartland.*

But the raid proved costly for the squadron, with eight of the nineteen Lancasters failing to return and the loss of fifty-three lives. A total of thirty-four gallantry awards were made to the survivors, including the Victoria Cross to 24-year-old Wing Commander Guy Gibson for leading the raid. His citation includes:

> *Under his inspiring leadership, this squadron has now executed one of the most devastating attacks of the war – the breaching of the Möhne and Eder dams. The task was fraught with danger and difficulty. Wing Commander Gibson personally made the initial attack on the Möhne dam. Descending to within a few feet of the water and taking the full brunt of the anti-aircraft defences, he delivered his attack with great accuracy. Afterwards he circled very low for thirty minutes, drawing the enemy fire on himself in order to leave as free a run as possible to the following aircraft which were attacking the dam in turn. Wing Commander Gibson then led the remainder of his force to the Eder dam where, with complete disregard for his own safety, he repeated his tactics and once more drew on himself the enemy fire so that the attack could be successfully developed. Wing Commander Gibson has completed over 170*

sorties, involving more than 600 hours operational flying. Throughout his
operational career, prolonged exceptionally at his own request, he has shown
leadership, determination and valour of the highest order.

A week later Bomber Command resumed the Battle of the Ruhr with
a second attack on Dortmund. With the Main Force having enjoyed
something of a rest from ops, an all-out effort was ordered for the night of
23/24 May. The mixed force of Lancasters, Halifaxes, Stirlings, Wellingtons
and Mosquitos – a total of 826 aircraft – was the largest since the Thousand
Bomber raids a year before and the largest to attack a single target during
this latest campaign. It was also a new record for the number of Lancasters
taking part; a total of 343. The raid was a success. Many industrial buildings
and factories were hit during the attack, so much so that Bomber Command
was able to leave this target alone for another year.

Amongst the many stories of the Dortmund raid that night is the
extraordinary tale of 21-year-old Sergeant Stuart 'Scotty' Sloan, an
Englishman serving with a Canadian squadron. Sloan was the bomb aimer
of a Wellington Mk X of 431 (Iroquois) Squadron RCAF based at Burn
in Yorkshire. Having completed its attack the Wellington became coned by
searchlights and was badly damaged after being hit several times by flak.
Despite taking evasive action, the pilot could not shake off the searchlights
and remained under sustained heavy fire. The situation had become so
critical that the pilot ordered the crew to bale out but by the time Sloan was
about to leave the aircraft he realized that two of the crew members had not
heard the order and were still on board.

With the pilot having already left the aircraft, Sloan took the controls
and managed to get the Wellington under control. Still harassed by flak and
searchlights, he carried out a number of manoeuvres to escape the enemy
defences. Then, once they were out of immediate danger, he set course for
home. He then discussed with his two colleagues still on board whether they
should abandon the aircraft or not, but they all decided to stay.

Inside the Wellington a gale was blowing through the fuselage from where
the escape hatch had been left open. It could not be closed and the rear
turret door was also open. The lights had been extinguished, making it very
dark inside the fuselage, but the navigator, Sergeant George Parslow, still

managed to plot a course for home. Throughout the return flight he and the wireless operator, 22-year-old Flying Officer John Bailey, assisted Sloan in every way and eventually the badly damaged bomber was back over the Norfolk coast. They again discussed whether Parslow and Bailey should abandon the aircraft while Sloan attempted a landing, but they both decided to stay. Then, having found an airfield, Sloan displayed great skill and determination in nursing the aircraft down to make an emergency landing.

The Wellington had landed at Cranwell in Lincolnshire. In appalling circumstances, Sloan, Parslow and Bailey had displayed great courage, determination and fortitude of the highest order for which Sloan was awarded the Conspicuous Gallantry Medal (CGM), while Parslow received the DFM and Bailey the DFC. When the facts unfolded about the events that night, Sloan's senior officers were so impressed that he was instantly commissioned and posted for pilot training; he later returned to Bomber Command as a Halifax pilot and survived the war, adding a DFC to his earlier decoration. Unfortunately, though, George Parslow and John Bailey were not so lucky. After their ordeal during the Dortmund raid that night they were crewed with the squadron commander, Wing Commander John Coverdale, but the crew were reported missing just a month later.

With Bomber Command regularly putting large numbers of aircraft over a single target, there were concerns, not least amongst the crews, about the risk of a collision with a friendly aircraft or from being hit by bombs or incendiaries dropped from another aircraft above. But a report looking into the instances of aircraft being hit by ordnance from other bombers concluded that the risk was small; less than 1 per cent. Although these risks could be kept to a minimum, by separating the bombers in time and space, they could never be removed altogether as highlighted in the next raid on the Ruhr, just two nights later, when the target was Düsseldorf.

The raid involved more than 750 aircraft but was a failure, largely due to the amount of cloud over the target. One aircraft to be hit by a small incendiary dropped by another bomber above was a Lancaster of 106 Squadron. The crew were lucky. The incendiary had passed straight through the rear fuselage, causing little damage.

A second aircraft, however, a Stirling of 149 Squadron, suffered far more damage after being hit by five incendiaries dropped from above. One incendiary passed through the cockpit roof and out through the bomb doors, just missing the aircraft's controls, while another passed through the fuselage and bomb bay, severing the bomb fusing and release cables. A third passed through the wing root into the fuselage, destroying three batteries and damaging control cables. The fourth had torn away the corner of a fuel tank and passed into the undercarriage bay, tearing and puncturing a tyre, while the fifth had hit the starboard outer engine, tearing away the corner of an oil tank and causing the engine to seize due to the lack of oil. The Stirling was not lost though. Somehow, the crew managed to get it back to Lakenheath.

It was not just over the target area that the risk of collision existed. The risk was seemingly just as great over the eastern part of England where hundreds of bombers took off from their airfields and then climbed through layers of cloud to form up into the main bomber stream for the transit across the North Sea and onwards to the target. While the risk of collision could be reduced by choreographing the departure to some extent, for example by staggering take-off times for each squadron and by issuing altitude blocks for crews to fly in, the recovery at the end of the raid could not be planned. Aircraft staggered home in the dark at all altitudes and at any time. The risks were more than obvious.

By the end of May 1943 there had been two further large-scale attacks on the Ruhr; against Essen and Wuppertal. These latest raids brought the number of individual sorties flown against the Ruhr in the past five nights to 2,000, with the attack against Wuppertal on the 29th/30th resulting in five of the city's six largest factories destroyed. It proved to be the outstanding success of the Battle of the Ruhr.

There were, however, losses that night with thirty-three bombers failing to return. For one young Nachtjagdflieger, Heinz-Wolfgang Schnaufer, it was a night of double-success. Schnaufer had been posted to the night fighter force straight from training at the age of nineteen, and while serving with NJG 1 had claimed his first victim, a Halifax of 76 Squadron, during the second of the RAF's Thousand Bomber raids. For the following year he had scored steadily, but not spectacularly, and his two claims during the early hours of 30 May 1943, a Stirling of 218 Squadron and a Halifax of

35 Squadron, brought his total to eleven. A translation of part of his combat report for that night reads:

> *At about 0035 hours I was directed on to an incoming enemy aircraft at an altitude of 3,500 metres [approximately 11,500 feet]. It was located on the radar and after further instructions I made out a four-engined bomber at 0045 hours, about 200 metres away above and to the right. I attacked the violently evading bomber from behind and below at a range of 80 metres, and my rounds started a bright fire in the left wing. The blazing enemy aircraft turned and dived steeply away, hitting the ground and exploding violently at 0048 hours."*

Increasing losses imposed a growing strain on Bomber Command. The majority were put down to the growing strength and efficiency of the German defences, not least the improved technical capability of the Luftwaffe's night fighters. The RAF had its own AI-equipped night fighters but they were unable to differentiate between an enemy night fighter and a friendly bomber. However, by the middle of June, advances in technology had seen the introduction of *Serrate*, a radar detection and homing device designed to track Luftwaffe night fighters equipped with the *Lichtenstein* radar.

Developed by the TRE, *Serrate* was fitted to the Bristol Beaufighter VIfs of 141 Squadron at Wittering under the command of 23-year-old Wing Commander Bob Braham. The son of a Methodist minister, Braham was an outstanding and highly decorated night fighter pilot with a DSO and a DFC and Bar. His squadron was allocated the role of bomber support and flew its first operations with *Serrate* on the night of 14/15 June when escorting nearly 200 Lancasters to Oberhausen. Flying with his trusted radar operator, Flying Officer Bill 'Sticks' Gregory, Braham claimed a Bf 110 that night to the north of the Dutch town of Stavoren on the coast of the Ijsselmeer. It was his fourteenth success of the war.

The squadron's first use of *Serrate* that night was the start of a series of operational trials lasting for nearly three months. Although *Serrate* could not give the Beaufighter crew the range of an enemy night fighter, it did give its bearing and elevation, and from this information they could get into a position from where their own AI radar could be used to detect the enemy night fighter. However, because the two pieces of equipment shared the same displays in the cockpit, they could not both be used at the same time.

The tactic generally employed when using *Serrate* was for the Beaufighter to fly just off the main stream while mimicking the characteristics of a bomber. When its rearward-facing *Serrate* picked up the radar emissions of an enemy night fighter, the radar operator would direct the pilot until it was estimated that the enemy night fighter was about a mile behind. At that point the Beaufighter would swiftly turnabout to a position where it was now astern the enemy aircraft, at which point its own forward-looking AI radar would be used to locate the enemy night fighter. It was then a case of trying to shoot it down.

By the end of the trial the squadron had flown more than 200 operational sorties during which its crews succeeded in achieving more than a thousand *Serrate* contacts. But less than 10 per cent of these had been converted into AI radar contacts and of these just thirty led to visual sightings, with only twenty resulting in an actual intercept. But once an intercept did take place success was often achieved, with fourteen enemy night fighters claimed as shot down for the loss of three Beaufighters.

While the number of *Serrate* contacts was encouraging the fact that less than 2 per cent were ever converted into actual intercepts was less so, although this was put down more to the Beaufighter's lack of performance than any technical problems with the equipment, an analysis that would soon lead to the fitting of *Serrate* into Mosquito night fighters.

Meanwhile, June 1943 had seen the campaign against industrial targets in the Ruhr step up another gear: Düsseldorf (the night of 11/12 June); Bochum (12th/13th); Oberhausen (14th/15th); Cologne (16th/17th); Krefeld (21st/22nd), Mülheim (22nd/23rd); Wuppertal (24th/25th); Gelsenkirchen (25th/26th); and Cologne again (28th/29th). It was relentless. These nine raids alone, carried out in the space of just over two weeks had seen another 4,650 individual sorties flown against the Ruhr. By the time Bomber Command flew its last raid of the campaign, against Gelsenkirchen on the night of 9/10 July, a further 1,300 sorties had been flown. It was a huge effort.

There were two final raids against the Ruhr before the end of July; one against Essen and the other Remscheid, which had previously been left alone during the campaign, to mark the end of the Battle of the Ruhr. The campaign had lasted more than four months with Bomber Command having flown nearly 20,000 individual sorties. At its peak it had been able to send more than 800 bombers to a target with 80 per cent being four-engine heavies. It had also been a costly one, with 900 aircraft lost in all.

The campaign had produced mixed results but there was no doubting that key industrial premises in the heartland of the Ruhr had been left in ruin, as were many military establishments and government buildings. Life in the cities had often been brought to a halt during the heavy air raids because the German defences had been unable to identify the intended target until the raid was in progress. With air raid sirens wailing across cities throughout the Ruhr on a regular basis, production in many factories was severely disrupted or came to a halt. Inevitably, though, there were civilian casualties in the thousands while the number bombed out of their homes was reported to be in the hundreds of thousands. One raid alone, against Cologne on the night of 28/29 June, had left a reported 4,377 dead, higher than in any previous Bomber Command raid of the war, and another 10,000 injured, while an estimated 230,000 had been forced to leave their homes.

For the Pathfinders, the campaign against the Ruhr led to No. 8 Group being given additional resources; 97 Squadron's Lancasters were provided by No. 5 Group while the newly formed No. 6 Group provided Halifaxes of 405 Squadron RCAF. The PFF had also gained a new met unit, 1409 (Meteorological) Flight, tasked with carrying out daily weather reconnaissance flights ahead of the night's operations.

As the RAF shuffled its pack there were other changes to Bomber Command. With planning for an Allied landing in north-west Europe now well underway, No. 2 Group was transferred to the newly created 2nd Tactical Air Force. Through all that had been going on in the night war over occupied Europe, the light and medium-bomber squadrons of No. 2 Group had courageously continued to take the fight to the enemy, with countless daylight attacks against some of the most heavily defended targets; the last taking place on 31 May 1943, the day before No. 2 Group left Bomber Command.

The end of the campaign against the Ruhr brought a temporary halt to large-scale raids against targets in Germany as, for now, Bomber Command turned its attention elsewhere.

Chapter Eleven

Gathering Pace

It is better to cause a high degree of destruction in a few really essential industries than to cause a small degree of destruction in many industries.

The height of the Ruhr offensive had seen yet another directive land on Harris's desk. It had come following the Allied Conference held in Washington in May 1943, during which discussions had taken place about the progress of, and future plans for, the Combined Bomber Offensive. One plan under consideration was that put forward by the commander of the American Eighth Air Force, General Ira Eaker, an advocate of daylight precision bombing of military and industrial targets, and the words above are taken from his so-called Eaker Plan.

The directive that emerged from all this, issued in June, brought into effect a Combined Bombing Strategy called 'Pointblank', ordering Bomber Command and the Eighth Air Force to bomb specific targets with the intention of destroying, or at least crippling, the German aircraft fighter strength. This was to reduce its effectiveness and ensure that it would not become an obstacle for the forthcoming Allied landings and breakout into north-west Europe.

Until that point Bomber Command and the Eighth Air Force had mostly been attacking German industry in their own way, but the overall strategic plan now called for the Americans to attack stated targets by day and for Bomber Command to hit the same area by night. As far as attacks on the German aircraft industry was concerned, it was pointed out that:

If the growth of the German fighter strength is not arrested quickly it may become literally impossible to carry out the destruction planned and thus to create the conditions necessary for ultimate decisive action by our combined forces on the Continent.

There was now the realization that air superiority was a basic pre-requisite for a successful bombing campaign. There was nothing particularly new in this as Harris had earlier asked Fighter Command to consider using Mosquito fighters as escort to the main bomber stream. But this concept was only just becoming practicable as Fighter Command introduced offensive patrols against German night fighter airfields. Codenamed *Flower*, these patrols coincided with the main bomber stream crossing the enemy coast. This idea was then further developed under *Mahmoud* patrols when the RAF's AI-equipped night fighters patrolled the vicinity of the Luftwaffe's night fighter airfields.

The night war over Germany had moved on. It was no longer just about mass bombing and all-out efforts, although this concept would always remain, but the Dams raid, for example, had shown that success against targets of both tactical and strategic importance could be achieved in different ways. Another example of how effective a specialist raid could be was Operation *Bellicose*, carried out on the night of 20/21 June 1943. While Bomber Command's Main Force was carrying out its campaign against targets in the Ruhr, a small force of sixty Lancasters, mostly from No. 5 Group, were tasked with attacking the Zeppelin works at Friedrichshafen where *Würzburg* radar sets were being made.

The city of Friedrichshafen lies on the northern shore of Lake Constance (the Bodensee) in southern Germany. It had become an important industrial area with companies such as Zeppelin, Dornier and Zahnradfabrik employing hundreds of prisoners from concentration camps, such as Dachau, nearby. In addition to attacking the Zeppelin works at Friedrichshafen, Operation *Bellicose* was also to be the first shuttle raid of the war, meaning that after the attack the bombers were to fly on to land in North Africa, where they would refuel and re-arm before mounting another attack on their way home.

Operation *Bellicose* would also see the concept of the Master Bomber tried once again. Guy Gibson's successful co-ordination of the Dams raid, the month before, had shown just how effective this idea could be and chosen to be Master Bomber for the Friedrichshafen raid was Group Captain Leonard Slee, the former CO of 49 Squadron. He was to fly on board one of the squadron's Lancasters flown by Squadron Leader Gerry Fawke, while four Lancasters of 97 Squadron were to mark the target.

On 16 June the Pathfinder crews left their home base at Bourn for the short flight to Scampton where they reported for 'special duties'. There they gathered with crews from 49 Squadron (based at Fiskerton) and the Australians of 467 (RAAF) Squadron (Bottesford) to be briefed for the raid. The crews were told the raid needed to be carried out by the end of the month, during the next period of full moon. They were also told that because of the excessively long transit and the short summer nights they would have to fly on to Allied airfields in Algeria – at Maison Blanche and Blida – rather than risk returning across France in daylight. Once in Algeria their aircraft would be refuelled and re-armed ready to carry out another attack on the way home.

With the main target being the dirigible factory at the Zeppelin works, the Pathfinder crews worked out the best tactics to employ and practised for the raid using the airship sheds at RAF Cardington in Bedfordshire. Then, on the evening of 20 June, sixty Lancasters took off from Scampton to carry out the raid. After crossing the coastline of northern France, the force headed towards the Rhine. Gerry Fawke's crew report reads:

Approaching the French coast at 19,000 feet, we encountered heavy cloud and electric storms up to 24,000 feet. We therefore decided to come down below the front and lost height to 5,000 feet. We were suddenly engaged by the defences of Caen or the outer defences of Le Havre – owing to technical difficulties with navigation instruments we were then uncertain of our exact position. Four 4-gun heavy flak positions engaged us for about four minutes. During this time we altered course by about 30 degrees every eight seconds, alternately losing and gaining height by 1,000 feet. The flak bursts were mainly 300–500 feet behind and about the same distance above us. It was noticed that the rate of fire of the guns was extremely high. We flew on below cloud at 2,500–3,000 feet across France and encountered no further opposition.

It was while crossing France that Fawke's aircraft then suffered a technical problem. His crew report describes what happened:

Three-quarters of an hour's flying time from Lake Constance it was necessary to feather the port engine, which was emitting showers of sparks, so we continued on three engines until we sighted the lake. By that time we had increased height to 6,000 feet. As the port–inner engine is essential for the Mark XIV bombsight, it was un–feathered and allowed to windmill, but shortly afterwards the engine caught fire. We were unable to feather it or extinguish the fire, which grew in intensity. The captain then jettisoned the bombs, told the Deputy Leader to take over and gave the order to prepare to abandon the aircraft, first diving across the lake into Switzerland and subsequently turning the aircraft towards Germany. We were about to bale out, expecting the petrol tanks to explode, when the engine seized and the fire went out. By this time we had descended to 4,000 feet but were able to maintain height.

Although he was able to carry on with just three engines providing power, Fawke was unable to climb to a suitable altitude from where Slee could co-ordinate the attack and so responsibility for directing the raid was passed to the nominated deputy, Wing Commander Cosme Gomm, the Australian commander of 467 (RAAF) Squadron.

Having arrived in the target area the plan was for two of the Pathfinders to run-in at 5,000 feet, dropping a line of flares from the city of Friedrichshafen to the Zeppelin works. The two remaining Pathfinders were to use these flares to find the sheds and then mark the target using a mix of red and green TIs, offset slightly to avoid covering the target in smoke.

As soon as the Pathfinders began their run-in the sky lit up with searchlights and flak. But the crews remained at their specified height to successfully mark the approach and target. Bombing was then carried out in two parts. While some bombed the TIs dropped by the Pathfinders, others ran in from Lake Constance to attack, using time and distance calculations from the shore to arrive overhead the works.

To ensure the greatest accuracy, bombing should have been carried out in bright moonlight at a height somewhere between 5,000 and 10,000 feet but because of the intense searchlights and heavy flak in the target area, Gomm directed the force to bomb from higher instead. Holding over Lake Constance and watching the raid take place was Fawke and his crew. Their report describes what happened next:

Whitleys of 58 Squadron at Linton-on-Ouse pictured at dusk waiting for the night's op. The squadron was involved on the opening night of the war when seven of its aircraft dropped leaflets over German cities. Although the Whitley was still relatively new in service, it would soon equip eight squadrons of No. 4 Group based in Yorkshire and was the RAF's only twin-engine medium bomber in service at the time to have been designed with night operations in mind. (*58 Squadron records*)

Hampdens and crews of 49 Squadron at Scampton. The Hampden served with No. 5 Group, mostly in Lincolnshire, and played an integral part in the full range of Bomber Command's operations during the early period of the war, but it did not take long for the limitations of this aircraft to become apparent. (*via the Lincolnshire Echo*)

Flight Lieutenant Rod Learoyd, a Hampden pilot serving with 49 Squadron, was awarded Bomber Command's first Victoria Cross of the Second World War for his courage while attacking the Dortmund-Ems Canal on the night of 12/13 August 1940. (*AHB*)

Major Wolfgang Falck, the son of a priest, was given command of the Luftwaffe's first night fighter wing, NJG 1, in the summer of 1940. It had been his tactical appraisal on how to intercept enemy aircraft at night that led to his appointment. It turned out to be an inspired one as Falck quickly became an early influencer of Germany's night war. (*Chris Goss collection*)

During the early stages of the war it was the twin-engine Messerschmitt Bf 110 that offered the Luftwaffe the most potential as a night fighter. The aircraft initially used in this role were standard daytime Bf 110s painted in an all-black scheme with additional modifications such as the fitting of flame dampers to the engine exhausts and modified cockpit lighting for night operations. (*Chris Goss collection*)

Josef Kammhuber, a Luftwaffe career officer in his forties, was the pioneer of Germany's night war and set up the first truly successful night fighter defence system. The system he put in place became known to the RAF's bomber crews as the Kammhuber Line. (*Chris Goss collection*)

Wellington crews of 149 Squadron at Mildenhall walk out to their aircraft ahead of another trip to the Reich. It is believed the picture was taken during the evening of 10 May 1941. If so, the target that night was Hamburg. (*AHB*)

As the war entered its second year the Luftwaffe sought other ways of hitting the RAF bombers and one idea was to fly intruder missions over eastern England. Despite some success, these missions never really impacted on Bomber Command's night war on Germany and also proved costly for the Luftwaffe. For one Ju 88 crew their lives were cut short during the early hours of 12 May 1941 when their aircraft was shot down by Scampton's anti-aircraft defences. They were given a military funeral in the local village. (*RAF Scampton*)

St John the Baptist churchyard at Scampton today. The two nearest graves (front row) and the two immediately behind in the second row are those of the Ju 88 crew killed on 12 May 1941. The furthest right (second row) is a double plot and includes the remains of a fifth member on board that night – one of the ground crew who had gone along for the experience, whose remains were not discovered until the aircraft was dug up in the 1960s. The two graves on the left of the front row and the two immediately behind are those of a Ju 88 crew killed in the early hours of 4 May 1945 during Operation *Gisela*. (*Author*)

Sergeant Jimmy Flint, a Hampden pilot serving with 49 Squadron at Scampton, had the unique distinction of being awarded two gallantry awards (the Distinguished Flying Medal and George Medal) for separate acts of bravery during the same mission against Osnabrück on the night of 5/6 July 1941. He would later add a DFC to his awards. (*via Bill Flint*)

In February 1942 Bomber Command acquired at its head the man who was to inspire and lead it for the rest of the war. That man was Air Marshal Arthur Harris whose appointment was welcomed amongst the squadrons as it came at a time when the command's fortunes and spirits were at a low ebb. (*AHB*)

Wellingtons of 12 Squadron pictured at Binbrook on the evening of 25 February 1942. The target that night was the German naval dockyards at Kiel. (*RAF Wickenby Memorial Collection via Anne Law*)

Hauptmann Helmut Lent, a holder of the Knight's Cross, pictured in March 1942 while Kommandeur of the recently formed II./NJG 2 based at Leeuwarden in Holland. At this time the 24-year-old ace had been credited with shooting down thirty aircraft, all but five being RAF bombers. Many more would follow. (*Chris Goss collection*)

Flying Officer Leslie Manser, a 20-year-old Manchester pilot serving with 50 Squadron, was posthumously awarded the Victoria Cross following Bomber Command's first Thousand Bomber raid against Cologne on the night of 30/31 May 1942. (*50 & 61 Squadrons' Association via the Manser family*)

Oberleutnant Egmont Prinz zur Lippe-Weissenfeld (left), a 23-year-old Austrian of royal descent and the Staffelkapitän of 5./NJG 2, pictured after his award of the Knight's Cross for shooting down four RAF bombers in a single night on 26/27 March 1942 to take his total to twenty-one. In the centre is Oberfeldwebel Paul Gildner and on the right is Feldwebel Müller. (*Chris Goss collection*)

Lancasters pictured at dusk waiting to take-off for another night raid on Germany. The Lancaster was the third of Bomber Command's four-engine heavies to enter operational service and finally gave Harris the aircraft he needed to carry out his strategic bombing offensive against the Reich. (*Author's collection*)

Lancaster Is of 83 Squadron pictured at Scampton during June 1942. The aircraft in the foreground (R5620) 'OL-H' went missing soon after this photo was taken. Flown by 20-year-old Pilot Officer Jim Farrow from New Zealand, it failed to return from a raid against Bremen on the night of 25/26 June. (*RAF Scampton*)

Spectacular night image of Bremen on the night of 2/3 July 1942, taken by a 97 Squadron crew at Woodhall Spa. (*via Ken Delve*)

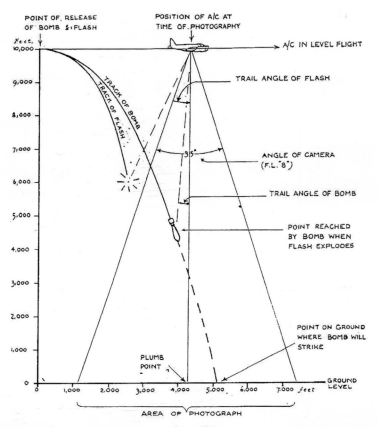

POINT OF RELEASE
OF BOMB & FLASH

POSITION OF A/C AT
TIME OF PHOTOGRAPHY

Feet.
10,000

A/C IN LEVEL FLIGHT

9,000

TRACK OF BOMB
TRACK OF FLASH

TRAIL ANGLE OF FLASH

8,000

7,000

35°

ANGLE OF CAMERA
(F.L. 8")

6,000

TRAIL ANGLE OF BOMB

5,000

POINT REACHED
BY BOMB WHEN
FLASH EXPLODES

4,000

3,000

2,000

POINT ON GROUND
WHERE BOMB WILL
STRIKE

1,000

PLUMB
POINT

0

0   1,000   2,000   3,000   4,000   5,000   6,000   7,000 feet

GROUND
LEVEL

AREA OF PHOTOGRAPH

Getting good aiming pictures at night was essential to the overall bombing strategy to verify (or not) whether the bombers were actually attacking the right place. But it was a procedure not liked by the crews. The camera ran from bomb–release until the calculated moment of bomb impact, which required the bomber staying on the attack heading for (typically) another thirty seconds after bomb release. Light was provided by a photoflash and from any ambient source, but any manoeuvring while the camera was running would result in the photograph being unusable. (*Author's collection*)

Night photography was not without its problems, both in the air and on the ground. This Lancaster I of 97 Squadron at Woodhall Spa was written off as a result of a photoflash going off on the ground. (*via Ken Delve*)

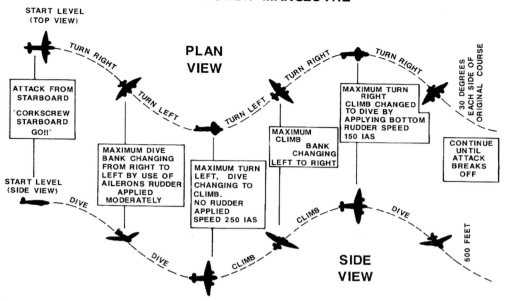

CORKSCREW MANŒUVRE

START LEVEL (TOP VIEW)

PLAN VIEW

TURN RIGHT — TURN LEFT — TURN LEFT — TURN RIGHT — TURN RIGHT — TURN RIGHT

ATTACK FROM STARBOARD
"CORKSCREW STARBOARD GO!!"

MAXIMUM DIVE BANK CHANGING FROM RIGHT TO LEFT BY USE OF AILERONS. RUDDER APPLIED MODERATELY

MAXIMUM TURN LEFT, DIVE CHANGING TO CLIMB. NO RUDDER APPLIED SPEED 250 IAS

MAXIMUM CLIMB
BANK CHANGING LEFT TO RIGHT

MAXIMUM TURN RIGHT CLIMB CHANGED TO DIVE BY APPLYING BOTTOM RUDDER SPEED 150 IAS

CONTINUE UNTIL ATTACK BREAKS OFF

30 DEGREES EACH SIDE OF ORIGINAL COURSE

START LEVEL (SIDE VIEW)

DIVE — DIVE — CLIMB — CLIMB — DIVE

SIDE VIEW

500 FEET

The method taught to try and throw off an attacking night fighter was a manoeuvre called the corkscrew. It consisted of a series of steep diving and climbing turns in alternate directions to make it difficult for the attacker to bring his guns to bear. (*Author's collection*)

When the Path Finder Force formed in August 1942 the man chosen by Harris to lead it was 31-year-old Donald Bennett, a talented, energetic and pioneering Australian aviator and former squadron commander. (*AHB*)

Having moved to Elvington in October 1942, 77 Squadron exchanged its Whitleys for the Halifax II. Shown about to get airborne for another night op is 'KN-W William'. (*AHB*)

Pilots of IV./NJG 1 pictured in late 1942. Sitting in the centre is the Gruppenkommandeur, Helmut Lent, while standing at the far right of the bench is Ludwig Becker (Kapitän of the 12th Staffel). Stood immediately behind Lent is Paul Gildner and to his right is Prinz zur Lippe-Weissenfeld. None of these four notable night fighter pilots would survive the war. Becker and Gildner would both fall in combat soon after this picture was taken while Lippe-Weissenfeld and Lent would be killed in 1944. (*Chris Goss collection*)

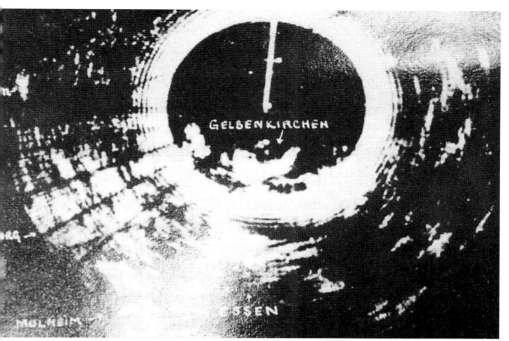

H2S picture of Gelsenkirchen. H2S was the first airborne ground-scanning radar system and was introduced to Pathfinder aircraft at the end of 1942. It allowed the operator to map the ground below by identifying notable navigation features such as coastlines, towns, lakes and rivers. From these known features, general navigation was relatively easy, although using H2S as a bombing aid was far more difficult. (*via Ken Delve*)

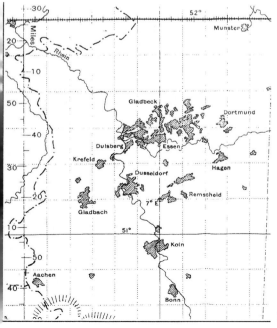

H2S map of the Ruhr. (*Author's collection*)

Pyrotechnic companies had been hard at work to develop a new target-marker for the PFF and the result was the Target Indicator (TI), a bomb casing filled with pyrotechnic candles. These purpose-built TIs could be dropped from any height and by using a barometric fuse, they could then fall to the ground in a mass of bright colours; red, yellow and green being the standard variants. They certainly produced a spectacular image. (*Author's collection*)

The silhouette of a Halifax captured by the light of TIs over the target. (*AHB*)

The Junkers Ju 88R–1 night fighter entered service in early 1943. Fitted with the FuG 202 *Lichtenstein* radar it was soon inflicting heavy casualties amongst the RAF bomber crews. The *Lichtenstein* series was the most widely used airborne radar installed into the Luftwaffe's night fighters but its complex arrangement of antennas at the forward end of four forward-projecting masts was not always liked by the crews as it reduced aircraft performance. (*Chris Goss collection*)

King George VI views post-raid aerial reconnaissance photos of the Ruhr dams during his visit to Scampton in May 1943 in the immediate aftermath of the raid. Stood alongside the King is Wing Commander Guy Gibson who was awarded the Victoria Cross for leading the raid. (*AHB*)

Oberfeldwebel Günther Bahr (centre) and his Bf 110 crew pictured in 1943 at Juvincourt in northern France. Bahr claimed his first night success (a Stirling) in August 1943 while serving with 3./NJG 6 and went on to survive the war having been credited with shooting down thirty-seven aircraft. (*Chris Goss collection*)

Hans-Joachim 'Hajo' Herrmann, a former bomber pilot and blind-flying expert, was one of the Luftwaffe's leading tacticians. It was his idea to form a new unit equipped with single-engine fighters and flown by experienced night fighter pilots who were given the freedom to visually hunt RAF bombers in the target area using any form of illumination available; such as searchlights, flares, fires on the ground, or simply the moonlight when the conditions allowed. It was a tactic known as *Wilde Sau*. (*Chris Goss collection*)

When Rudolf Schönert took command of II./NJG 2 he instructed his armourers to mount two 20 mm cannon in the rear compartment of his Bf 110G-4 and designed to fire upwards through the canopy. His first success using the idea came in May 1943 and within a year of its introduction one-third of all German night fighters were fitted with the upward-firing installation known as *Schräge Musik*. Unsurprisingly it was feared by the RAF's bomber crews once word of its existence had spread. (*Chris Goss collection*)

A Lancaster of 101 Squadron dropping *Window*. The bundles of thin strips of coarse paper were cut to a specified size to confuse the German defences by producing multiple radar contacts. It was a simple yet extremely effective idea and was first used during a raid against Hamburg on the night of 24/25 July 1943. (*101 Squadron records*)

For 20-year-old Arthur Orchard, a Lancaster rear gunner serving with 101 Squadron, the raid against the V-weapons research establishment at Peenemünde on the night of 17/18 August 1943 was his first operational experience. He would have a lucky escape the following month when he was the only member of his crew to survive a crash-landing after being hit by flak during a raid against Bochum. (*Author's collection*)

Bombing photo of Nuremberg taken by a 97 Squadron crew on the night of 27/28 August 1943 (*97 Squadron records*)

Jimmy Mann of 61 Squadron was the 22-year-old wireless operator of Flight Lieutenant Bill Reid['s] crew. Reid was awarded the Victoria Cross for his courage during a raid against Düsseldorf on th[e] night of 3/4 November 1943 but Mann was fatally wounded that night when their Lancaster wa[s] attacked by a night fighter for a second time; he died two days later. (*via Deborah Mitchelson*)

Lancasters of 50 Squadron heading for the Big City during November 1943. It was the start of the Battle of Berlin, the hardest-fought and costliest campaign of them all. (*Les Bartlett*)

An ABC-equipped Lancaster of 101 Squadron following a crash-landing in February 1944 after supporting a raid on Augsburg. Based at Ludford Magna in the Lincolnshire Wolds, 101 was a specialist squadron of No. 1 Group and in a war that had become highly technical on both sides, Airborne Cigar was designed to jam communications frequencies used by the German night fighters. Two of the ABC aerials are visible on top of the fuselage; a third was under the nose. (*101 Squadron records*)

Born of aristocratic descent, Major Heinrich Prinz zu Sayn-Wittgenstein, the Kommodore of NJG 2, was one of the most complex characters in the Luftwaffe, having earlier been a cavalryman, an observer and a bomber pilot. There were few, if any, better Ju 88 night fighter pilots than Sayn-Wittgenstein. His death in January 1944 was a huge blow for the Nachtjagd as he was the highest scoring night fighter pilot at the time with eighty-three aerial successes to his name, for which he was posthumously awarded the Swords to his Knight's Cross with Oak Leaves. (*Chris Goss collection*)

Neptun was the name given to a new series of airborne intercept radars installed in German night fighters. Shown here is the FuG 218 *Neptun* fitted to a Bf 110G, although the 'stag's antlers' installation added more weight to the aircraft and so reduced its overall performance. (*Chris Goss collection*)

Bomber crews preparing for another night raid. This time the target is Frankfurt and the night is 22/23 March 1944. (*via Ken Delve*)

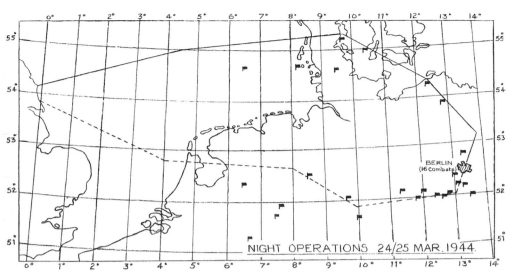

The long northern route taken to Berlin and the recovery plan for the attack against Berlin on the night of 24/25 March 1944. It was the last raid against the Big City during the hard and costly campaign against the Nazi capital. (*Author's collection*)

FIDO (standing for 'Fog Investigation and Dispersal Operation') was an ingenious method of dispersing fog at airfields. The system was based around a network of pipes filled with fuel and laid along the edges of the runway. When the fuel was ignited the effect was to lift the fog up to 300 feet; high enough, and for long enough, to enable bombers to land. (*via Ken Delve*)

Sergeant Norman Jackson, a Lancaster flight engineer serving with 106 Squadron at Metheringham, was awarded the Victoria Cross for a quite extraordinary act of bravery during a raid against Schweinfurt on the night of 26/27 April 1944 when he climbed out of the aircraft to try and stop a fire spreading along the starboard wing. Although he was thrown clear when the aircraft was again attacked by a night fighter, Jackson survived his ordeal to be taken as a prisoner of war. (*AHB*)

The morning after the night before. This Lancaster of 83 Squadron was lucky to make it home having been hit by flak while over the target. (*83 Squadron records*)

The Beetham crew of 50 Squadron pictured in April 1944 at Skellingthorpe towards the end of their tour. Standing L–R: Sergeant Jock Higgins (air gunner); Flight Lieutenant John Blott (air gunner); Flight Lieutenant Mike Beetham (pilot); Flying Officer Frank Swinyard (navigator); and Pilot Officer Les Bartlett (bomb aimer). Sitting L–R: Flying Officer Ted Adamson (flight engineer); Sergeant Reg Payne (wireless operator). (*Les Bartlett*)

After being awarded the Victoria Cross and recovering from his wounds, Bill Reid (left) was posted to 617 Squadron at Woodhall Spa. He took with him his trusted bomb aimer, 22-year-old Les Rolton, and the two men are pictured in front of the Petwood Hotel (used in the war as the Officers' Mess) in the spring of 1944. Soon after, they were taking part in a 'Tallboy' attack against a V-weapons storage dump in France when their Lancaster was hit by a bomb dropped from an aircraft above. Reid was one of only two to get out of the aircraft to be taken as a prisoner of war but Rolton died in the wreckage. (*Bill Reid*)

Wing Commander Bob Braham (right) pictured with his radar operator Flying Officer 'Sticks' Gregory. The battle of the night fighters over Germany was hard fought. By the time Braham was shot down in June 1944 to become a prisoner of war, nineteen of his twenty-nine successes had been achieved at night, earning him a DSO and two Bars and a DFC and two Bars, making Braham the RAF's most highly decorated fighter pilot of the war. (*AHB*)

Oberleutnant Georg Hermann Greiner was awarded the Knight's Cross in July 1944 while Staffelkapitän of 11./NJG 1. By then he had been credited with shooting down thirty-six aircraft and he would later add the Oak Leaves at the end of the war having taken his total to fifty. (*Chris Goss collection*)

One of Bomber Command's most notable losses of the war was that of 26-year-old Wing Commander Guy Gibson VC DSO and Bar DFC and Bar, the legendary leader of the Dams Raid, who was killed on the night of 19/20 September 1944 while acting as Master Bomber for a raid against Rheydt and Mönchengladbach. He and his navigator, Squadron Leader James Warwick DFC, were killed when their Mosquito came down in flames at Steenbergen in Holland. (*AHB*)

Significant losses came on both sides and, at the time of his death in October 1944, 26-year-old Helmut Lent was the Nachtjagd's highest scorer, having been credited with shooting down 103 aircraft at night (110 overall). He was the first of only two night fighter pilots to be awarded the coveted Diamonds, Germany's highest recognition for gallantry. (*Chris Goss collection*)

Leonard Cheshire commanded 617 Squadron during 1944 and was awarded the Victoria Cross having completed 100 operational sorties. It was the only occasion when a VC was awarded for a prolonged period of operations rather than for a specific act. (*AHB*)

A staged image of ED860 'QR–N Nuts' of 61 Squadron at Skellingthorpe in August 1944. At this stage of the war the aircraft was the mount of Flying Officer Norman Hoad and most operations were being flown in support of the Allied advance on Germany, but this legendary Lanc had already completed 119 ops since its first mission just over a year ago, mostly to heavily defended targets of the Reich. (*50 & 61 Squadrons' Association*)

Heinz-Wolfgang Schnaufer (centre) pictured with his crew colleagues in late 1944. On the far right is his long-term *Bordfunker* (radar operator), Friedrich 'Fritz' Rumpelhardt, and second left is his *Bordschütze* (air gunner), Wilhelm Gänsler. Second right is Georg Hermann Greiner and far left is Hans-Heinz Augenstein who was killed in December 1944 having been credited with shooting down forty-six aircraft, all at night. (*Chris Goss collection*)

Heinz-Wolfgang Schnaufer survived the war having shot down 121 aircraft, all at night, making him the highest scoring night fighter pilot in the history of air warfare. At the age of twenty-two he was the Luftwaffe's youngest Commodore and after Helmut Lent was the only other night fighter pilot to be awarded the coveted Diamonds. (*Chris Goss collection*)

Flight Sergeant George Thompson was awarded the Victoria Cross in January 1945 while serving with 9 Squadron. Single-handedly, he courageously fought a fire aboard his Lancaster to rescue crew colleagues trapped at the rear of the aircraft but he later succumbed to his own awful injuries. (*AHB*)

The impressive Me 262B-1a/U1 night fighter was fitted with the FuG 218 *Neptun* radar and the *Naxos* radar-homing device. While its performance was awesome for the time, the 262 had entered the war at too late a stage to influence its outcome and only a few of these specialist variants were in operational service by the end of the war. Pictured here is Red 10 of 10./NJG 11, the Luftwaffe's only jet night fighter unit, based at Burg-Magdeburg. (*Chris Goss collection*)

Capable of carrying a 4,000 lb bomb load, the de Havilland Mosquito light-bomber proved to be a highly versatile addition to Bomber Command's inventory. This aircraft is about to embark on the last raid of the war against Kiel on 2 May 1945. (*AHB*)

We stayed over Lake Constance for thirteen minutes and had an excellent view of the attack. There were approximately 16–20 heavy flak guns and 18–20 light flak guns, and 25 searchlights, within a radius of 6–8 miles of the target. Several aircraft were coned but not for any length of time. Heavy guns were firing both predictor-control and unseen. As the defences were heavier than expected, the Deputy Leader gave the order for all aircraft to increase height by 5,000 feet, so that the attack was actually delivered from 10,000–15,000 feet.

It was a difficult run-in but bombing was accurate, after which the bombers headed south to cross the Alps to land in Algeria just as dawn was breaking. Fawke's crew report concludes:

Leaving the target area, we commenced to fly over the Alps. By skirting the peaks we eventually crossed, gradually gaining height to 14,000 feet. The 600-mile flight over the Mediterranean was slow, as we had to fly at 140 mph to prevent over-heating. Eventually we sighted the Algerian coast and landed safely at Maison Blanche at 0752, after a flight of 10 hours and 13 minutes.

All the Lancasters made it safely to Algeria. Then, on the night of 23/24 June, fifty-two of them returned home having bombed the Italian port at La Spezia on the way. Of the eight Lancasters left behind in Algeria to undergo repairs from the previous raid, a handful returned to England soon after while other crews eventually returned home via Gibraltar.

Operation *Bellicose* had been a success, resulting in severe damage to the Zeppelin works with a significant impact on radar production. It was the first of several Allied bombing attacks against the facility and over the course of the war about two-thirds of Friedrichshafen would be destroyed. The fact that the raid had been conducted without casualties shows just how a well-planned and well-executed raid by a specialist force could achieve great success.

As the number of night attacks against the Reich increased a new Luftwaffe fighter unit, JG 300, was introduced. Equipped with single-seat, single-engine fighters, and using a new tactic called *Wilde Sau* (Wild Boar), this new unit operated for the first time on the night of 3/4 July during a raid against Cologne. Its introduction had been brought about because of the inflexibility of *Himmelbett*. Because *Himmelbett* could only ever employ a fraction of the night fighters available at any one time, it was a system that had long had its critics and with new ideas being tried and tested, its days were numbered.

Wilde Sau had been developed by Major Hans-Joachim 'Hajo' Herrmann, a former bomber pilot and a blind-flying expert who had gained a reputation as one of the Luftwaffe's leading tacticians. It had been his idea to form a new unit equipped with single-engine day fighters but flown by experienced night fighter pilots. They were to be given the freedom to visually hunt the bombers in the target area by using any form of illumination available to them, such as searchlights, flares, fires on the ground, or simply the moonlight when the conditions allowed.

Standard Focke-Wulf FW 190As and Messerschmitt Bf 109Gs were borrowed from day fighter units to test the theory. Because the fighters had no specialist equipment fitted that could assist the pilot at night, he was required to fly to a pre-briefed radio beacon from where he would orbit at a nominated height until an attack commenced. He would then be ordered to the target area where he would look for the bombers, and once seen he would carry out his attack visually.

Although a rather simplistic idea, *Wilde Sau* was an effective tactic and took the bomber crews by surprise. During its first use that night, in early July 1943, twelve bombers were shot down in the target area, although some of these were jointly claimed by the anti-aircraft batteries on the ground.

One to achieve his first *Wilde Sau* success that night, a Halifax near Cologne, was Friedrich-Karl Müller. Known as 'Nasen', and not to be confused with the day fighter ace Friedrich-Karl 'Tutti' Müller, he was a pre-war pilot with the German airline Lufthansa and had flown transport aircraft during the early years of the war. His experience of blind flying meant that he was ideal for Herrmann's experimental unit.

Nasen Müller's score would soon rise into double figures, after which he would go on to serve as a Gruppenkommandeur with NJGr 10. He was also given responsibility for evaluating all technical and tactical aspects of the Nachtjagd's single-engine night fighters and in particular how to counter the RAF's Mosquito. His work would earn him the Knight's Cross and he would survive the war having been credited with shooting down thirty aircraft, all but seven using *Wilde Sau* tactics, making him the Luftwaffe's most successful pilot in this role. Hajo Herrmann, meanwhile, went on to become the Luftwaffe's *Inspekteur der Nachtjagd* (Inspector of Night Fighters) and was awarded the coveted Swords to his Knight's Cross with Oak Leaves. When he was elevated to his new appointment, command of JG 300 passed to Kurt Kettner and from the success of JG 300 would come two more specialist units, JG 301 and JG 302, all under the overall command of Kettner.

The initial *Wilde Sau* idea was enhanced by the addition of flare-equipped Ju 88s. The crews were tasked to position themselves at the rear of the bomber stream to help guide the night fighters onto their targets. To reduce the risk of falling to their own anti-aircraft guns on the ground, the batteries were instructed not to fire higher than a specified height, leaving the night fighters the freedom to operate above.

Back in England, Harris warned his group commanders to prepare for his next onslaught. This time against Hamburg. This historic shipyard and transport hub in northern Germany was the country's second largest city. It was well beyond the range of Oboe but its location on the southern point of the Jutland Peninsula, where continental Europe meets Scandinavia, as well as being situated on the River Elbe, meant that Hamburg would be a good target for H2S.

Hamburg would not only attract attention from Bomber Command in the days ahead. For the first time the bombing campaign was to be a truly combined Anglo-American effort, with the Eighth Air Force carrying out daylight raids in between those by Bomber Command at night.

Called Operation *Gomorrah*, the Battle of Hamburg began on the night of 24/25 July with a large and mixed bomber force of nearly 800 aircraft taking part. Conditions were good and the first bombs fell on the city just after midnight. By the time the attack finished, less than an hour later, more than 90 per cent of the bombers had found the target with more than 2,200 tons of bombs falling on the city. The raid also marked the operational debut of a new radar countermeasure called *Window*, a simple device yet one that would turn out to be one of the most effective of the Second World War.

The idea of producing spurious radar returns stemmed back to the pre-war days but the introduction of *Window* had only come after much delay and many heated discussions at the highest level. Although it had been ready for use a year before, the internal arguments about whether it should be used had raged on; the argument against its use based on the concern that the Germans would start using the idea themselves. Eventually, though, Harris got his way when the doubters were finally convinced that introducing *Window* might reduce bomber losses by as much as 30 per cent.

The tactic involved bombers dropping bundles of thin strips of coarse paper, cut exactly to a specified size (27 cm in length and 2 cm wide), equivalent to half the wavelength of the German *Würzburg* ground radars and *Lichtenstein* air intercept radars. The bundles were dropped from around 60 miles to the target at a rate of one bundle a minute, and continued until the bombers reached the same distance on their way home. The idea was to swamp the German defences on the ground by producing multiple radar contacts, as well as confusing the night fighter crews by producing numerous false returns on their radar sets.

The introduction of *Window* during the raid against Hamburg had certainly presented the night fighter crews with a scene of utter confusion. Their radar displays showed contact after contact, making it all but impossible to differentiate between a genuine radar return from a bomber and this new piece of deception. One to be caught up in the confusion that night was 21-year-old Wilhelm 'Wim' Johnen, flying a Bf 110 of 3./NJG 1, who already had a handful of successes to his name. Part of his combat report is included in Mike Spick's book *Luftwaffe Fighter Aces*. Johnen reported:

> … *my sparker [radar operator] announced the first enemy machine on his Li [Lichtenstein]. I was delighted. I swung round on to the bearing in the direction of the Ruhr, for in this way I was bound to approach the [bomber] stream. Facius [his radar operator] proceeded to report three or four pictures on his screens. I hoped that I should have enough ammunition to deal with them! Then Facius shouted 'Tommy flying towards us at great speed. Distance decreasing … 2,000 metres; 1,500…1,000…500.*

There was, of course, nothing there. The rapidly reducing distance to what appeared like a target was merely the closing speed of the night fighter on the bundles of *Window* drifting down to earth, with no velocity other than the effect of the wind. The relative speed when closing on the radar return of a genuine bomber would, of course, be much less. And it was not long before Facius was shouting again but, as before, nothing was to be seen. Initially, there was some joking between the two men but Johnen later reported:

But soon I lost my sense of humour, for this crazy performance was repeated a score of times and finally I gave Facius such a rocket that he was deeply offended. This tense atmosphere on board was suddenly interrupted by a ground station calling 'Hamburg, Hamburg. A thousand enemy bombers over Hamburg.'

Despite the confusion caused by *Window*, a number of night fighters from NJG 3 still managed to get into the main bomber stream. One was a Bf 110 flown by Hans Meissner. After a number of spurious contacts and fruitless chases, it was just after 1 a.m. when his *Bordfunker*, 21-year-old Josef Krinner, gained yet another contact. This time the young Krinner showed he had a cool head for someone so young. To him the radar return was behaving exactly as it should for another aircraft and not at all like those seen earlier that night. Meissner could soon make out the shape of a heavy bomber, a Stirling, and having closed down the range he promptly shot it down.

The Stirling came down to the north of Neumünster in the northernmost part of Germany. With thirteen more claims by the crews of NJG 3 it had been a successful night for some, although Bomber Command figures show twelve RAF bombers lost that night; just 1.5 per cent of the attacking force.

For the British, *Window* was a technological success and now gave Bomber Command two main tactical advantages. Firstly, it could be used to confuse the German defences by hiding the real attacking force amongst multiple radar returns and, secondly, it could be used to simulate a much larger force than was actually present.

German night fighter crews would become familiar with seeing *Window* on their radar displays. They would even use it to their advantage as its trail would lead them to RAF aircraft. But they were never able to totally remove the problems it caused. Also, Bomber Command would become very clever in its use. For example, spoof raids could be created by just a handful of aircraft dropping *Window*, while the Main Force bombers made large and rapid changes to head off in another direction.

Gomorrah continued with the Americans following up the opening raid on Hamburg with a daylight attack, although less than a hundred bombers reached the city. But a planned second consecutive night attack by Bomber Command had to be cancelled because fires were still burning from the night before, and smoke over the target area would make accurate bombing difficult. And so Bomber Command went to Essen instead, although a handful of Mosquitos did carry out minor operations over Hamburg.

Harris's force returned to Hamburg on the night of 27/28 July, just three nights after the first raid had taken place. Again, nearly 800 bombers took part and although the tonnage of bombs dropped was similar to the previous raid, the outcome was total devastation. The lack of any rain for some time meant that everywhere was very dry and the resulting firestorm was triggered by the combination of a high ground temperature and low humidity. A vortex and whirling updraft of super-heated air created a tornado of fire up to 1,000 feet in height, with winds reported to reach up to 150 mph and temperatures in the huge inferno reaching 800 degrees Centigrade; it was a totally unexpected effect.

The fire burned for several hours, incinerating 8 square miles of the city, including three-quarters of Hamburg's closely built-up residential areas. An estimated 40,000 people died, many from the lack of oxygen that had been totally consumed by the fire. More than a million survivors of the raid fled Hamburg in fear of further raids. And there were, indeed, further raids. Bomber Command returned just two nights later. Again, nearly 800 bombers took part. Then a fourth raid took place on the night of 2/3 August, involving 750 bombers, although bad weather and thunderstorms encountered over Germany meant this last raid was a failure.

Bomber Command had flown more than 3,000 sorties in its four raids against the city and had dropped nearly 10,000 tons of bombs. After the raid of 29/30 July, German reports stated:

The port was severely hit, the damage was gigantic. The failing of the water system, and the fighting of fires which remained from earlier attacks, hampered all work severely. The whole of Hamburg was on fire. Rescue, evacuation, clearing of vital roads, fire-fighting etc, asked the impossible from the available forces. Economically, Hamburg was knocked out, as even the undamaged parts had to stop work on account of the destruction of water, gas and electricity supplies.

Even the Reich Minister of Propaganda, Joseph Goebbels, commented on the damage as a *'catastrophe, the extent of which simply staggers the imagination'*. And Albert Speer, the Minister of Armaments and War Production, expressed the opinion that if another six big German cities were similarly destroyed he would not be able to maintain armaments production. These were significant comments from key Nazi officials. In many ways, these raids against Hamburg were the fulfilment of what bomber chiefs had been saying for a long time.

Although it had lasted for just eight days and seven nights, the Allied bombing of Hamburg was the heaviest assault of air power at the time. All parts of the city and dock, including all four shipbuilding yards, were shattered. More than a third of the city's large factories were totally destroyed and hundreds of smaller industrial buildings were either damaged or destroyed. Industrial losses were so severe that Hamburg would never recover to full production. Furthermore, its transport systems were completely disrupted and half of the city's dwellings were destroyed. More than 42,500 of Hamburg's population had been killed, the vast majority during the second raid, and nearly as many again injured. It would be a long time before anything like a normal way of life could resume.

Hamburg has since been described by some as the 'Hiroshima of Germany'. In particular, the firestorm resulting from the second raid has continued to cause outrage and criticism. It has even been suggested that Bomber Command had dropped an excessively high proportion of incendiary bombs. This is not true. In fact, the proportion of incendiaries dropped on Hamburg was lower than what was dropped on many industrial targets in the Ruhr. But no subsequent city raid shook Germany as much as that on Hamburg.

Chapter Twelve

More Precision Required

Ask anyone if he remembers his first bombing operation – he will. It's a kind of high adventure one never forgets. Even the smallest detail stays fresh in the mind long after most other operational flights have slipped away into memories limbo.

The words belong to Arthur Orchard who later recalled his first op on the night of 17/18 August 1943 when Bomber Command launched Operation *Hydra* against the German V-weapons research establishment at Peenemünde on the Baltic coast. With growing evidence the Germans were building and testing new V-rockets at the site, the destruction of the facility had become one of the War Cabinet's highest priorities.

Harris had initially delayed the raid until conditions were favourable for his attacking force. The moon period had offered some welcome respite for his squadrons but now was the time, and so he ordered the attack. The plan put in place was one of Bomber Command's most complex yet. The precision attack against this small target was to be carried out at night, the aim being to hit specific buildings rather than to bomb the whole area. To make marking and bombing easier the raid was to take place under bright moonlit conditions and, to further increase the chances of success, it would involve a Master Bomber to control the attack.

This was the first time the Master Bomber concept was to be used for a large-scale attack and the man chosen for the task was 30-year-old Group Captain John Searby, the commanding officer of 83 Squadron. He would direct the large attacking force of nearly 600 bombers – a mix of Lancasters, Halifaxes and Stirlings – with three main aiming points specified: the factory, the experimental testing site and the living accommodation.

For one young Lancaster crew of 101 Squadron based at Ludford Magna up in the Lincolnshire Wolds, Peenemünde was to be their first op. At twenty-six, Flight Sergeant Fred Ray was the oldest of his crew. The rest were all under the age of twenty-one and included 20-year-old Sergeant Arthur Orchard, the rear gunner and a former employee of the Vauxhall Motor Company in his home town of Luton. Orchard later recalled his feelings that night:

> *The first op is a long awaited consummation of hundreds of hours of flying training between seven young men. That afternoon the station was buzzing with pre-ops gossip. Since the petrol load was a relatively large one we knew it was going to be a long trip, but we hadn't the least idea where. Not till briefing time did we know and the news was not conducive to the morale of a sprog crew. The target was Peenemünde, a long way on the German Baltic coast. Our intelligence had discovered their highly secret research and development complex. We were told they wouldn't be expecting us and so this could be a once only attack and had to be effective. But that night was chosen particularly because it was a full moon. We gasped. We would be seen by every German night fighter between the Channel and the Baltic. Worse, we were to bomb from only 7,000 feet.*

As things were to turn out the Pathfinders found Peenemünde without any problems, their route having been devised to confuse the German defences as to the true location of the target. Eight Pathfinder Mosquitos of 139 Squadron had also managed to draw enemy night fighters away from the Main Force in a spoof tactic towards Berlin, leaving the target clear for at least the first half of the attack. Both these ideas worked. The German commanders initially believed the target to be either Stettin or Berlin.

After taking off from Ludford Magna at 9 p.m. and climbing slowly out into the early night sky, Fred Ray followed the track to the specified turning points and approached Peenemünde without encountering any problems. Arthur Orchard later recalled what it was like as they made their final run-in to bomb:

> *As we neared the target the Lancaster started to heave and pitch in the slipstream of other aircraft, which we could see clearly in the full moon. An unholy mess of flak came up from the target area below. Small bits clattered*

against our aircraft but our bomb aimer got the load away successfully and
we headed for home. There were fighters in the offing, so we jinked about a
bit in the usual evasive action, and finally settled down to the long trip back.

Ray safely touched down back at Ludford Magna in the early hours of the
following morning, exactly seven hours after getting airborne.

Meanwhile, nine Hercules-powered Lancaster IIs of 426 Squadron RCAF
based at Linton-on-Ouse had been in the third wave of the attack. It was the
squadron's first operation with the new type, making 426 the first Canadian
squadron to operate the Lancaster. Flight Lieutenant Shaw was the skipper
of one of the squadron's aircraft. His crew report reads:

Excellent visibility and green TI markers guided this aircraft to the
target. Rügen Island turning point was plainly marked with green TIs and
bombing was done with green TIs in the bombsight. The whole peninsula
wall appeared ablaze and smoke was rising to 4,000 feet. Bombed at 0036
from 8,000 feet.

The raid, overall, had gone well with the factory and the experimental site
receiving the brunt of the attack. The original markers had gone down a
little off the aiming points but this had soon been corrected; the Master
Bomber concept had again proved a success.

The Peenemünde raid set the V-weapons programme back by an estimated
two months but it had also come at a cost to Bomber Command. Forty
aircraft were lost that night, mostly from the third wave after the Luftwaffe's
night fighters had arrived. The worst of the losses, in percentage terms, were
suffered by the Canadian No. 6 Group. Of the group's fifty-seven aircraft
taking part, twelve did not return; more than 20 per cent. Two of those shot
down were from 426 Squadron RCAF. One was 'OW-M' flown by Flight
Lieutenant Doug Shuttleworth, an experienced pilot from Saskatchewan
with a DFC and twenty ops already behind him. Having just converted from
the Wellington most of Shuttleworth's crew were of similar experience but
they had picked up a new flight engineer for the Lancaster, Sergeant Syd
Barnes, who was on his first op. Nothing was heard from the crew again.

The second of the squadron's aircraft lost that night was 'OW-V' flown by the squadron commander, 33-year-old Wing Commander Leslie Crooks DSO DFC. Crooks was on his second operational tour but only one of his crew, the bomb aimer Sergeant K W Reading, survived to be taken as a prisoner of war. It was a tragic end for the crew and sadly typical of so many similar stories. The bodies of Crooks and four of his crew were found in the wreckage. It appears that the navigator, 21-year-old Flight Sergeant Alfred Howes, had managed to get out of the aircraft only to fall to his death when his parachute failed to open; he was on his third op. The flight engineer, Sergeant John Hislop, a young Scot, was also just twenty-one. He was flying his first op, as was the mid-upper gunner, 20-year-old Pilot Officer Theo Dos Santos from Trinidad. Leslie Crooks was the squadron's second CO to be killed in action and he is buried with his crew colleagues in the Berlin 1939–1945 War Cemetery.

Despite the losses the British press were quick to pick up on the raid. One newspaper ran the headline '*RAF hit new target in Germany – 41 bombers missing from moonlight raid on aircraft centre.*'

The reported number of aircraft lost was one more than actually the case and the target was referred to as an aircraft centre, such was the difficulty of factual reporting at the time and the classification of the target. The opening words of the article that followed reported:

Our home-based bombers found a new German target on Tuesday night. It was Peenemünde, on the German Baltic coast, in the Bay of Pomerania, and 60 miles north-west of Stettin. The research establishment here is the largest and most important of its kind in Germany. First reports indicate that the attack, which was made in bright moonlight, was heavy and well concentrated.

Another newspaper reported the outstanding courage and performance of Bomber Command's crews that night, but again the reporter would have had no understanding of the establishment's real use at the time of the attack:

Bomber Command attacked one of the most important research plants for radio-location in the whole Reich. To find and hit a single building in a small place required conditions of moonlight which virtually amounted to those needed for precision bombing. Yet so far into Germany was the target that to attempt the sortie in such conditions meant, in the absence of incredibly good fortune, a higher proportion of losses than usual. This mission, therefore, must rank as one of the most courageous our bomber crews have ever undertaken.

Although not immediately evident to the bomber crews at the time, the night had seen the Nachtjagd's first operational use of an upward-firing twin-cannon installation known as *Schräge Musik*. Taken from the German colloquialism for 'Jazz Music' (with the word *schräg* meaning slanted), the installation was mounted just above the rear cockpit of the night fighter, meaning it could now make an attack from below the bomber and outside the scan of its gunners.

The idea of upward-firing guns was not entirely new. It had first been trialled during the First World War but the concept was taken forward during the Second World War by Rudolf Schönert. He had first experimented with upward-firing guns in 1942 and although his idea was initially rejected by his superiors, he eventually managed to get approval to conduct further trials. When given command of II./NJG 2, Schönert instructed his armourers to mount two MG FF 20 mm cannon in the rear compartment of the upper fuselage of a Bf 110G-4, and designed to fire through the canopy. His first success using the idea came in May 1943 and the following month modifications were authorized for other night fighters, such as the Ju 88 and Do 217. Schönert was eventually credited with shooting down sixty-four aircraft, including eighteen using *Schräge Musik*, earning him the Oak Leaves to his Knight's Cross.

While the Luftwaffe's night fighters had enjoyed success during the Peenemünde raid, so too had the RAF Beaufighters sent over northern Germany to offer some protection to the raiding force. Bob Braham, for example, scored his first double of the war when he downed two Bf 110s of IV./NJG 1 in quick succession.

Braham had come across three 110s that had been vectored on to the main bomber stream as they were crossing the Frisian Islands on their way to the target. One was flown by 22-year-old Oberfeldwebel Georg Kraft. Kraft had already been credited with shooting down at least fourteen aircraft and was now in a gentle turn to port and closing on another intended victim when his aircraft was suddenly raked by 20 mm cannon shells from Braham's Beaufighter. Kraft quickly went into a dive but Braham hit it again. The 110 then burst into flames and was last seen plunging vertically towards the sea.

Kraft's demise had also been witnessed by Feldwebel Heinz Vinke, another of the Nachtjagd's high-scorers with twenty confirmed successes at the time. By the time Vinke spotted Braham's Beaufighter it was already behind and slightly below Kraft's aircraft. In a desperate attempt to save his colleague, Vinke broke hard towards the Beaufighter but it was already too late. Braham had also seen the 110 and turned hard inside it, firing from extremely close range and narrowly avoiding a collision.

Braham's short burst had been devastating. The *Bordschütze* (air gunner), Unteroffizier Johann Gaa, and *Bordfunker*, Feldwebel Karl Schödl, were both hit and the 110 was soon out of control. Facing no option other than to abandon their stricken fighter, the three crew members decided to bale out. Whether Gaa and Schödl managed to get out is unclear. They were never seen again. Vinke did manage to escape and after spending eighteen hours in his dinghy was picked up by a German float plane of the air-sea rescue unit. However, Heinz Vinke would also lose his life just six months later having then been credited with shooting down fifty-four aircraft.

Braham's double that night had taken his personal score to eighteen, the last four of which had all been Bf 110s. Georg Kraft and Heinz Vinke were two of three 110 aces that fell to his guns. His third victim was 23-year-old Hauptmann August Geiger, the Gruppenkommandeur of III./NJG 1, who then had fifty-three successes to his name. Geiger fell victim to Braham over the Zuiderzee in Holland on the night of 29/30 September; it was Braham's twentieth success. Although Geiger managed to bale out, he drowned when his parachute dragged him under the water.

Braham was awarded a second Bar to his DFC and days later he was rested from operations having also been awarded a Bar to his DSO. He was later appointed Wing Commander Night Operations at HQ No. 2 Group but continued to fly on operations whenever he could, although he was restricted to flying just one operation a week. Flying with Sticks Gregory and his other preferred radar operator, Flight Lieutenant Henry 'Jake' Jacobs, Braham would soon take his total to twenty-nine, nineteen of which were achieved at night, earning him a second Bar to his DSO to make him the RAF's most highly decorated fighter pilot. Bob Braham's war came to a sudden end in June 1944 when he was shot down by FW 190s, although he survived to become a prisoner of war.

The night fighter versus night fighter battle had taken the air war over Germany to another level but the fact remained that the Luftwaffe was still some way behind the RAF when it came to the technological war. However, the introduction of a new and improved airborne radar, the FuG 220 *Lichtenstein SN-2*, in late 1943, as a response to *Serrate* as well as being impervious to *Window*, would go some considerable way towards closing the gap, and would prove to be one of the most important technical improvements for the Nachtjagd of the war.

Operating in the 85-90 MHz low-VHF band, *SN-2* worked in the same part of the frequency spectrum as the *Freya* early-warning radar and so it remained unfamiliar to British intelligence officers for some time. Even when operators on board specialist RAF aircraft first detected its transmissions as part of their routine search of the electronic spectrum, they put the returns down to the more familiar *Freya*. When *SN-2* eventually fell into Allied hands it was found to be vulnerable to *Window* of a longer length, sometimes referred to as *Long Window*, but for now it remained unknown and the majority of German night fighters were soon upgraded with the new installation.

The combination of *SN-2* and *Schräge Musik*, together with *Flensburg* and *Naxos*, now made the German night fighter an extremely effective weapon. It could approach a bomber from the rear and below, completely independent of any ground control, and without the need to pull up sharply to make its attack. The Nachtjagdflieger learned to slow down his approach and once positioned underneath the bomber he would then gently rise up beneath it. He would then hold close formation with the bomber about 65–70 degrees above. The gunsight was modified with a reflecting mirror fitted above his head, in line with a similar mirror behind the actual gunsight. It was complicated in theory but the final positioning was achieved by his *Bordfunker* giving commands until he could clearly see the bomber above. He could then adjust his final movements until in a position to open fire.

A well-practised crew could complete the manoeuvre in seconds rather than minutes. The only real hazard was that they had to get out of the way quickly once they had carried out their attack. Being at such close range meant the firing solution was simple and their guns were so accurate. Any debris or parts of the bomber falling off or, worse still, its bomb load exploding, presented a real risk to the night fighter crew. And so, many crews chose to aim at the wing to cause structural damage and to hit the wing fuel tanks rather than aim at the central part of the underside of the fuselage where the risk of hitting the bomb bay was too great.

When *Schräge Musik* was first introduced it came as a complete surprise to the unsuspecting crews of Bomber Command. The RAF was slow to react, claiming initial losses to be due to flak rather than anything else. It was only when detailed analysis was done of returning bombers that the damage was acknowledged to have been caused by enemy night fighters firing from below.

Within a year of its introduction, a third of all German night fighters were fitted with *Schräge Musik* and later installations included more powerful 30 mm cannons. While these heavier calibre weapons meant that only a handful of hits were required to bring a large bomber down, their low muzzle velocity meant the night fighter had to get even closer to its intended target before opening fire.

Understandably, *Schräge Musik* was feared by the bomber crews once word of its existence had spread, but because of the installation's weight and drag not all Nachtjagdflieger were sold on the idea. Hauptmann Hans-Joachim Jabs, for example, then the Kommandeur of IV./NJG 1 and an experienced Bf 110 pilot with a Knight's Cross for his thirty-plus successes, had it removed from his aircraft so that he could retain its performance. Nonetheless, *Schräge Musik* was one of the Luftwaffe's greatest successes in the night war over Germany and remained a constant worry to the crews of Bomber Command.

Chapter Thirteen

Road to Berlin

The progressive destruction of the German military, industrial and economic system, the disruption of vital elements of lines of communication, and the material reduction of German air combat strength by the successful prosecution of the Combined Bomber Offensive from all convenient bases is a pre-requisite to 'Overlord'. This operation must therefore continue to have the highest strategic priority.

Yet another Allied conference, this time at Quebec, brought renewed discussion on the best way to pursue the strategic air offensive. Thoughts were already turning towards the Allied landings in north-west Europe, codenamed Operation *Overlord*, now less than a year away. A new directive, containing the statement above, was issued just days after Harris had ordered a return to Berlin.

The return to the Nazi capital on the night of 23/24 August 1943 was the first major raid against Berlin for five months but with the loss of fifty-six bombers, some 8 per cent of those taking part, it was a costly one. An analysis of the raid showed the Halifax units had suffered particularly badly, with nearly 10 per cent of its numbers lost, including six of the thirty-four Pathfinders taking part. Losses amongst the Stirling crews, which had made up the third wave, had also been high with sixteen aircraft lost (13 per cent of those taking part).

A more detailed look into the losses suggests that thirty-three of the bombers were shot down by night fighters, twenty of them over the target area. The losses attributed to flak were put down to bombers straying off their intended course, particularly around the defences of Bremen. In fact, things might have been considerably worse had the night fighters not been recalled to their bases around midnight because fog was beginning to form at their airfields. Until that point the German ground control system had worked very well, with the night fighter crews being fed a continuous commentary of the whereabouts of the main bomber force:

2133 [hours] – bombers approaching Amsterdam; 2155 – bombers flying east; orbit searchlight beacons; 2217 – bombers approaching Bremen; 2238 – Berlin is possible target; 2304 – all fighters proceed to Berlin; 2332 – bombers over Berlin.

With this information the night fighter crews had been able to decide where and when to make their attack, taking into account their own position and other factors such as the weather and how long they could remain in the air.

It was a similar story just a week later, when Harris ordered another raid on Berlin. Of 622 aircraft sent to the target, forty-seven were lost (7.6 per cent). This time it was the Stirling force that had suffered the most with seventeen of the 106 aircraft taking part failing to return (16 per cent).

Just three nights later, on 3/4 September, Harris ordered a third raid on Berlin. Because of the losses suffered by the Halifax and Stirling squadrons in the earlier raids, this was an all-Lancaster effort with just over 300 aircraft taking part. The Lancasters took a longer track to approach Berlin from the north-east while four Mosquitos dropped flares well away from the main bomber route in an attempt to draw away the night fighters; even so, twenty-two aircraft were lost (7 per cent).

Not only were the Luftwaffe's night fighter crews being aided by information and control from the ground, they were helping each other by marking the position of the bombers with flares once they managed to locate the main stream. And with Bomber Command sending its aircraft over the target in concentrated numbers, all the night fighter crew had to do was to find one bomber. They would then often stumble across three or four more. On a good night, a night fighter crew could claim two or three successes in a matter of minutes.

With bomber losses running at double the 'acceptable' or 'sustainable' 4 per cent, these three raids were a costly reminder that the German defences remained very strong. While the planners went away to decide how best to improve tactics against this particularly difficult nut to crack, Bomber

Command spent the remainder of September 1943 going elsewhere; to Mannheim twice, Munich, Hannover twice and Bochum.

The first of the two raids against Hannover took place on the night of 22/23 September and was the first against this major centre in northern Germany for more than two years. It was also the chance for Bomber Command to introduce a new tactic to try and reduce its losses. A small Pathfinder force of twenty-one Lancasters and eight Mosquitos carried out a spoof raid against Oldenburg, to the north-west of the main target. Dropping *Window* and flares the hope was that the German defences would be deceived into believing it was the main attack while more than 700 bombers went to Hannover.

As things were to turn out for the main raid, stronger than forecast winds made marking difficult and caused most of the bombs to fall to the south-east of the city. However, the spoof part of the plan seemed to work well with overall losses that night below 4 per cent, a considerable improvement over previous weeks.

An attempt to repeat the spoof tactic the following night was not so successful. While the Pathfinders carried out a deception raid against Darmstadt, the Main Force went to Mannheim, 30 miles further south. The main problem was that the two towns were too close together. The German controllers were quickly able to identify the likely area of attack, and the combination of the bomber route taken to the target and Mannheim's location in the south-west of Germany meant the raiding force felt the full weight of the Nachtjagd. As the bombers made the long transit across Europe they were continuously hassled by up to 200 night fighters along the route; from units based in Holland (from Jagddivision 3), north-west Germany (Jagddivision 2) and central Germany (Jagddivision 1). Although bombing went well, thirty-two of the Main Force were lost (5.1 per cent).

Amongst the horrors of the night war came an extraordinary act of chivalry during the second of the raids against Hannover that month (flown on the night of the 27th/28th). Georg Hermann Greiner, now attached to 10./NJG 1, had just claimed his thirteenth victim, a Halifax, when he came across another of the same type over the North Sea. As he closed in on what should have been his next victim he could see the Halifax was flying on just its two port engines and with some six feet of its starboard wing missing. Closing alongside the stricken bomber on its port side, the young Greiner observed the scene. In *Hunters of the Reich: Night Fighters* by David P Williams, Greiner recalled his feelings that night:

What encounters had it been involved in? How serious was its overall damage? And how long had it already been flying in that condition? When one takes all this into consideration it had been a great achievement by the crew, and especially that of the pilot, who one could only show the utmost respect. After flying alongside the badly damaged Halifax it was clear to me that the crew of the bomber had performed a unique achievement which had to be rewarded. Without a moment's hesitation I rocked my wings a few times in time-honoured tradition, a conciliatory and peaceful gesture even among enemies. We then turned for home.

The decision to leave the crippled bomber that night would not have been an easy one for Greiner. Although few and far between, such acts of humanity, on either side, were extremely welcome during what had become a war of attrition in which thousands of men were losing their lives.

For the young men locked in battle in the night sky over Germany death came in all sorts of ways, an example being that of 24-year-old Hans-Dieter Frank, a holder of the Knight's Cross, whose life was cut short that same night. Including his day successes earlier in the war, Frank was credited with shooting down fifty-five aircraft and for such a young man he had been an outstanding leader, first as the Staffelkapitän of 2./NJG 1 and then as the Gruppenkommandeur. But his luck ran out when his He 219A collided with another night fighter, a Bf 110, near Celle.

Frank's death marked the beginning of a bad week of notable losses for the Nachtjagd. Just two nights later August Geiger fell to the guns of Bob Braham. Then Hauptmann Rudolf Sigmund, the high-scoring Kommandeur of III./NJG 3, was killed. Sigmund had only just been awarded the Knight's Cross for shooting down twenty-eight aircraft but his Bf 110 was shot down near Göttingen in central Germany while intercepting a raid on Kassel. And just days later another ace fell. This time it was Leutnant Heinz Grimm of IV./NJG 1. He had twenty-seven successes to his name but succumbed to his wounds after falling victim to his own flak over Bremen. Both Frank and Geiger were posthumously awarded the Oak Leaves while Grimm was posthumously awarded the Knight's Cross. And so it went on.

The story was similar across the North Sea but one young airman had a lucky escape while returning from the raid on Bochum on the night of 29/30 September. That lucky man was Arthur Orchard, the rear gunner of Fred Ray's crew. The crew had now been transferred to the Pathfinders of 156 Squadron at Warboys in Huntingdonshire. Flying that night in Lancaster 'GT-E Easy' the Bochum raid was their eighth op. Orchard later recalled the night he would never forget:

Briefing said it was the Ruhr valley again or as we called it Happy Valley – Flak Happy Valley! Already in one week we had been to Mannheim and Hannover and that night it was to be Bochum. The route – straight in and straight out. No diversions in attempt to fool enemy night fighters. A lightning strike! Duration – 3½ hours. We were downing our egg and bacon to a backcloth of brittle cheerfulness and idle chatter – this prelude the worse of all – and we were thankful when the Bedford truck arrived to take us out to the aircraft. We looked a strange motley crew piling into those trucks dressed in our various garb – boys really appearing to be men with their bulbous flying jackets and heavy boots distinguishing the frames within. Our Lanc stood there in its drab camouflage paint stained with oil, threadbare in parts through erosion, as if waiting for this truck load of unruly beings who would alone make it live again. Within the hour we were off over the flat Huntingdonshire countryside but climbing as fast as our heavy load would permit – eager to join the protection of the bomber stream before reaching occupied territory. Only a scare from very heavy and accurate gun fire over the Dutch coast diverted us slightly and we were still climbing and flying fast into the comfort of the ever darkening sky.

The crew arrived over Bochum to find the target partially covered with slightly broken cloud. Orchard continued:

Our function was to drop four flares visually to build up those dropped earlier by other Pathfinders and to add for good measure 10,000lb of high explosive bombs. Over the target area it was a three minutes run-up to the aiming point, straight and level.

Having marked the target the crew released their bombs. Ray immediately turned for home, jigging and weaving as he went, just as an orange glare lit the dark sky just fifty or so yards away. A Lancaster nearby had been hit by flak. The crew pressed on, putting the horrific sight to one side, but moments later their own Lancaster was hit. A blinding flash illuminated the inside of the aircraft. Before they had time to fully take stock of what was going on, they were going down fast but Ray eventually managed to get the Lancaster under control. They had been hit by flak. The aircraft's instruments, including the altimeter, had been taken out but with all his skill Ray nursed the stricken bomber back towards England. The radio had also packed up and so there was no way of communicating with anyone else or to know their height. Finally, having estimated they were somewhere over south-east England, Ray took the Lancaster down in the hope of breaking cloud. Orchard's account reveals what happened next:

Met reports had told us before we left that there would be cloud cover on return but no lower than 3,000 feet. So we continued to descend – still no break and still down we went and by now we had no alternative as we were fast running out of fuel. Suddenly we were through – airfield lights could be seen on the port side but to our horror the giant aircraft could not have been flying more than fifteen feet off the ground as we could see tops of trees above us. Met were wrong. Cloud cover was down to the floor but we would have diverted if we had been able to make [radio] contact. I had the feeling the old plane was trying to claw its way back into the sky – but alas the next thing I remember was opening my eyes, unable to move, looking up into that black night sky that was a comfort to us not many hours before. I heard people. I called and asked 'where am I?' and the guttural reply sounded ominous. I despaired we had crashed and were still in Germany.

The Lancaster had, in fact, come down in Norfolk and the rear turret of the Lancaster had broken away from the rest of the fuselage on impact with the ground. Orchard had been thrown clear and was later found. He was then rushed to hospital and was remarkably lucky to get away with just a broken leg, concussion and a bruised spine. A week or so later he was informed that he had been the sole survivor of his crew. Orchard summed up in his own words:

> *Little did any of us know at tea time there would be no supper for any of us that night.*

Bomber Command was learning some hard and costly lessons, but it was not all about large-scale raids against German cities. There was still the potential of small–scale low–level night precision raids against specific targets by the Lancasters of 617 Squadron.

Since carrying out the Dams raid the squadron had moved to Coningsby in Lincolnshire as a specialist unit. It was now under the command of 30-year-old George Holden, a highly decorated pilot with a DSO and a DFC and Bar, and on the night of 15/16 September the squadron carried out an attack against the notoriously tough and heavily defended Dortmund–Ems Canal. An attempt the previous night had to be aborted because of bad weather but eight of the squadron's Lancasters finally carried out the attack using a new 12,000 lb bomb. However, the combination of misty conditions and improved defences meant the raid was a failure. Not only had the canal not been breached but five of the Lancasters were lost.

Amongst those killed was Holden and his crew, which included four of Guy Gibson's crew who had taken part in the attack against the Ruhr dams: the navigator, Flight Lieutenant Torger Taerum DFC; the bomb aimer, Flying Officer Fred Spafford DFC DFM; the wireless operator, Flying Officer George Deering DFC; and Flight Lieutenant Robert Hutchison DFC and Bar, one of the air gunners. Also killed that night was 22-year-old Flight Lieutenant Les Knight DSO, another of the legendary 'Dambusters' who had breached the dam on the Eder, while another survivor of the Dams raid, 23-year-old Squadron Leader Dave Maltby DSO DFC, lost his life when his aircraft crashed into the North Sea during the aborted attempt the night before.

The raid on the Dortmund–Ems Canal had been a disaster for 617 Squadron and after these terrible losses the squadron was rested from operations. It needed time to recover. It also meant the end of low-level attacks by its Lancasters as from now on the squadron was to be trained as a specialist high-level bombing unit.

The night war went on and during the first week of October 1943 Bomber Command spread its effort across a number of German cities: Kassel on the night of 3rd/4th; Frankfurt (4th/5th); and Stuttgart (7th/8th). This latter raid against Stuttgart saw the introduction of ABC-equipped Lancasters of 101 Squadron. The squadron had been selected for the role of RCM to help counter the night fighter threat and its aircraft modified to carry the highly secret Airborne Cigar equipment, simply known as ABC.

ABC had been designed to jam the VHF communications frequencies being used by the German night fighters. To operate ABC meant an additional crew member, a German-speaking special duties operator who sat at a table just above the bomb bay. His task was to listen to the night fighter radio frequency in use and then cause confusion by broadcasting erroneous information at the appropriate point.

Not all of the squadron's aircraft were ABC-equipped but those that were could be easily identified by additional transmitter and receiver aerials; two fitted on top of the fuselage and a third under the nose. These modified Lancasters still carried a bomb load but typically 1,000 lb less than the Main Force bombers to take into account the weight of the specialist equipment and the operator.

In the early days of ABC the operator transmitted false information to the night fighter crews in German but the German defences soon became aware of this spoof tactic and countered it by broadcasting information across several different frequencies. The next tactic, therefore, was for the special duties operator to jam all the frequencies in use to prevent the night fighter crews receiving any transmitted information from the ground.

At that stage of the war, the aircraft and crews of 101 Squadron were all that Bomber Command had to fulfil this role and these specially equipped aircraft were considered so vital that the squadron was tasked to support every major Bomber Command raid until the end of the war. It is hardly surprising that the ABC-equipped Lancasters soon became prime targets for the German night fighters as they were able to home-in on the jamming frequency being used, which often led to high losses amongst the squadron's crews.

The night after the operational debut of ABC during the Stuttgart raid, Bomber Command returned to Hannover for its third major raid on the city in just two weeks. It was the last time Wellingtons took part in a Main Force raid after four years of war. Twenty-six Wellington Xs from the Polish 300 'Mazowiecki' Squadron at Ingham and the Canadian 432 Squadron RCAF from East Moor took part in the raid with all aircraft returning safely.

The development of technology continued and because of its operational limitations much effort had gone into improving Oboe. This led to Oboe Mk II of which four versions were produced: *Penwiper* (using the klystron tuneable valve, albeit unsuccessfully); *Pepperbox* (a modified *Penwiper* but also unsuccessful); *Fountain Pen* (the first successful modification using a magnetron and designated Oboe Mk IIF, which entered service in early 1944 and was also known as *Aspen*); and *Album Leaf* (more sophisticated than *Fountain Pen* and designated the Mk IIM, which became the standard variant with a theoretical accuracy of 0.01 mile).

Oboe's earlier problem of each aircraft having to fly the same approach path to the target had been solved by a technique known as the Delta Approach. This allowed several aircraft to use the system while running in to the target. Moreover, an increased number of pulse frequencies and the use of more than one wavelength meant that up to forty aircraft could use the system in the target area at any one time. These developments would, in turn, lead to the Mk III system, which entered service during mid-1944 with thirteen ground stations and ten mobile stations providing coverage across most of Bomber Command's target areas.

The latter weeks of 1943 saw the introduction of another new radio navigation aid called 'Gee-H', a 20–80 MHz transponder-based navigation system and blind-bombing device designed to replace Oboe. Given the technical designation AR.5525, the name Gee-H referred to the system's use of the existing Gee system as well as the use of the H-principle (twin-ranging) to determine the aircraft's location.

Because Gee already included a receiver unit and display, all that was needed was a broadcasting unit to trigger the ground station transceiver making it, in effect, a reverse Oboe. The new transmitter sent out pulses around 100 times per second, with the timing deliberately advanced or retarded slightly from other users; a technique known as jittering. This gave each aircraft a slightly different timing so that the system had a theoretical capacity of 100 users, although, in practice, it was typically used by seventy to eighty aircraft at a time. Only the signals originating from the aircraft were presented on the navigator's display, so that he could direct the pilot onto the right path. By knowing the range of the release point from the station, which had been computed and dialled into the equipment in advance, the navigator was then able to determine the point at which the bombs were released.

Like Gee, and all the other VHF and UHF systems, Gee-H was reliant on line-of sight and so was limited in range to around 300 miles from the ground station, although its accuracy of 150 yards was very good. Furthermore, with each aircraft determining its own timing, and by the use of jittering, it made the system less susceptible to jamming. Turning off the aircraft's transmitter simply reverted the system to straightforward Gee.

Gee-H made its operational debut during a raid against Düsseldorf on the night of 3/4 November 1943. Thirty-eight Lancasters were fitted with the equipment but less than half were able to use it to find the designated target, the Mannesmann tubular-steel works on the northern outskirts of the city. Twenty-one sets did not function correctly, forcing the crew to either return early or manage without it, and two aircraft did not return at all. As for the raid itself, nearly 600 aircraft took part with most bombs falling in the centre and to the south of the city. Eighteen aircraft failed to return (3 per cent of the force).

One Lancaster fortunate to make it back from Düsseldorf that night was 'QR-O' of 61 Squadron from Syerston flown by 21-year-old Flight Lieutenant Bill Reid, a young Scot flying his tenth op. Soon after crossing the Dutch coast at 21,000 feet the Lancaster was shot up by a Bf 110. The windscreen was shattered and Reid wounded in the head, shoulder and arms. The aircraft was difficult to control and its compasses and communications systems put out of action. The rear turret was also badly damaged, leaving Flight Sergeant Joe Emmerson exposed and freezing cold.

Having ascertained that his crew were unscathed, and saying nothing of his own injuries, Reid pressed on. But soon afterwards the Lancaster was attacked again, this time by a FW 190. Cannon shells raked the fuselage from stem to stern, killing the navigator, Pilot Officer John Jeffreys, while the young wireless operator, 22-year-old Flight Sergeant Jim Mann, collapsed on top of him, fatally wounded. The flight engineer, Flight Sergeant Jim Norris, had also been hit.

It had been a devastating blow. The Lancaster's mid-upper turret, where Flight Sergeant Cyril Baldwin had somehow managed to escape the carnage inside the fuselage, was now out of action and the Lancaster's oxygen and hydraulics systems ruptured.

Despite his own wounds, Norris went to the assistance of Reid, providing him with a portable emergency oxygen bottle and helping him steady the aircraft. Without the use of his main aircraft compass, with two turrets out of action and with two of his crew either dead or seriously wounded, Reid would have been fully justified in turning the aircraft back towards home but he later recalled:

In my mind, to turn round was not an option. We would have been turning back into the Main Force bombers, all heading in our direction and at different heights. I felt we stood a better chance if we carried on to the target. Besides, that's what we were there to do.

With Reid using the stars to aid navigation, Düsseldorf was reached an hour later. Down in the bomb aimer's position, Flight Sergeant Les Rolton had been almost oblivious to much that had gone on elsewhere. With the aircraft's communications system out of action he had been left totally isolated from the rest of the crew and all that had been going on back in the main fuselage. He knew they had been hit but he was unaware of how bad. All he knew was that they were now overhead Düsseldorf and that it was his job to deliver the bombs on target.

Reid used all his strength to hold the bomber steady, his arms wrapped around the aircraft controls. Then, with the bombs gone, he turned for home. Their bombing photos would later show that the Lancaster had been right over the centre of the target when the bombs were released.

With the windscreen shattered it was intensely cold inside the aircraft. Reid was steadily getting weaker through the loss of blood. Nonetheless, with the support of Norris, and again using the stars to aid navigation, he nursed the bomber homewards. Crossing the Dutch coast for a second time they ran into flak but escaped further damage.

Reid was now lapsing into semi-consciousness but somehow he managed to get the bomber back over the English coast where an airfield was sighted. Ground mist partially obscured the runway lights but Reid was not going to give up. Not now. With the aircraft's hydraulics out of action, the undercarriage had to be lowered using the emergency hand pump. Using all his strength, and with blood flowing from his gaping head wound and into his eyes, Reid expertly touched the aircraft down. He held it steady for as long as he could before the leg of the damaged undercarriage collapsed and after sliding across the concrete runway the Lancaster finally came to a halt.

The Lancaster had landed at the American base at Shipdham in Norfolk. It was just after 10 p.m.; five hours after they had taken off. Reid was rushed to hospital and it was there that he later learned of his award of the Victoria Cross. His citation concluded:

Wounded in two attacks, without oxygen, suffering severely from cold, his navigator dead, his wireless operator fatally wounded, his aircraft crippled and defenceless, Flight Lieutenant Reid showed superb courage and leadership in penetrating a further 200 miles into enemy territory to attack one of the most strongly defended targets in Germany, every additional mile increasing the hazards of the long and perilous journey home. His tenacity and devotion to duty were beyond praise.

Also recognized for his courage that night was Jim Norris; he was awarded the CGM. The rear gunner, Joe Emerson, would later be awarded the DFM. Sadly, though, Reid's wireless operator, Jim Mann, succumbed to his wounds two days later. It was a sad and personal loss to Reid. His crew had always been made so welcome during their visits to Mann's family home in Liverpool. While recovering in hospital at Ely, Reid wrote to Mann's parents:

Jim's loss must be still such a great shock to you and so hard to understand. It is hard for me to express myself in sympathy to you. But, having known and flown with Jim well over a year now, it just seemed we were part of a family, and I know you will understand the deep regret I have for this sad bereavement. At the time I never thought Jim was so badly wounded since he said not a word about it…. I was glad to hear that the others did manage to attend Jim's funeral and am sorry I was unable to pay my respects to such a fine member of our crew as Jim was. When I get my sick leave however, I'll most certainly visit you and let you know anything you want to hear about. If I can possibly help you in any other way please don't be afraid to ask me. Should you have any trouble about Jim's personal kit I'll see what I can do.

Just days after the Düsseldorf raid a new special duties group, No. 100 (Bomber Support) Group, was formed within Bomber Command to consolidate the increasingly complex world of electronic warfare and countermeasures within one organization.

Led by Air Vice-Marshal Edward Addison, the group was based in East Anglia and given four main tasks. Firstly, it was to give direct support to night bombing and other operations by carrying out attacks on enemy night fighter aircraft in the air or by attacks on ground installations. Secondly, it was to employ airborne and ground RCM equipment to deceive or jam enemy radio navigation aids, enemy radar systems and wireless signals. Thirdly, it would examine all intelligence on the offensive and defensive radar, radio and signalling systems of the enemy, with a view of future action within the scope of the first two tasks. And fourthly, the group was to provide immediate information, additional to normal intelligence information, as to the movements and employment of enemy fighter aircraft to enable the tactics of the bomber force to be modified to meet any changes.

Included in the new group were the *Serrate*-equipped Beaufighters of 141 Squadron, now based at West Raynham, tasked in a roving night fighter role. A crew report, typical of the squadron's latest activities, is that of 22-year old Flight Lieutenant Ron MacAndrew and his navigator Flying Officer Wilk, on the night of 19 November. The crew were patrolling the area of the German night fighter airfield of Bonn-Hangelar. The report reads:

Two distant 'Serrate' contacts to the north-east were ignored; one contact followed by AI contact at 19,000 feet near Aachen [to the west of their position] but enemy aircraft worked into a stern position and a 30-minute dogfight ensued. Followed enemy aircraft down to 3,000 feet before abandoning the chase near Eindhoven. During the descent the enemy aircraft was able to get into stern position three times and Beaufighter evaded only with difficulty.

Specialist equipment such as *Serrate*, *ABC*, *Monica*, *Mandrel* and *Tinsel* were just some of the new advances in technology that had been introduced. Others included: *Boozer* (designed to pick up enemy radar signals); *Grocer* (to jam enemy AI radars, primarily the FuG 202 and FuG 212); *Corona* (voice jamming of night fighter control frequencies); *Drumstick* (to jam HF transmissions); *Jostle* (to jam radio frequencies); *Piperack* (a radar jammer); *Shiver* (to jam ground-control intercept frequencies and gun-laying radars); *Tuba* (to jam electronic warfare); and *Perfectos* (homing in on to the German IFF).

The specialist crews of No. 100 Group would become experts in countering what had become a formidable German defence system. This was achieved by using the group's own night fighters as well as its own squadrons of heavy bombers, which included American-built B-17 Fortresses and B-24 Liberators, as well as Halifaxes and Stirlings, all modified with electronic devices and operated by highly trained specialists to detect enemy night fighters. They were to play an increasingly important part in helping to reduce the number of enemy night fighters engaging the main bomber stream. It was a battle that would last for the rest of the war and become ever more complex as more systems were introduced.

The Nachtjagd had moved forward too. The introduction of airborne radar had brought an end to *Wilde Sau*, but from this tactic came another, *Zahme Sau* ('Tame Boar'), a similar concept but one that gave freedom to the twin-engine, multi-crew, radar-equipped night fighters to operate alone rather than under any close direction.

Pioneered by Oberst Viktor von Lossberg, a former bomber pilot, the idea behind *Zahme Sau* was for the ground-based radars to detect a raid and for the night fighters to then be scrambled to designated holding points. Once on station the crews would wait for further instructions and to be directed towards the main bomber stream in large numbers. Having then got amongst the bombers the night fighter crews were left to use their own AI radars to detect their targets and press home their attacks.

Zahme Sau had not quite brought an end to the idea of operating single-engine fighters at night. A number of Bf 109Gs were fitted with better radio equipment to improve communications with the ground controllers and *Naxos* Z to home in on the H2S transmissions of bombers. Some 109G-6s and FW 190A-6s were also fitted with an early version of the FuG 216 *Neptun* to operate as radar-equipped night fighters with NJGr 10 and NJG 11.

Neptun was the codename given to a new series of airborne radars being developed by Flugfunkforschungsinstitut Oberpfaffenhofen (FFO – the German airborne radio research institute in Bavaria). Although the *Lichtenstein* series remained the most widely used radar equipping German night fighters during the war, *Neptun* would eventually supersede it.

Operating in the low to mid-VHF band, *Neptun* would soon be fitted to several types of night fighters. The FuG 217 and the mass-produced FuG 218, for example, operating on six mid-VHF frequencies between 158 and 187 MHz, were fitted to the Ju 88G-6 and Ju 88R-1, as well as the He 219 and Bf 110G-4. The transceiver used a *Hirschgeweih* ('stag's antlers') eight-dipole antenna array, an improvement on earlier designs with shorter elements, but still adding considerable weight to the aircraft and reducing its overall performance. Furthermore, the night fighter's own radar transmissions could be picked up, meaning the *hunter* also became the *hunted* as more RAF night fighters entered the combat arena.

As 1943 drew towards a close the stage was set for what would be the greatest concerted strategic air offensive yet mounted by Bomber Command – the Battle of Berlin; the hardest-fought and costliest campaign of them all.

Chapter Fourteen

The Big City

We can wreck Berlin from end to end if the USAAF will come in on it. It will cost between 400–500 aircraft. It will cost Germany the war.

Bomber Command had now expanded into a force capable of causing mass destruction and the statement above comes from a Minute from Harris to Churchill in early November 1943. The long nights now favoured sending large forces deep into the heart of Nazi Germany, including Berlin, and with the Americans on board, Harris believed that a combined all-out effort against the Nazi capital might just bring the war to an end, and so prevent a prolonged offensive on the ground.

The origins of this historic city date back to the early thirteenth century when it was part of German expansion east of the River Elbe. The two founding towns, Kölln and Berlin, affiliated soon after and when Friedrich III declared himself as King Friedrich I of Prussia, Berlin rose to become the royal capital. During its more recent history, the industrial revolution of the nineteenth century transformed it and led to its dramatic economic expansion and growth in population. Berlin soon became the main transport hub and economic centre of Germany and, in 1871, became the capital of the newly founded German Empire. At the end of the First World War, the Weimar Republic was proclaimed in Berlin and it was not long before all the suburban areas had been brought under Berlin's administration, taking the capital's population to about four million. Then, following the rise of Hitler and his National Socialists, Berlin became the capital of the Third Reich with the Reichstag becoming the centre of Hitler's power.

Berlin was, and still is, a large city by any standards. Not only was it Germany's largest city by some considerable margin during the war, it was the third largest city in the world. Its total area covered some 400 square miles with the main city centred on five central districts: Tiergarten, with its marvellous zoological garden and famous landmarks of the Reichstag, the Victory Column and the Brandenburg Gate; Mitte; Kreuzberg; Wilhelmsdorf; and Charlottenberg. Being the centre of Nazi Germany, and geographically lying midway between the Western and Eastern Fronts, Berlin was the big one as far as the crews of Bomber Command were concerned. To them it was known as the Big City.

It had been more than two months since Harris had sent his Main Force to Berlin. The results of the three most recent raids, carried out during August and September, had meant there were two main factors to take into consideration when deciding upon a new and sustained campaign. First, losses would have to be maintained at an economic level and second, the bombing would have to be concentrated around specific aiming points.

Regarding the first point, the losses, it was optimistic to expect losses to be maintained at an economic level. It should have been no great surprise to the planners that the three previous raids against Berlin had each resulted in losses exceeding 7 per cent. Yes, this was nearly double what was considered to be an acceptable and sustainable loss rate but then Berlin was that much further away than, for example, the Ruhr. Bombers going to Berlin had to spend far longer over enemy territory than when attacking the Ruhr, typically by as much as two or three hours depending on the route. This gave the German defences more time to locate and then intercept the main stream. It also gave the night fighter crews two bites of the cherry; first when the bombers were on their way to the target and then again on their way home.

While the desire to maintain losses to an economic level might have been optimistic, the second factor, that of concentrating the bombing around specific aiming points, was far more achievable. This was an area where Bomber Command had become very good. Navigation and target-marking had improved considerably over the past year. Furthermore, in the Lancaster, Bomber Command not only had an aircraft that could deliver a heavy bomb load over such a long distance, it now had them in large numbers, with half of the sixty-eight squadrons available to Harris so equipped.

While the Americans seemed uninterested in a bombing campaign against Berlin by day, Harris felt the time was right for an all-out offensive at night. Morale in Germany was supposedly low, with the war against the Russians not going well in the east and with Italy having turned against them in the south.

Morale in some parts of Germany might well have been low but the fact was that the bomber crews would be facing a formidable German defence system that now included a new night fighter wing, NJG 6. Around Berlin alone there were an estimated 600 flak units, of which 350 were heavy, and 200 searchlights. There was also a comprehensive arrangement of decoy sites around the Nazi capital, the best example being at Nauen in Brandenburg, some 20 miles to the west of the city centre, where more than 9 square miles had been turned into supposed industrial complexes and other buildings. A vast array of pyrotechnic devices had been installed to simulate all the aspects of Berlin's defences as well as Pathfinder target-marking at various stages of an attack. It was clever, very clever, and is known to have fooled many crews.

For historical purposes, the Battle of Berlin can be broken down into four distinct phases, with the opening round played out on the night of 18/19 November 1943. For this return to the Big City Bomber Command decided to split its resources with an all-Lancaster force of more than 400 aircraft going to Berlin while a second and slightly smaller force, mostly Halifaxes and Stirlings, went to Ludwigshafen.

The route to the Nazi capital took the Lancasters across the North Sea and Dutch coast, but the weather was not as good as had been hoped and the forecast winds proved unreliable. There were also problems with some H2S sets, which all amounted to a number of the Pathfinders failing to drop their markers. The Main Force did manage to bomb the city but bombing was scattered, making an assessment of the damage all but impossible. The long return route took the bombers south of Berlin and then to the south of the Ruhr, before crossing Belgium and northern France to make their way home. The one positive fact from the night was that few enemy night fighters were encountered. Only nine Lancasters were lost (2 per cent) but this first raid was generally considered a failure.

Four nights later the weather was considered near-perfect for a return to the city and so Harris ordered a maximum effort. To enable a greater tonnage of bombs to be dropped the route was almost direct to the target. For one new 50 Squadron crew based at Skellingthorpe near Lincoln, skippered by

20-year-old Flying Officer Mike Beetham, it was to be their first bombing op. Beetham's wireless operator, Sergeant Reg Payne, also only twenty years old, recalls his reaction during the briefing when he first found out that the target for the night was Berlin:

> *A single piece of red tape stretched from Lincoln, over the North Sea and all the way to Berlin. I felt my stomach turn over and my chest tighten. Not Berlin, surely not for our first op.*

After the squadron commander's briefing there followed the meteorological brief. It was then the turn of the squadron specialist leaders – navigation, bombing, wireless operator and gunnery – before the squadron's Intelligence Officer added his piece.

From the seemingly endless number of briefings the crews picked up all the information they needed for the raid. Beetham's bomb aimer, Sergeant Les Bartlett, kept a diary throughout his tour of operations. An extract from his long entry for Monday 22 November 1943 records in detail his first raid and provides a marvellous insight into what it was like to fly on a bombing op to the Nazi capital:

> *At 9,000 feet and still climbing we break cloud. It is almost dark yet all around we can see shapes, vague yet resolute, all moving in the same direction. It is rather comforting to know you are not alone in your effort, and from figures given us at briefing we know that for every kite we can see there must be a hundred we can't. Up and up we go, again in cloud, and finally at 20,000 feet we level out and settle down to a steady cruising speed. Already we can see the futile attempts of the enemy to stem the attack, all along the Dutch coast the bright flashes of the German 'heavy stuff' light up the clouds. Their prediction is bad though and the shells burst way below us. Now I get busy setting up my bomb panel – 'bombs selected', fusing switches 'on', distributor set – and I start my regular bit of jamming to the German radio direction finding apparatus codenamed 'Window'. They love it! From now on things begin to liven up. Far away on the port the defences of Bremen are in action against some poor sod off-track. Then, Hannover, they shoot up all they can but to no avail, our route, which we rigidly adhered*

to thanks to the skill of Frank [Swinyard], our navigator, takes us out of range of their flak. Searchlights try to pick us up, but that's useless, they can't get through the cloud. On and on we roar passing an occasional track marker put down by the Pathfinders. They quickly improve on that and follow up with 'REDS' cascading into 'GREENS' gradually descending into the clouds. These are the ones we bomb. Already I can see the first wave unloading their bombs. At the same time a line of fighter flares goes down, brilliant and bright, parallel to our track about 2 miles away, but don't panic, it's a decoy laid down by our Mosquito boys. Things are getting larger and clearer as we approach the target. Then the final turn in – this is it! I crane my neck in an excited attempt to see everything at once. It is my job to decide in my own mind which of all the target indicators is the most accurate. This done I give the necessary correction to Mike [Beetham] to get the TIs lined up in my bombsight. At last – 'bomb doors open', but look! Way down below us I see a Halifax, shouldn't like to prang him with my bombs, so we do a quick weave ending up on a parallel course, and with a final 'left, left, steady' to Mike, I press the 'tit' and up lurches the kite as 4,000lb of death shoot down and, can-by-can, our incendiaries scatter. Quickly I throw the jettison bars across to ensure we have no 'hang-ups' in the bomb bay, then we straighten up while the camera operates to photograph our aiming point. 'OK, camera operated, bomb doors closed' I shout. Now I have time to survey the scene. Below us is the capital of the Third Reich at our mercy. The clouds are too thin to hide the destruction which is taking place. Everywhere below us for miles around is burning, throwing up pink and scarlet through the clouds, making it so bright that I could have read a newspaper in my bombing compartment. The vivid yellow explosions of 'cookies' [4,000 lb bombs] bursting are so numerous that the figure of forty a minute must be a gross understatement. When we bombed in the fifth wave, they seemed to be bursting all over the target simultaneously. As far as flak is concerned it was very moderate and all fell short bursting about 3,000 feet below us. Across the port bow I saw a plane out of control, falling down to earth with smoke pouring from it, but no fire as far as I could see, so the crew had a fair chance to bale out. Another disconcerting sight was a 'scarecrow' fired by the German 'ack-ack', which burst about 1,000 yards starboard of us. They are supposed to represent a kite on fire, and believe me I was fooled, not having seen one before. It seemed to hang there. Numerous minor explosions followed and clouds of black smoke poured out, after which it just dropped to earth in a mass of flames. By now we are tearing speedily out of the target area, and ahead everything looks black, offering very inviting cover. This is the danger area really, where fighters usually wait. The red 'Very' signals, which they use to attract one another's attention in the air, were all around us, so, to avoid being 'jumped', Mike did a steady weave for about five minutes. Time passes rather slowly now. I suppose it's because we are keen to get back to base having accomplished our task. However, there are 600 miles to go so there is no need to get over-anxious. Cloud is still our greatest advantage. We pass near the defences of many German cities but the searchlights just can't break through the clouds; consequently, the flak is very dispersed and spasmodic. Finally, we pass the last track marker in enemy territory, and we alter course for the Dutch coast. Things begin to get quieter, but to be on the safe side we do an occasional banking search to ensure that no enemy night fighters are able to get us from underneath. Now all is quiet and Frank gives us the glad news that according to his calculations we are now crossing the Dutch coast. However, our presumed safety is rather premature, because 'wuff' and bang under our nose bursts three rounds of heavy stuff – obviously predicted at us. Away we go into violent evasive tactics while I pile on the agony by jamming their radio location with 'Window'. Again all is quiet – this time for good I hope – as we start letting down from the height of 25,000 feet, which we managed to attain after getting rid of our bombs. Half an hour later at 8,000 feet we are able to release our oxygen masks and breathe more freely once more. That is a relief that can be appreciated only after wearing one for seven hours. Now the fun starts. Don [Moore], our engineer, gets busy passing round to the rest of the crew flasks of hot coffee which refresh us no end, even to the extent of chatting a little on the intercom. Now we can see other kites as they switch on their navigation lights. As the English coast is reached we are in the centre of a great armada, there are hundreds and hundreds of little red, green and white navigation lights – actually, of course, the kites have been there all the time but without lights we couldn't see them. Now there is the problem of finding base. We are well below cloud now and can see kites weaving off in all directions, to their various 'dromes – luckily we haven't far to go. We are in our own circuit in no time, passing the usual message, 'Hello Black Swan [call-sign for RAF Skellingthorpe]. This is Pilgrim [50 Squadron call sign] D-Dog [aircraft identification]'. This is acknowledged by the friendly voice of the WAAF radio operator and we heave a sigh of relief as our wheels finally touch down on the runway.

For the record, Beetham's crew had been airborne for seven hours and fifteen minutes. They had been one of a mixed force of 764 aircraft – Lancasters, Halifaxes, Stirlings and Mosquitos – that went to Berlin that night, and it would prove to be the most effective raid against the Nazi capital of the war. Fortunately for the raiders, poor weather in some parts of Europe prevented a number of night fighters from getting airborne, and although Berlin had been found to be covered in cloud, marking was excellent, as was the bombing. But for the Stirling force it was to be the end of the road. More technical problems and high losses, percentage-wise, meant they were now withdrawn from the battle.

In view of the success of this second raid, Harris ordered another the following night. But mounting a third raid against Berlin in the space of just six nights meant that numbers were down. Less than 400 bombers took part, all but eighteen being Lancasters. The force arrived over the target to find it covered in cloud. Nonetheless, the sky-marking was again very good and the bombing accurate, and so the raid was considered a success.

There were two further raids against the Big City in the next ten nights. The first of these, on the night of 26/27 November, again involved the Beetham crew. It was their third trip to Berlin that week. An excerpt from Les Bartlett's diary describes what it was like over the target:

The first signs of Berlin were the searchlight belts of the outer defences. As we approached two kites were 'coned', one on either side of us, so we had a more or less unmolested passage through the inner belt. Those two kites took terrific punishment from the flak, which was 'spot on', yet they were both weaving frantically to escape when we lost sight of them. We were now close enough to the target to see the effect of our predecessors in the first wave and it really was terrific. The whole of the target area was a sea of flames, with two particular spots rather like volcanoes. Even when 4 miles high the glare was so intense you could clearly see streets and buildings amid the inferno. I opened our bomb doors and down went the whole load on a cluster of ground markers in the centre of Berlin. Whilst all this was taking place our wireless operator Reg reported two combats, and I was just in time to see the second, a Lancaster, going down in flames. As it began to spin, four parachutes very smartly appeared. I'm afraid the rest of the crew went down with the kite.

Twenty-eight Lancasters were lost that night but that was not all. Those bombers that did return home faced mist and fog over their bases in eastern England. Bartlett's diary entry covering the latter stages of the raid for that night continues:

As far as the enemy was concerned they gave us a few more rounds of heavy stuff at the Dutch coast and that was that. Fighters – nil. Little did we know it but here our troubles really began. First of all we ran into dense cloud. Then a message came through from base diverting us to RAF Pocklington near York because Skellingthorpe was fog-bound. After a spot of quick thinking by Frank, our navigator, we altered course for our new destination. Then the old kite starts icing up and we start losing height hand over fist. Luckily freezing height was 5,000 feet and we found that nearer the deck we thawed out and at 1,000 feet we crossed the coast near the Humber. From there Frank directed us on radar straight to RAF Pocklington. Visibility was bad but we could see the flare path, and Mike called them up in double-quick time. This was where we got our first shock. They wouldn't take us; said visibility was not good enough and they diverted us to the next 'drome, RAF Melbourne. Things were really serious now. Obviously the weather was deteriorating rapidly, and we were running short of fuel, so off we went – no messing about! We got into Melbourne circuit and called them up. There was much more fog here than at previous 'drome, but we just HAD to get down here so in we went. The glow of the flare path was just visible through the fog and by a miraculous combination of good piloting by Mike and good luck, we lined up on the runway first shot to touch down on our first attempt. There's no doubt about it; this was our lucky night. We were the first of the squadron to land here, and judging by the messages passing on RT [radio] things were really chaotic. We had already heard two of the squadron ordered out to sea and bale out because their fuel was down to nil, so we parked the kite as instructed by air traffic control and piled out, getting as far from the runway as possible and only just in time. Immediately behind us 'A–Able' [JB485 flown by Pilot Officer Toovey] came in and swerved off the runway, becoming bogged down in the soft ground, then down came 'X-Xray' [DV377 – Pilot Officer Weatherstone] who missed the runway completely, hit a van then slap into 'A–Able'. Both kites caught fire. However, the crews were prepared for anything at this stage and were all out in a flash and no one was even injured. The usual RAF Standard 8 van was on airfield duty. Sadly the driver of the van was killed. Actually a wheel had passed over the vehicle and the van's engine was partly buried in the ground. While all this had been taking place, 'K-King' [ED393 flown by 20-year-old Flight Sergeant Joseph Thompson DFM] had been trying to land and, after many unsuccessful attempts, hit a farmhouse. The only survivor was the rear gunner. The poor farmer and his wife were also killed.

In addition to the squadron's three aircraft written off at Melbourne, 50 Squadron had lost a fourth Lancaster that night; DV178 'N-Nan', flown by Pilot Officer J C Adams, was missing over Germany. In all, fourteen Lancasters were forced to crash-land at various airfields, taking the overall loss rate amongst the Lancaster force for the night to an unacceptable 9.5 per cent.

The last raid against Berlin of this opening phase took place on the night of 2/3 December. It was planned to be a maximum effort but fog in Yorkshire meant that many Halifaxes were unable to take part. Many other aircraft turned back after encountering bad weather and icing over the North Sea. Those crews that did continue found the weather to be bad all the way to the target, causing the Main Force to become scattered. Worst still, the German night fighters were waiting for them. The raid ended up a failure with only slight damage caused to the city and forty aircraft lost (8.7 per cent), many of which were shot down on their way home.

Although the Nazi capital had been the focus of attention during the past two weeks, there had been other large raids as well – to Leverkusen, Frankfurt and Stuttgart – but following this latest disappointment, it would be two weeks before the next raid was ordered against the Big City.

The end of this initial phase had already brought many questions but Harris was determined for the campaign against Berlin to be a success. He had no doubts that by April his command could achieve '*a state of devastation in which surrender is inevitable*' just as long as he was given priority in certain areas, such as the production of Lancasters and operational equipment.

The second phase of the Berlin offensive began on the night of 16/17 December. Favourable weather conditions, including fog over some of the German night fighter airfields, meant that Harris could send an all-Lancaster force of nearly 500 aircraft to the Nazi capital, plus some Mosquitos to mark the target and to drop decoy markers to the south of the city. Although some night fighters managed to get airborne to harass the Main Force, conditions proved mostly favourable. Even though Berlin was covered by cloud, accurate sky-marking meant that bombing was a success. But again, many bombers returned to find their own bases covered by low cloud and fog. In addition to the twenty-five Lancasters lost during the raid, a further twenty-nine crashed on landing or had to be abandoned because of the weather. One Pathfinder unit, 97 Squadron based at Bourn, lost seven aircraft that night.

With the Lancaster force having suffered an overall loss rate in excess of 11 per cent, it was a bad start to the second phase and so it was a week before Harris ordered a return to the city. There was in between an unsuccessful raid against Frankfurt (on the night of 20th/21st) by a large mixed force of 650 aircraft. Forty-one aircraft failed to return (more than 6 per cent), eight of which fell to a Ju 88 flown by Hauptmann Wilhelm Herget, the Kommandeur of I./NJG 4, a record number of successes in one night.

For the next raid against Berlin on the night of 23/24 December, a longer and more southerly route was planned and with fewer bombers taking part. It was essentially an all-Lancaster force of 364 aircraft, supported by a handful of Halifaxes and Mosquitos carrying out a diversionary raid on Leipzig to the south-west. The longer route and diversion plan seemed to work well with overall losses for the raid at a little over 4 per cent.

These were fewer losses than before and came as some welcome news, but the raid also resulted in the lowest tonnage of bombs dropped on the Nazi capital. Damage was assessed as only slight and overall it had not been one of Bomber Command's most effective raids.

Six nights later, Harris ordered another maximum effort against Berlin. It was a bitterly cold day as the crews waited at their bases across eastern England. Reg Payne recalls what it was like at Skellingthorpe in those final moments before climbing aboard the aircraft:

It seemed particularly cold out on the dispersal pan as we waited underneath the wings of our new aircraft LL744 'VN-B Baker' (soon to be more affectionately known to the crew as 'B-Beetham'). The lazy wind blew gently enough, but coming across the open expanses of the aerodrome it cut straight across our clothing. This final waiting outside the aircraft, despite the cold, had its purpose as it gave us all, especially the gunners, a last opportunity to take care of the calls of nature in the dark at the side of the dispersal.

The short days and long transit to the target meant that take-off was early; soon after 5 p.m. More than 700 aircraft (two-thirds being Lancasters and the rest Halifaxes) took a long southerly route to Berlin. The initial part of the route towards Leipzig and a diversionary tactic by Mosquitos, succeeded in confusing the German defences and so the Main Force reached Berlin with relative ease. They had been helped by some bad weather over many night fighter airfields restricting the number able to get airborne, which kept the losses for the raid to below 3 per cent. But Berlin had again been found covered in cloud and so bombing was scattered.

There was to be no rest for the crews as three nights later, on the opening night of 1944, Berlin was again the target. This time an all-Lancaster force of more than 400 aircraft took part but a combination of factors meant the night was not one of the best. The Main Force was picked up soon after crossing the Dutch coast and many bombers were shot down without reaching the target. Those crews that did reach Berlin again found the city covered in cloud. Target-marking was hampered by a strong wind and the overall result was scattered and ineffective bombing. Losses were high, with twenty-eight Lancasters failing to return (6.6 per cent).

Despite these latest losses, Harris ordered another all-Lancaster attack on Berlin the following night. With the squadrons having less than twenty-four hours to recover and prepare for the next raid, it was a slightly smaller force of 362 Lancasters that went to the Nazi capital that night. The route taken was near-direct and so it did not take the German controllers long to work out where the target was most likely to be. The Pathfinders suffered particularly badly. Out in front of the Main Force they were the first to be intercepted by German night fighters. Nearly one-third were shot down or forced to return to base with the Warboys-based Lancasters of 156 Squadron losing five of its fourteen aircraft during the raid. With the Pathfinders having been mauled on their way to the target the result of the Main Force bombing was scattered with no specific damage caused. Another twenty-seven Lancasters were lost (7.5 per cent).

Despite the best efforts of all those who took part, this last effort was yet another ineffective raid and brought to an end the second phase of the battle. In the ten raids flown against Berlin since the opening night of the campaign six weeks before, nearly 5,000 individual sorties had been flown and more than 16,000 tons of bombs dropped. The vast majority of these sorties, 86 per cent in fact, had been flown by the Lancaster crews. But the offensive had already come at a high cost; 239 aircraft had been lost so far, 212 of which were Lancasters.

The combination of the hard winter weather and a period of full moon brought to a close what had been a series of unsuccessful raids against the Big City. History tells us this was only half-time in the Battle of Berlin but there were already many reasons for the lack of success. The long transits in the height of winter and the amount of time the crews had to spend over enemy territory was certainly a factor, as was the fact that the German defence system had ample warning of where the target was most likely to be, giving the night fighters plenty of opportunity to intercept the raids. Furthermore, the frequency of the raids and the decision to withdraw the Stirlings, and then the Halifaxes, had also meant the number of bombers dispatched for each raid were lower than might have been expected at the start of the campaign. Only twice had the so-called maximum efforts produced more than 500 aircraft.

With Bomber Command's crews given little time to rest between these long missions, fatigue must also have been a contributing factor. As for the results of the bombing, poor weather and plenty of cloud over Berlin during the winter had made marking difficult; not helped by the losses suffered by the Pathfinders on the way to the target. Morale amongst the crews of Bomber Command was dropping in the face of high losses for little positive result.

Studies showed that at this stage of the campaign less than a quarter of Berlin had been destroyed, a figure that compares less favourably with other major cities at the time: Hamburg – 70 per cent devastated; Wuppertal (70 per cent); Mannheim and Hannover (both estimated to be 55 per cent destroyed); Düsseldorf and Essen (40 per cent); and Dortmund (33 per cent).

All these factors had resulted in an ineffective and costly campaign so far. For the campaign to be more successful, Harris clearly had to bring greater numbers of aircraft into his plans and this meant the Halifax squadrons rejoining the battle. There would be other plusses as well. More Mosquitos were now available and more of the Pathfinder's Lancasters were equipped with the latest H2S sets.

For the next two months, more aircraft, more bombs and more lives would be thrown into the mix, and after visits to Stettin and Brunswick, the Berlin offensive resumed on the night of 20/21 January 1944. Nearly three weeks had passed since the previous raid on the Nazi capital and once again Harris ordered a maximum effort. This time a large force of 769 aircraft was made available, including 264 Halifaxes. Planning did away with the direct-line approach to the target, but large amounts of cloud over Berlin meant that it was difficult to assess the results of the raid.

The Nachtjagd had again enjoyed a night of success, mainly at the expense of the Halifax force with twenty-two of the type failing to return, more than 8 per cent of those that had taken part. Pocklington's 102 Squadron, in particular, had a bad night with five of its sixteen Halifaxes lost during the raid.

Although the defenders had enjoyed much success, not all night fighter crews had things their own way. Werner Hoffmann, for example, now a Hauptmann and acting Kommandeur of I./NJG 5, owed his life that night to his parachute. He was patrolling over Berlin and had just shot down his twentieth victim but then found himself up against a most determined Lancaster rear-gunner. His starboard engine was soon on fire. In David P Williams' book *Hunters of the Reich; Night Fighters*, Hoffmann described what happened next:

As I couldn't extinguish it [the fire] the only thing my crew and I could do was to jump out using our parachutes. We got out of the aircraft without any trouble...after the jerk of my parachute opening I was suspended at about 5,000 metres [16,500 feet] with the British aircraft and the German night fighters flying all around me. From above the bombs were falling and from below the flak was firing – it was not a pleasant situation to be in.

As he descended to earth amidst the chaos of Berlin, Hoffmann's next hazard was a large building on fire, but although bombs were still falling and flak was still firing he drifted to safety and came down away from danger.

Three RAF bombers were claimed that night by the Luftwaffe night fighter ace, Major Heinrich Prinz zu Sayn-Wittgenstein, the 27-year-old Kommodore of NJG 2. Often referred to as the Prince of Darkness, Sayn-Wittgenstein was one of the most complex characters in the Luftwaffe. Born of aristocratic descent in Denmark but raised in Switzerland, he was a former cavalryman and then bomber observer before qualifying as a bomber pilot. He then transferred to the night fighter force and by early 1944 was in command of NJG 2 having taken his personal total into the sixties for which he had been awarded the Knight's Cross and Oak Leaves.

There were few, if any, better Ju 88 night fighter pilots than Sayn-Wittgenstein. He preferred the type over the Bf 110 and had formed a strong partnership with his trusted *Bordfunker*, Herbert Kümmritz. But Kümmritz had recently gone on leave and so he was flying with Feldwebel Friedrich Ostheimer that night when they had intercepted the Main Force near Berlin. But while shooting down their third victim that night they almost collided with the Lancaster they were in the process of shooting down. In Spick's *Luftwaffe Fighter Aces*, the author gives Ostheimer's account of what happened:

... a burst from Schräge Musik blew a big hole in the wing and started a blazing fire. This time the British pilot reacted unusually: he remained at the controls of his burning machine and dived down on top of us. Our Prinz, too, whipped the Ju 88 into a dive, but the blazing monster came closer and closer and hung in visual contact over our cabin. I had only one thought: 'We've had it!' A heavy blow staggered our aircraft, Prinz Wittgenstein

lost control of the machine and we went into a spin, plunging down into the night.

It took all of Sayn-Wittgenstein's experience and skill to recover the Ju 88 several thousand feet lower and to then belly-land it safely, only to find that a large part of the starboard wing was missing and to discover a large hole in the rear fuselage. Although Sayn-Wittgenstein was fortunate on this occasion, his luck ran out the following night when he was shot down during a *Zahme Sau* mission after intercepting a raid on Magdeburg. Sayn-Wittgenstein had already claimed four Lancasters in less than forty minutes but during an attack on a fifth his Ju 88R was hit and caught fire. The crew baled out but the wreckage of the night fighter was found in a forest the following day. The body of Sayn-Wittgenstein was nearby, his parachute unopened. He may have caught part of the aircraft, possibly the vertical stabilizer, as he jumped out.

At the time of his death Sayn-Wittgenstein was the Luftwaffe's highest-scoring night fighter pilot, having been credited with shooting down eighty-three aircraft. He was posthumously awarded the coveted Swords, making him only the eighteenth member of the Luftwaffe at that time to have been so recognized. On 25 January 1944 his death was announced in the *Wehrmachtbericht*:

The commodore of a night fighter wing Major Prince zu Sayn-Wittgenstein found, engaged in combat with enemy terror fliers, after achieving his 83rd nocturnal aerial victory, after destruction of five British bombers, a heroes death. The Führer honoured the fallen night fighter with the presentation of the Oak Leaves with Swords to the Knight's Cross of the Iron Cross. With him the Luftwaffe loses one of their most outstanding night fighter pilots.

It is possible that Sayn-Wittgenstein had fallen to a Mosquito night fighter. Many were now patrolling over enemy territory, particularly around the Nachtjagd's airfields, while the main raids were taking place. In an attempt to counter this mounting threat the Bf 110 units increased the number of patrols, but the truth was that the heavily laden 110 was too slow to be effective against the fast and highly-manoeuvrable Mosquito.

The death of Sayn-Wittgenstein had been a huge blow for the Nachtjagd and came on the same night and just a few miles from where another night fighter ace had fallen in combat. This was Hauptmann Manfred Meurer, the Kommandeur of I./NJG 1. Having shot down sixty-five aircraft he was the Luftwaffe's fifth highest-scoring night fighter pilot but he and Oberfeldwebel Gerhard Scheibe, the first *Funker* to have been awarded the Knight's Cross, were killed after their He 219A was hit by debris falling from a Lancaster they were attacking to the east of Magdeburg. Both aircraft fell to earth in flames.

Given the way the Luftwaffe operated at night, with the high-scorers always at the forefront of the action while others new to the game were left to mooch around in the dark, such losses were inevitable. Nonetheless, these losses had a psychological effect on the crews as did the sight of German cities seemingly endlessly ablaze under the weight of attacks, knowing that their citizens were taking a severe pounding. But while such sights might have demoralized some, others were driven on; more determined than ever to make Bomber Command pay for the death and destruction being caused.

The Nachtjagd was fighting the air war over Germany under the direction of Wolf Falck. Now an Oberst and holding the title *Einsatzleiter Nachtjagd* (Head of Night Operations) he was responsible for the fighter defence of the Reich. From his headquarters in Berlin Falck was updated each night on the developing air war by using a large map, divided into a system of grid squares, so that he could direct the air battle as it evolved. Using this simple but effective system he was able to determine the likely target for that night and how many bombers were involved, so that he could direct the German defences accordingly.

Meanwhile, for Bomber Command, the raid against Berlin on the night of 20/21 January had not been a good return to the campaign for the Halifax squadrons. In view of the losses suffered that night Harris decided to leave them out of the next raid a week later when an all-Lancaster force of over 500 aircraft, supported by fifteen Mosquitos, went back to the city.

Once again, an indirect route was taken to confuse the enemy defences. Diversionary operations also seemed to work well as few night fighters were encountered on the way to the target. But the crews again arrived over Berlin to find the city covered by cloud. However, marking was good, as was the bombing, and so the raid was assessed to have caused reasonable damage to the city, although a number of bombers were intercepted on their way home by prowling night fighters. Thirty-three Lancasters were lost during the raid (6.4 per cent).

Just twenty-four hours later the Main Force was on its way back to Berlin. Harris again ordered a maximum effort and this time a mixed force of 677 aircraft (two-thirds Lancasters and one-third Halifaxes) were involved. As with the earlier intense phases of the campaign, there had been no rest for the Lancaster crews of Bomber Command. The late night of the previous raid was followed by a day of preparation and then waiting for the op that night.

The Beetham crew of 50 Squadron had flown against Berlin the night before on what was their longest sortie of the war – five minutes short of nine hours. They were now to take part in their ninth raid against the Nazi capital, and their fourteenth op overall. Les Bartlett's entry for Friday 28 January 1944 reads:

Although we didn't get to bed until 0430 hrs we had to get up at 0900 hrs to go to RAF Waddington to collect a Lanc, the rest of the squadron being able to stay in bed until lunchtime. On return to base we went straight to the mess and found we were down on the operational list so the usual procedure was followed; briefing was tannoyed for 1415 hrs and we found that it was Berlin once more. Things were rather uncertain at flight planning, and although everything was prepared, take-off time was not decided, but was provisionally fixed for 2345 hrs. Of course, we all intended to get about three hours' sleep in the mess during the evening, but the inevitable card game started and we played until 2130 hrs, following up with an operational supper of ham and eggs. At 2230 hrs we donned our flying gear, got transport out to the aircraft and passed a leisurely hour doing final checks on engines and equipment. There is none of the usual glamour attached to a midnight take-off compared with a daylight flight.

The route taken for this latest raid on the Big City was a long north-easterly transit across Denmark and then south-east towards Berlin; then returning in the opposite direction. It was a good route in some respects as it took the bombers too far north for many of the Luftwaffe's night fighters, while others were drawn away by diversionary raids. However, the route taken by the bombers, and the pattern of the winter thus far, made the target predictable and so the German controllers had managed to concentrate the night fighters around Berlin.

Despite all that was going on around them, the Pathfinder crews accurately marked the target. The cloud over the city was broken and so some ground-marking was possible. It was the most concentrated attack by Bomber Command of this period and as far as the bombing was concerned, the raid was a success. But the biggest hazard for the returning force turned out to be the weather, with severe icing and strengthening headwinds, causing some aircraft to crash on their way home. Forty-six aircraft failed to return (6.8 per cent).

The Combat Report submitted by 50 Squadron to HQ No. 5 Group for this raid includes an account relating to the Beetham crew:

At 0323 hours, on the bombing run, position target, height 21,300 feet, speed 146 [knots] rectified, on a course of 100 magnetic, a Ju 88 was sighted by Captain on starboard down, and rose to ahead, crossing from starboard to port at 500 yards. The front and mid–upper gunners [Sergeants Les Bartlett and 'Jock' Higgins] both opened fire allowing 1 1/8 rads deflection, strikes were observed. 'B'- 50 [VN-B of 50 Squadron] executed a corkscrew to starboard and enemy aircraft flew down on the port beam. The Ju 88 is claimed as damaged. Monica did not indicate. Weather – clear; Front gunner – 50 rounds; Mid-Upper – 100 rounds.

As with all combat reports, the crew is then listed and the report signed by the Gunnery Leader [in this case Flight Lieutenant A Gray], the squadron commander [Wing Commander T W Chadwick] and the station commander [Group Captain D Christie].

Two nights later the Main Force returned to Berlin once more. It was the third raid in just four nights. More than 500 aircraft took part, mostly Lancasters, with the route being the familiar northern track across Denmark. The return route, however, was direct so that a greater tonnage of bombs could be dropped.

The weather encountered over Europe, though, was bad, with thick cloud and icing. It was again mainly around Berlin that most of the aerial combats took place with several bombers shot down. More thick cloud over the target area made an assessment of the raid difficult, although it is believed that bombing was concentrated and caused significant damage to the city. Thirty-three bombers failed to return; all but one were Lancasters (6.2 per cent).

There were, however, some successes for the RAF that night. One crew flying a *Serrate*-equipped Mosquito II of 141 Squadron claimed their first victim of the war. Flight Lieutenant Graham Rice and his young radar operator, 21-year-old Flying Officer Jimmy Rogerson, had been together for a while having first flown the Beaufighter in a defensive role, but they had only converted to the Mosquito earlier that month. After spending many night hours searching for the enemy over southern England without any luck, they now had the freedom to fly over occupied Europe and hunt down the enemy over their own territory.

To cover the raid against Berlin, Rice and Rogerson were patrolling the Hamburg area. It was still early evening but the time of year meant they had been able to make the long transit from their base at West Raynham under the cover of darkness. Rogerson first obtained an AI contact to starboard at an estimated range of 40–50 miles. Other contacts started to appear but these were ignored; to be dragged so far away from the area of patrol would have negated their reason for being there. Then, at 7.30 p.m., a *Serrate* contact was obtained. Rice manoeuvred the Mosquito into position and after chasing the contact for a couple of minutes, Rogerson picked it up on his AI set at 20,000 feet.

Climbing gradually, the Mosquito gave chase. The enemy aircraft was flying an orbit, searching for its own prey, and seemingly unaware the Mosquito was even there. The range started to close and approaching the enemy aircraft from below, Rice and Rogerson stared out into the dark night sky. They were still closing. Then a silhouette appeared. They could now see it more clearly. It was a Bf 110.

The range suddenly reduced as the 110 peeled away to starboard and began to descend, possibly in response to the Mosquito closing. But it then settled again at 18,000 feet and started an orbit to port. Maintaining visual or radar contact during a descending turn in the dark was never easy, and the Bf 110 might have got away, but Rogerson again picked it up on his AI set and so Rice took the Mosquito in closer. The crew's combat report states what happened next:

> *Our aircraft obtained another visual at 600 feet and opened fire in a 5-6 second burst. E/A's [enemy aircraft's] port engine burst into flames and it reared up and blew up, parts of it flying past our aircraft, which pulled out of the way. Mosquito watched it spiral down in flames with thick black smoke pouring out and crew saw a dull reflection through cloud where E/A had crashed. It is claimed as one Me 110 destroyed.*

The crew landed back at West Raynham after more than four hours in the air. In all, 120 rounds had been fired and the aircraft was confirmed as destroyed. It was the first of their eventual total of three aircraft shot down together.

The RAF's own radar-equipped night fighters of No. 100 Group were proving a menace for the Nachtjagd. They were difficult to intercept and shoot down, as were the Pathfinder Mosquitos. In fact, the RAF Mosquitos had become such a problem that two of the Luftwaffe's specialist units, JG 300 and NJGr 10, were given the task of countering their growing threat.

The winter weather was continuing to be a problem all along the eastern part of England, making it difficult for the bomber squadrons to maintain the high operational tempo demanded by Harris. The harsh conditions made it particularly hard for the ground personnel. Day after day and night after night they were left to work in freezing cold temperatures to keep the runways, taxiways and hard standings free of heavy snow and ice just to keep the airfield operational. They also had to maintain the aircraft in bitterly cold temperatures as best described by Sergeant John 'Buck' Rogers, a Fitter II serving with 100 Squadron at Grimsby, when later recalling what it was like to carry out an engine change:

> *The kite was towed to the hangar where, overnight, working high up on the servicing platforms in chilling sub-zero wind, we struggled with spanners and hand torches. Our eyes watered and our noses ran. Our frozen fingers fumbled. After what seemed to be a lifetime we reached the stage for a test-*

run. The kite had to be serviceable by dawn but the hangar doors were immovably frozen open at both ends. The wingtip clearance at each side was about a foot or so and with a couple of 'bods' on the towing arm we could keep her straight until clear of the hangar doors. But outside the apron was smothered with frozen, rutted snow and glazed ice on a falling gradient. I would also have to blast her round to port towards the perimeter track. I had visions of losing her in a colossal broadside. There were no volunteers so I decided to run-up in the hangar. The noise was shattering and in moments the watchers stationed at critical positions around the aircraft had stepped outside. I need not have worried. The air pressure and brakes held; the tail arm kept the tail wheel straight and the chocks did not move whilst I feathered and un-feathered the prop, checked the magnetos and finally went through to full power as the exhaust glowed cherry red. All indicated serviceable and OK. However, any loose equipment which happened to be in the slipstream was soon removed some fifty yards outside the hangar! As a result I was offered a severe reprimand, with no further questions asked, or a court martial!

A severe reprimand it was to be. There followed a short break as the combination of bad weather and early February moon temporarily prevented further attacks against the Big City. For everyone involved the rest was most welcome. In this latest series of raids, spanning just eleven nights, more than 2,500 individual sorties had been flown and over 8,000 tons of bombs dropped.

Although it had been an intense period of operations, the offensive against the Nazi capital was now yielding success. An assessment of this third phase revealed that damage to Berlin was significant. Large areas of the city were in ruins and the effect on its population must have been devastating. Although bomber losses remained high, and still above what was considered to be sustainable for that stage of the war, these past few raids had produced far better results.

After two weeks of minor operations, Bomber Command returned to Berlin for its fourth and final phase of the campaign. In reality it was not a phase as only two raids, separated by more than five weeks, were flown against the city. Nonetheless, they were both huge efforts.

The long lay-off meant the first of these, flown on the night of 15/16 February, produced nearly 900 aircraft for the raid, of which 561 were Lancasters. It was another record for the type and was the largest force assembled for a single attack since the Thousand Bomber raids nearly two years before. It was also the heaviest raid on Berlin of the war with more than 2,500 tons of bombs dropped, resulting in extensive damage to the city, although another forty-three bombers were lost (4.8 per cent).

With the Air Staff demanding attacks against other German targets, which were considered to be far more important to the overall war effort than Berlin, it would be some time before Harris was able to return to the Nazi capital. Although he had been issued with a new directive in January, calling for attacks against primary targets such as Schweinfurt, Leipzig and Brunswick, it had taken Harris until the end of the third week of February before one of these cities was attacked. In this case it was Leipzig. Schweinfurt, meanwhile, listed as the priority target because of its production of ball-bearings, was not bombed until even later in the month.

The night war being fought above the Reich was as intense now as it was at any stage of the war. For one young Nachtjagdflieger, 23-year-old Oberleutnant Paul Zorner, the large raids provided a perfect opportunity to rack up his personal score. A former transport pilot, Zorner was now Kapitän of 8./NJG 3 and an accomplished marksman. He was also a master of multiple successes in one night.

Like many junior night fighter pilots, Zorner had to wait patiently for his first success but he had been fortunate to learn from men like Prinz zur Lippe-Weissenfeld, his Gruppenkommandeur, and it was now that Zorner blossomed. With his Bf 110G fitted with the deadly combination of *SN-2* and *Schräge Musik*, his most notable period was in February 1944 when he was credited with shooting down nine RAF bombers in just two nights of fighting. He first claimed four Lancasters during the early hours of the 20th while intercepting the Leipzig raid and then five nights later he took off from Lüneburg to meet a strong bomber force heading across northern France towards southern Germany. It was the opening phase of the Schweinfurt raid.

Transiting to the east of the Ruhr at 5,500 metres (18,000 feet), Zorner headed south towards his designated patrol area near Stuttgart. To be a successful night fighter pilot required many attributes, not least patience and an ability to strike quickly when the opportunity presented itself. This particular night was to be no different. Loitering for two hours and listening to commentary coming from the ground could be tedious, and at times disorientating, but the better night fighter crews learned how to build and then maintain an air plot in their mind. This required patience and an appreciation of what was going on around them.

When further reports came through that the main bomber stream had turned east instead of continuing south, Zorner felt it might not be their night. But when his *Bordfunker*, Oberfeldwebel Heinrich Wilke, suddenly reported a radar contact crossing in front of them, Zorner demonstrated the ability to react and strike quick. In David P Williams' book *Hunters of the Reich: Night Fighters*, Zorner later recalled what happened next:

> *I saw, left of me and a little higher, a four-engine bomber. I went down a little lower and took my aircraft astern and below the bomber, a Lancaster. I intended to attack with my Schräge Musik. With my first attack I saw the explosive shells above me, but with no effect on the bomber. So I decided to attack again, this time with 'Spray Fire' – that is, I wouldn't fire one exact burst but fly my aircraft in such a way that a long burst of fire would be located in and around the bomber in a sort of funnel shape. The result came about unexpectedly quickly. The bomber began to burn in both wings, and we were able to move off to one side and watch. The bomber went into a flat turn to the left, then into a steeper dive, finally going down vertically south-west of Stuttgart.*

Zorner was amongst the main bomber stream and in the next fifteen minutes he shot down two more Lancasters in quick succession. It was still only 10.30 p.m. and with three successes already that night he headed for the airfield at Echterdingen to refuel and re-arm.

Thirty minutes later he was back in the air. Bombs had already started falling on Schweinfurt but a second wave of bombers was now being tracked across Belgium. Zorner headed straight for them, climbing as he went, and minutes later Wilke picked up a number of radar returns heading towards them and above. By the time they were to the north of Stuttgart they had climbed above 6,000 metres (21,000 feet). Zorner then spotted a lone bomber ahead and off to the right. He attacked and in no time at all the Lancaster was on its way earthwards in flames.

Zorner then took up a heading towards Schweinfurt. It took twenty minutes to chase down the second wave of bombers heading for their target. Wilke then picked up a radar contact below. The sky was clear, making it easy for Zorner to spot his next victim, another Lancaster, and moments later he had taken up a position just 100 metres (300 feet) beneath the bomber. It was clear to him that they had not been seen, but Zorner's first burst with *Schräge Musik* did not hit, nor did the bomber react. It simply flew on. Easing the nose of the 110 upwards to get closer still, Zorner's next burst was deadly, sending the Lancaster to earth in flames.

His latest victim, his fifth that night, had taken Zorner's total to thirty-five. It had been his most successful night so far. Promotion to the rank of Hauptmann followed, as did the award of the German Cross in Gold, but he would have to wait until June, when his score had reached forty-eight, before he was finally awarded the Knight's Cross. He would later add the Oak Leaves while Heinrich Wilke received the Knight's Cross.

More bad weather and unfavourable moon conditions during the first half of March 1944 restricted Bomber Command to a series of minor operations, but the heavy raids resumed on the night of 15/16 March when more than 850 aircraft went to Stuttgart with minimal success. Two large raids on Frankfurt followed and then Harris decided to have one last crack at Berlin. He knew all too well that the Allies were looking ahead towards a landing in north-west Europe, with targets in northern France considered to be a higher priority, and so he would have one final go at Berlin. It would give him one last chance to finish off the Big City before his squadrons were needed for other tasks.

The opportunity to go back to Berlin for one last time fell on the night of 24/25 March with more than 800 bombers due to take part. The weather forecast predicted a warm front over the North Sea with colder air towards the Frankfurt area and across to Vienna. A belt of cloud was expected along the front but to the east there would be patchy cloud at medium altitude and little or no low cloud. Even further to the east of the Baltic coast there would be broken cloud and good visibility, while over Berlin there was a good chance of clear skies, although there was also a possibility that thick cloud would cover the target. Meanwhile, back at the bomber airfields, fog was forecast to develop during the early hours of the morning over Lincolnshire and East Anglia, and then across Yorkshire, although it was expected that half of the airfields would remain available for the crews to land until at least 2 a.m. with visibility of at least 1,500 yards.

Although not particularly special nor in any way unusual, the official Bomber Command Report of Night Operations for the night of 24/25 March 1944, titled Night Raid Report No. 562, provides a good example of the planning involved in a maximum effort, particularly against Berlin, at this stage of the war.

The Main Force was to take the northern route to Berlin. This well-trodden path took the bombers eastwards across the North Sea and once on the eastern side of Denmark they were to turn south-eastwards across the Baltic Sea to coast-in over northern Germany around Rostock, having stayed to the north of the Kiel defences. The bombers were then to maintain a south-easterly heading to pass to the north of Berlin before making one final turn south-westwards towards the target. Once off-target the bombers were to maintain a south-westerly course until well clear of Berlin and then return by a more southerly route, passing between the heavily defended areas of Hannover and Leipzig before turning north-west towards Holland and avoiding the defences of the Ruhr. Once over Holland it was a direct heading for home. It was, essentially, one long conveyor belt of bombers, all flowing in a clockwise direction.

The Pathfinder's plan over Berlin seems at first glance complicated. Essentially, it was Newhaven (visual ground-marking) with sky-marking as a back-up. The blind marker illuminators were to drop green TIs and white flares if there was less than 7/10ths cloud cover over the target, but if there was more cloud then the plan was to release green and R/P flares (red with yellow stars). If H2S was unserviceable then all markers were to hold their TIs and flares, and bomb with the supporting aircraft. Visual markers were to mark the exact aiming point with mixed salvos of reds and greens. Those blind backers-up detailed to attack before 'z+7 minutes' (where 'z' stood for 'zero hour', the time of the first Main Force bombers on target) were to aim at the centre of all the TIs, if Newhaven was in progress. However, if cloud had prevented this then they were to drop markers blindly. Later arrivals were to drop both reds and sky markers blindly. Visual backers–up were to aim reds at the centre of the mixed salvos, or at the centre of all TIs, with a two–second overshoot. Supporters were to bomb blindly, if possible; otherwise after visual identification or on good dead–reckoning if at the centre of all TIs, or sky markers on a heading of 217 degrees magnetic.

Instructions for the Main Force bomb aimers were less complicated. They were to aim at the centre of all mixed salvos in the early stages of the raid and at the centre of the reds if arriving during the later stages of the raid. If TIs could be seen then the Main Force was to bomb the centre of the sky markers on the same heading.

The timing of the attack was for 'zero' hour to be at 10.30 p.m., with the duration of the attack lasting from 10.25 p.m. ('z–5', i.e. the time of the first blind marker illuminators) until 10.45 p.m. ('z+15', the time of the last Main Force bombers over the target). Timings were broken down as: twenty–eight blind marker illuminators to mark at 'z–5'; six visual markers at 'z–3'; twenty blind backers–up at 'z–1' and 'z+14'; and seventy supporting aircraft to be available from 'z–5'. The Main Force had just fifteen minutes to complete the attack: 125 aircraft were to bomb between 'z' and 'z+3'; the next 125 were to bomb between 'z+3' and 'z+6'; 128 to then bomb between 'z+6' and 'z+9'; 125 between 'z+9' and 'z+12'; and the final 129 aircraft to bomb between 'z+12' and 'z+15'.

A further twenty–six ABC–equipped Lancasters of 101 Squadron were to support the raid and eleven Mosquitos were tasked with dropping *Window* ahead of the Main Force over Denmark, at a rate of four bundles per minute before they bombed Kiel. Once off–target the Mosquitos were to continue dropping *Window* at a rate of two bundles per minute, as well as dropping spoof fighter flares to the south–west of Berlin. The bombers of the Main Force were also to drop *Window* at the rate of two bundles per minute once within 50 miles of Berlin and one bundle per minute for the rest of the route. As a further part of the deception plan, nearly 150 aircraft from OTUs were tasked with flying towards Paris at the same time as the Main Force was on its way to Berlin.

With the planning and briefing over, 811 aircraft took off for Berlin. The actual weather encountered *en route* was almost complete cloud cover with tops at 5,000 feet until reaching Denmark, after which the cloud broke to small amounts with the sky clear as far as Rostock, after which the cloud built up again. But it was not the cloud that caused the problems, it was the wind. The forecast had proved inaccurate, with crews instead reporting winds of more than 100 mph, causing bombers to become scattered instead of being able to maintain one concentrated stream.

Those crews that did manage to find their way to Berlin arrived to find differing cloud conditions, depending on where and when they arrived. Squadron Leader Keith Cresswell, for example, a flight commander serving with the Pathfinders of 35 Squadron at Graveley, was the skipper of ND648 'TL-B Baker', one of the squadron's fourteen Lancasters taking part in the raid. Cresswell arrived over the target just before 10.30 p.m. An excerpt of his crew's account is included in *The Bomber Battle for Berlin* by John Searby, himself a former Master Bomber, which includes:

Weather 9/10ths cloud, tops 8 to 10,000 feet; released marker flares at 2227 ½ hrs from 18,000 feet, course 222 magnetic – A/S [airspeed] 155 knots indicated. Identified and bombed on H2S. Two markers seen on arrival. Attack very scattered at first improving in later stages with better concentration of markers. Attack seemed to be a tremendous overshoot. A large bunch of reds and greens seen about 10 miles south-west of target on way out.

The marking was punctual but searchlights were busy sweeping the night sky in the hope of catching a glimpse of the raiders. However, their search was mostly in vain, although the bomber crews still reported plenty of heavy anti-aircraft fire over the target. But many crews found they had been blown too far south and with no option other than ditching their bombs, they turned for home.

Amongst all that was going on over the target, a handful of *Serrate*-equipped Mosquitos were orbiting over Berlin to fend off any enemy night fighters loitering in the area. They included a 141 Squadron Mozzie flown by a 23-year-old Londoner, Flight Lieutenant Howard Kelsey. Despite his young age, Kelsey was already an experienced campaigner with a DFC and Bar. He and his long-term radar operator, Flying Officer Edward Smith, had crossed the enemy coast soon after 9.30 p.m. On the way to the target area Smith had picked up a number of weak *Serrate* contacts but had chosen to ignore them. Their mission was to orbit over the Brandenberg area of Berlin to cover the main attack and so they could not afford to be distracted elsewhere. An hour later they arrived at their designated position to set up their holding pattern. It was now a matter of waiting while searching the night sky. The crew's combat report describes what happened next:

> *In the target area, at 2303 hours, an AI contact was chased and finally lost in a dive. This was followed immediately by another AI contact, which, after chasing the jinking target for twenty-five minutes to the east, resulted in the visual on a fuselage with lights underneath. The visual was lost in a diving turn to port, but AI contact was maintained and the chase continued.*

The target was weaving hard but this simply allowed the Mosquito to continue its heading and close down the range. It was not long before Kelsey and Smith could see their target once more. It was a FW 190. The crew's combat report continues:

> *After three bursts of cannon at 400 yards range, closing to 200 yards, the enemy aircraft exploded in the air and is claimed as destroyed.*

The FW 190 came down to the east of Berlin. It was Kelsey's first success in a Mosquito to add to his four while flying the Beaufighter. He would be awarded the DSO at the end of the war, his citation crediting him with having shot down ten enemy aircraft.

For Kelsey and Smith the rest of their sortie over Berlin that night was uneventful, but it was a different story for many bomber crews after coming off-target, as it was on the long journey home that the majority of losses occurred. Les Bartlett, now flying his nineteenth op, and his tenth to Berlin, recorded what it was like after leaving the target area:

> *Shortly afterwards things got hot. The enemy fighters put a ring of flares down across our path as we were leaving the target area. Luckily, although we saw a few fighters, none attacked us and all we had to do was to dodge*

the flak and keep out the defences of Leipzig, Brunswick, Osnabrück and Hannover. Along this leg we saw bags of combats, and kite after kite went down in flames so we were absolutely on the alert and ready for anything. The worst didn't happen, however, and we cleared the Dutch coast safely with a little cloud to help us. Back at base they had problems too. Fog again became dense and we received a message from base to say that it was out of the question to try and land there so we were diverted to Docking in Norfolk. We found the place OK and got safely into the circuit with the rest of the squadron. We were given number six to land, but this was our unlucky night. We were circling around the 'drome waiting to come in when number three pranged on the runway so landing was out of the question. We were given an alternate to make for RAF Coltishall. Mike was cheesed off by this time and when the first aerodrome lighting system came into view he called them up. It turned out to be RAF Fiskerton and we landed with the aid of FIDO.

The Beetham crew had been fortunate to get down safely. The fog had come down earlier than forecast and the term FIDO in Bartlett's diary entry stands for 'Fog Investigation and Dispersal Operation' (although it is also sometimes referred to as 'Fog Intense Dispersal Operation' or 'Fog, Intense Dispersal Of'). It was an ingenious method of dealing with fog at airfields. The system was based around a network of pipes filled with fuel and laid along the edges of the runway. The fuel was ignited and the effect was to lift the fog up to 300 feet, high enough and for long enough to enable aircraft to land.

The Berlin raid that night produced many remarkable stories, but perhaps none more so than the remarkable escape of 21-year-old Flight Sergeant Nicholas Alkemade, the young rear-gunner in Lancaster DS664 'KO-D' of 115 Squadron flown by Sergeant Jack Newman. While returning from the target at 19,000 feet, the Lancaster was overhead Schmallenberg in Westphalia when it was attacked by a Ju 88 of 1./NJG 6. Flown by Hauptmann Gerhard Friedrich, the 88's cannon shells tore through the bomber's rear fuselage, catching Alkemade in the leg, before the Lancaster caught fire and spiralled downwards out of control.

With the rear section of the fuselage on fire, Newman gave the order to bale out. Alkemade opened his turret door to reach for his parachute but the fire was too intense and the heat unbearable, and so he quickly closed the door. Now facing certain death, either by burning or being killed by crashing to earth, Alkemade decided to take the quick and relatively painless option rather than slowly burn to death. Rotating his turret sideways, he opened the door and fell backwards out of his turret; his parachute still inside the burning aircraft.

Three hours later Alkemade came to and opened his eyes. He had survived the fall, estimated to have been 3 miles, by plummeting through pine trees and landing into a large snow drift, which had cushioned his fall. He was subsequently found and taken as a prisoner of war, although his captors were naturally suspicious of his story. It was only when the wreckage of the Lancaster was found, including the bodies of Jack Newman and three other members of the crew, and still containing the charred remains of Alkemade's parachute, that his remarkable escape was confirmed.

Newman's aircraft was one of seventy-two lost by Bomber Command that night (8.9 per cent). It was the largest loss of the campaign, both percentage-wise as well as being the highest number of aircraft lost in a single night. The Bomber Command report for the night includes:

An exceptionally strong wind caused the Pathfinders to overshoot the aiming point and the bombing spread outside the southern suburbs. Considerable damage was, however, inflicted on the capital.

As far as Bomber Command's losses were concerned, the report goes on to say:

… it is estimated that nearly three-quarters were due to flak, the wind driving many bombers off their course over heavily defended areas.

The raid marked the end of the long and hard-fought campaign against the Nazi capital. The Battle of Berlin was over. During the sixteen raids, spanning four months, more than 9,000 sorties had been flown and nearly 30,000 tons of bombs dropped. At no other stage of the war was such a sustained bombing campaign against a single target carried out.

Berlin had been left in ruins but the campaign had come at a huge cost for Bomber Command with more than 500 aircraft lost; far more than had been expected. Furthermore, Harris's belief that a sustained bombing offensive against the Big City would cost Germany the war had not turned out to be the case, although the effect it had on German industry and the morale of the city's population may never be known. The discussions and debates about whether the Battle of Berlin was successful or not continue.

Chapter Fifteen

Disastrous Night

The bomber dived violently and turned to the north, but because of good visibility we were able to keep him in sight. I now attempted a second attack after he had settled on his course, but because the Lancaster was now very slow we always came out too far to the front. I tried the Schräge Musik again and after another burst the bomber fell in flames.

The words belong to Oberleutnant Helmut Schulte of II./NJG 5 as he describes the last moments of a Lancaster on the night of 30/31 March 1944. The target that night was the ancient city of Nuremberg, the shrine of Nazism, and flying a Bf 110G-4 fitted with *Schräge Musik* his success contributed to what turned out to be Bomber Command's worst night of the war.

The choice of target, deep in the heart of Bavaria in southern Germany, was an interesting one, as it was not considered to be of industrial importance. There were, however, several small factories around the city and it was a central link in rail and water communications. But any route taken to Nuremberg meant passing close to known heavily defended areas. Furthermore, the moonlight meant that it should have been a period of stand-down for the Main Force but a favourable weather forecast, with protective cloud cover all the way to the target and clear conditions over Nuremberg, led to the decision being made to go ahead with this distant raid.

The Bomber Command pump was again full-on with the squadrons producing aircraft and crews in large numbers. It had been less than a week since the last raid against Berlin (which had involved 800 aircraft) and just four nights since Essen (over 700), but, even so, 795 aircraft were made available for the Nuremberg raid.

For the Beetham crew of 50 Squadron it was to be their twenty-first op. Their experience that night is best told through the words in Les Bartlett's wartime diary:

Such a nice day today, little did we know what was in store for us. Briefing was getting later each day as the days grew longer, and today it was 5 pm, so we all had an afternoon nap. The target was Nuremberg. Where was that? 'Oh, this should be a nice quiet stooge', someone said, but that remained to be seen. At 10 pm we taxied out and were first airborne. Everything was quiet during the climb to 20,000 feet over the Channel. We crossed the enemy coast and it was eyes wide open. As we drew level with the south of the Ruhr Valley, things began to happen. Enemy night fighters were all around us and, in no time at all, combats were taking place and aircraft were going down in flames on both sides. So serious was the situation, that I remember looking at the poor blighters going down and thinking to myself that it must be our turn next, just a question of time. A Lancaster appeared on our port beam, converging, so we dropped 100 feet or so to let him cross. He was only about 200 yards or so on our starboard beam when a string of cannon shells hit him and down he went. We altered course for Nuremberg, and I looked down at the area over which we had just passed. It looked like a battlefield. There were kites burning on the deck all over the place – bombs going off where they had been jettisoned by bombers damaged in combat, and fires from their incendiaries across the whole area. Such a picture of aerial disaster I had never seen before and hope to never see again. On the way into the target, the winds became changeable and we almost ran into the defences of Schweinfurt but we altered course in time. The defences of Nuremberg were nothing to speak of, a modest amount of heavy flak which did not prevent us doing a normal approach, and we were able to get the target indicators dropped by the Pathfinders in our bombsight to score direct hits with our 4,000lb 'Cookie' and our 1,000lb bombs and incendiaries. We were able to get out of the target area, always a dodgy business, and set course for home. To reach the coast was a binding two-hour stooge. The varying winds were leading us a dance. We found ourselves approaching Calais instead of being 80 miles further south, so we had a slight detour to avoid their defences. Once near the enemy coast, it was nose down for home at 300 knots. Even then, we saw some poor blokes 'buy it' over the Channel. What a relief it was to be flying over Lincoln Cathedral once more. Back in debriefing, we heard the full story of the squadron's effort. It was the worst night for the squadron.

Bartlett and his crew had been lucky. It appears the weather forecast had been wrong and several wind-finding errors were made, causing the Main Force to become scattered. One-in-five bombers, it is reckoned, missed one of the turning points by at least 30 miles.

For the experienced crews who had spent the past few months clawing their way through varying densities of cloud to attack the major cities in Germany, including Berlin, the conditions just did not feel right. An attempt to deceive the German controllers of the intended target had failed; the lack of H2S transmissions coming from the Mosquitos carrying out spoof attacks against Cologne and Kassel making these attempts to deceive the defences easily recognized for what they were. And if this was not bad enough, a long straight leg of 270 miles to the target made the actual area of attack predictable.

Everything seemed to favour the defenders. Not only had the bombers become scattered over a wide area, the atmospheric conditions meant that condensation trails from their engines formed at a much lower height than normal. Also, there had been little or no cloud over much of Belgium and eastern France, and even where there was some cloud it was very thin and offered little or no protection. Over Holland and the Ruhr the sky was clear and the bright half-moon lit up the trails, making the bombers visible from many miles away.

The first night fighters appeared before many of the Main Force had even reached the Belgian border, enabling them to constantly harass the bombers for the next hour. Falling bombers merely presented a trail of fires as they crashed to earth. By the time the Main Force approached Nuremberg some eighty bombers had been shot down with dozens more having aborted their mission either because of damage sustained or for other technical reasons.

Helmut Schulte was one to get amongst the main bomber stream at 20,000 feet with ease. In Spick's *Luftwaffe Fighter Aces* Schulte described what happened next:

I sighted a Lancaster and got underneath it and opened fire with my slanting weapon. Unfortunately it jammed, so that only a few shots put out of action the starboard inner motor. The bomber dived violently and turned to the north, but because of good visibility we were able to keep him in sight. I now attempted a second attack after he had settled on his course, but because the Lancaster was now very slow we always came out too far to the front. I tried the Schräge Musik again and after another burst the bomber fell in flames.

For the bomber crews that did make it to Nuremberg they arrived over the city to find it covered by thick cloud, which extended up to 15,000 feet. It was not at all what had been briefed. Having expected the target to be clear of cloud, the Pathfinders carried mostly ground markers, which, of course, could not be seen through the cloud. Most of the bombs fell in residential areas, with only slight damage caused to industry.

Because of the problems caused by the wind, more than a hundred bombers had become so straggled that it is likely they bombed Schweinfurt, to the north-west of Nuremberg, instead. This belief is backed up by some post-raid reports of crews that had passed to the west of Schweinfurt on their way home. Pilot Officer John Chatterton of 44 Squadron, an experienced skipper flying his twenty-third op that night, later recalled what his crew had seen after leaving Nuremberg for the long journey home:

… after several minutes they [his air gunners] called our attention to another target away over to our right which seemed to be cloud free and with a lot of action. Tongue in cheek I asked Jack [his navigator] if he was sure we had bombed Nuremberg and received the expected forceful reply, with added information that the burning town was probably Schweinfurt.

Helmut Schulte, meanwhile, claimed three more bombers before coming across another Lancaster to the south of Nuremberg. When the bomber went into an immediate corkscrew he knew he had been spotted. With his *Schräge Musik* jammed, Schulte had no choice but to opt for his forward-firing guns but on this occasion his attack did not bring any success as he later recalled:

As soon as I opened fire he dived away and my shells passed over him. I thought that this chap must have nerves of steel: he had watched me formate on him and then had dived just at the right time. He had been through as much as I had – we had both been to Nuremberg that night – so I decided that was enough.

Schulte's performance that night was impressive but it was bettered by another Bf 110 pilot, Oberleutnant Martin Becker, the Staffelkapitän of 2./NJG 6, who claimed seven bombers during the raid. Six of his victims – three Lancasters and three Halifaxes – all came down over Wetzla and Fulda in central Germany in a matter of minutes while the seventh, another Halifax, was claimed over Luxembourg while Becker was returning to base. These latest successes took his score past twenty, thirteen of which had been claimed in just over a week, earning him the Knight's Cross and command of the 4th Gruppe.

Not only was the Nuremberg raid a failure, it turned out to be the worst night for Bomber Command of the war. Ninety-five aircraft were lost, of which seventy-nine fell to the night fighters. These figures might have been even higher had some Bf 110s not have been sent too far to the north. A further ten more bombers were written off after crash-landing back at base and a further fifty-nine had sustained considerable damage.

Leaving aside those aircraft that had been damaged, the overall loss rate for the raid was in excess of 13 per cent, with a reported 535 lives lost and a further 180 wounded or taken as prisoners of war. The Halifax force had again suffered the heaviest losses. Including the five written-off back in England, thirty-six of the 214 aircraft taking part in the raid had been lost (16.8 per cent). 51 Squadron based at Snaith in Yorkshire had suffered particularly badly with six of its seventeen Halifaxes failing to return, with the loss of thirty-five lives.

One young Halifax pilot to be killed that night was 22-year-old Pilot Officer Cyril Barton of 578 Squadron based at Burn in North Yorkshire. Flying Halifax 'LK-E Excalibur', Nuremburg was his nineteenth op. For most of the transit to the target he had been fortunate to avoid any trouble but the first he and his crew became aware of immediate danger was when they spotted pale red parachute flares, dropped by Ju 88s to mark the position of the bomber stream.

The sky was clear and the crew watched in horror as night fighters suddenly appeared. One by one their colleagues were picked off. They knew it would soon be their turn but they were now on the final leg towards the target and there was to be no turning back. Suddenly, two night fighters appeared in front. They were seen attacking head-on just as cannon shells ripped through the Halifax, puncturing fuel tanks and knocking out the aircraft's rear turret and all of its communications while setting the starboard inner engine on fire.

Barton threw the aircraft into a hard evasive manoeuvre just as a Ju 88 passed close by. Corkscrewing as hard as he dare, the Halifax went down. For a while it seemed the danger had passed but no sooner had Barton resumed his course towards Nuremberg than the Halifax was attacked once again. Shells raked the fuselage for a second time. Again, the Ju 88 broke away but it was soon back again, scoring more hits on the crippled bomber before eventually turning away.

Undaunted, Barton again resumed his course for Nuremberg. He was finally able to gather his thoughts and to assess the damage to his aircraft, only to find that three of his crew members had gone. Unable to communicate with their skipper, and with the bomber repeatedly under heavy attack while corkscrewing towards the ground, the navigator, bomb aimer and wireless operator had all abandoned the aircraft to become prisoners of war.

Left in a desperate situation, Barton decided what to do next. With a crippled bomber, one engine out, leaking fuel, his rear turret out of action, no communications or navigational assistance, and now with three of his crew missing, he would have been fully justified in aborting his mission. But he decided instead to press on to the target with just his two air gunners, Sergeants Freddie Brice and Harry Wood, and his flight engineer, Sergeant Maurice Trousdale, left on board.

The four airmen struggled on as best they could. By working together and using the stars to navigate, they eventually reached the target and completed their attack before finally turning for home. Remarkably, they managed to keep out of further trouble as Barton nursed the crippled Halifax back towards safety. It was an outstanding feat of airmanship for a pilot so young. But the crew were still not out of danger and although Barton was satisfied they had coasted-in somewhere over eastern England, they still had to find somewhere to land.

It was just before 6 a.m. and still dark but the Halifax was now desperately short of fuel. As Barton eased the bomber down he was all too aware that the remaining engines were about to give up. With his three crew colleagues braced behind the aircraft's rear spar, he was all alone in the cockpit. Visibility was extremely poor and suddenly a row of terraced houses appeared in front. Yanking the control column back in a desperate attempt to hurdle the obstacles before him, a wing first clipped the chimneys before the Halifax came crashing down, demolishing everything in its way.

The Halifax had come down in the yard of Ryhope colliery in County Durham. One miner on his way to work, 58-year-old George Dodds, was killed in the wreckage. Remarkably, though, the three crew members braced in the rear of the fuselage had survived; all to later receive the DFM. Fortunately for them, the rear section of the aircraft had broken away on impact. The forward section, however, still with the gallant young pilot inside, was a wreck of twisted metal. Barton was pulled from the wreckage and rushed to hospital but he died from his injuries the following day.

It was an extraordinary act of courage and words are difficult to find. A few weeks later came the announcement of the posthumous award of the Victoria Cross to Cyril Barton. The citation, which appeared in the Fifth Supplement to the *London Gazette* on Friday 23 June 1944, concludes:

> *In gallantly completing his last mission in the face of almost impossible odds, this officer displayed unsurpassed courage and devotion to duty.*

The disastrous raid against Nuremberg was yet another costly reminder that large-scale raids deep into Nazi Germany were still extremely hazardous and often resulted in heavy losses. Unfortunately for all the bomber crews lost during the long and hard winter of 1943/44, they had come up against the Luftwaffe's night fighter force at the peak of its effectiveness.

It was, for now, the last all-out offensive against the German homeland and brought to an end Bomber Command's long-employed tactic of massed attacks against major targets. Not until the Allies enjoyed air superiority over north-west Europe would Bomber Command employ such tactics again. If it had not been apparent before then it was certainly apparent now – the war would not end until Germany had been defeated on the ground. However, everything Germany needed to maintain both military and civil defence – water, electricity, transport and emergency services – as well as the raw materials to keep the factories going, had drawn heavily on its resources throughout that hard winter. In truth, Germany was slowly grinding to a halt. The Nuremberg raid had also marked the Nachtjagd's last great victory of the war.

Chapter Sixteen

Road to Victory

In view of the tactical difficulties of destroying precise targets by night, Bomber Command will continue to be employed in accordance with their main aim of disorganizing German industry.

The statement is part of a directive issued to Harris as he was forced to turn his attention to the support of Operation *Overlord*. With operational control of Bomber Command having passed to the recently-formed Supreme Headquarters Allied Expeditionary Force, under the command of the Supreme Allied Commander, General Dwight D Eisenhower, the directive was issued by Air Chief Marshal Sir Arthur Tedder, Eisenhower's deputy, to highlight Bomber Command's intended role throughout the operation.

In short, Bomber Command's role was to deplete the German fighter forces and to destroy and disrupt rail communications, particularly those affecting the movement towards the *Overlord* lodgement area. On the occasional nights when his command was not required to bomb targets in support of *Overlord*, Harris was able to revert to targets in Germany.

Ralph Cochrane's No. 5 Group was now often operating alone as an independent force. His group had become increasingly unhappy with various aspects of the Pathfinder techniques and how the Main Force was being employed. Bennett, on the other hand, saw Cochrane's experimentation with low-level target-marking, through 617 Squadron, as a direct threat to the reputation of his own specialist squadrons. The rivalry between the two AOCs had become so intense that, at times, it was verging on hostile.

617 Squadron was now commanded by Wing Commander Leonard Cheshire. With a DSO and two Bars and a DFC, Cheshire was one of the most experienced pilots in Bomber Command. A former station commander he had been the RAF's youngest group captain at the age of twenty-five,

but having become increasingly frustrated at being away from operations, Cheshire had taken a reduction in rank to command 617.

For some time Cheshire had wanted to prove his theory of marking a target at low level. There had been a number of recent examples where high-level marking had been unsatisfactory, particularly against targets in France, and had resulted in the loss of many French lives. But flying a Lancaster below 100 feet at night, particularly over built-up areas, was not easy and so Cheshire was granted his request for a handful of Mosquitos.

Cheshire put his new idea to the test in early April 1944 when he took a single Mosquito to an aircraft factory in France to provide marking for an attack by the group's Lancasters. The raid was a success and so the PFF was ordered to give up a Mosquito squadron, 627, so that it could be transferred to No. 5 Group to work alongside 617 at Woodhall Spa.

The two squadrons worked well together. They soon developed a group marking technique based on low-level identification of the target and subsequent marking by the Mosquitos, after which the Lancasters of 83 and 97 Squadrons, now based at Coningsby, provided back-up marking and dropped flares for the rest of the group's Lancasters to bomb. It was a tactic that would achieve much success, with bombing accuracy reported to be double that achieved when using Oboe and marking from higher altitudes.

The idea was tried again later in the month when it was first used against a heavily defended German city. While the rest of Bomber Command went to Düsseldorf and Laon, No. 5 Group went to Brunswick. However, although low-level marking by the Mosquitos was accurate, a layer of cloud hampered visibility over the target area, preventing more than 200 Lancasters carrying out the attack.

Not wishing to be put off by the disappointment of the Brunswick raid, No. 5 Group was given another chance to prove the concept of low-level marking just two nights later. While the rest of the Main Force were off to Karlsruhe, No. 5 Group was to go to Munich, with 234 Lancasters (including ten provided by No. 1 Group) and sixteen Mosquitos taking part; four from 617 Squadron to mark the target and twelve from 627 to fly ahead of the Lancasters to drop *Window*.

The raid offered 617 many challenges, not least the fact that the target was so deep in enemy territory, meaning the Mosquitos would be on the limit of their operational range. There would be no fuel to spare and so marking would have to be carried out quickly and accurately.

Cheshire flew one of 617's Mosquitos with the others flown by Gerry Fawke, Terry Kearns and Dave Shannon, a long-term member of the squadron and survivor of the Dams raid. The four Mozzies first flew to Manston to refuel before taking off to fly a direct route to the target. Having arrived during the early hours of the following morning, Cheshire was immediately 'coned' by searchlights. With no time to hang around he took the Mosquito down to low level and began his run-in to mark the target.

Despite the fact that all guns within range opened up against him, Cheshire flew in at 700 feet to drop his markers with great accuracy. Fawke, Kearns and Shannon then followed suit, marking the target with the same precision. As the Lancasters carried out the main attack, Cheshire remained overhead the city, where from a height of just 1,000 feet he was able to assess the accuracy of the marking and direct the bombing, despite his own aircraft being hit several times.

Finally, satisfied the attack had been a success, Cheshire turned for home, later landing back at Manston with hardly a drop of fuel to spare. A post-raid reconnaissance carried out the following morning showed the attack on Munich had been a success, with considerable damage caused to the railway installations and with many buildings having been destroyed.

For John Chatterton and his 44 Squadron crew the Munich raid that night was the last of their operational tour. Flying from Dunholme Lodge on some of Bomber Command's most costly raids of the war, his crew had endured a long and hard winter. Chatterton, awarded the DFC during the tour, later recalled:

> *I can't remember much about my last 'op' on the squadron except that it was a long haul to Munich (nearly ten hours) and that the Alps looked a splendid sight in the bright moonlight – a sharp contrast to the murky nights that had made up most of my tour. Although I knew it to be my last trip I had got into the habit of not looking too far ahead in life and it was the following day before I felt the warm feeling of relief and release of tension. Someone asked me, what was I going to do next? I hadn't even thought about it!*

As things were to turn out for Chatterton he would become an instructor at No. 5 Lancaster Finishing School and the aircraft he took to Munich that night, ND578 'KM-Y Yorker', his trusted mount since taking it on its maiden op to Berlin back in February, went on to become one of thirty-four Lancaster centurions; it survived the war having completed more than 120 ops.

The Munich raid had cemented No. 5 Group as a semi-independent force. Harris would later sum up this period:

No. 5 Group operated largely as an independent unit and developed its own techniques, including the original Master Bomber concept, also offset sky marking continued to develop, for example '5 Group Newhaven' using offset techniques 1,000 – 2,000 yards from the aiming point, any error in the red TIs being cancelled by yellows from the Master Bomber. Other techniques developed, including 'sector bombing' with each aircraft given a heading and overshoot setting. This gave a good bomb distribution but needed very accurate low-level marking.

It was this latter aspect that became the No. 5 Group trademark – going in at low level to put the TIs within feet of the aiming point. With men like Leonard Cheshire, Guy Gibson and Micky Martin leading the way, Ralph Cochrane had the men to make his group's ideas a great success and this started a trend towards more group individuality, although the other group commanders generally remained content with the tactics and techniques of Bennett's Pathfinders.

Two nights after the Munich raid, on 26/27 April, Bomber Command again split its resources. No. 5 Group sent more than 200 aircraft to Schweinfurt (including a handful of Lancasters provided by No. 1 Group), while nearly 500 went to Essen (a mixed force from across the other groups) and nearly 200 Halifaxes (from Nos 4 and 6 Groups), supported by the Pathfinders, went to bomb railway yards in the suburbs of Paris.

It was during the Schweinfurt raid that another Bomber Command VC was won. The recipient on this occasion was 24-year-old Sergeant Norman Jackson, a Lancaster flight engineer serving with 106 Squadron. Having volunteered to fly an additional sortie with another crew earlier in his tour, Jackson had already completed his thirty ops two nights before, but for his own crew, skippered by Sergeant Fred Miffin, Schweinfurt was to be their thirtieth and final op of their tour.

It was late in the evening when the crew had taken off from their home airfield of Metheringham in ME669 'ZN-O'. As they headed out across the North Sea a stronger than forecast headwind had made progress slow and caused many bombers to become scattered. By the time they arrived over the target they seemed to be all alone. Fortunately, flak was surprisingly light and having released their bombs Miffin turned for home.

No sooner had the aircraft turned to climb away at 20,000 feet, the wireless operator, Flight Sergeant E Sandelands, reported a blip on the aircraft's *Fishpond* receiver, signalling an enemy night fighter was close by and somewhere to their rear. Miffin immediately put the aircraft into a corkscrew manoeuvre to try and shake off the attacker, just as the two air gunners, Sergeant W Smith and Flight Sergeant Hugh Johnson, spotted what looked like a night fighter. But it was already too late. Just as the enemy FW 190 was seen to be breaking away its cannon shells riddled the fuselage.

The Lancaster had sustained many hits, particularly in the starboard inner engine. A fire had started near the fuel tank on the upper surface of the wing, between the fuselage and engine, and the tank was now in danger of exploding.

Jackson had been thrown to the floor during the attack and wounded in his right leg and shoulder, but despite his pain he decided to fight the fire. Clipping on his parachute and pushing a hand-held fire extinguisher into the top of his battle-dress jacket, he jettisoned the escape hatch above the pilot's head and started to climb out of the cockpit. His plan was to make his way back along the fuselage and out onto the starboard wing. He then pulled the ripcord of his parachute so that his colleagues could feed the rigging lines and canopy out of the aircraft. Should Jackson be unable to hang on, the parachute would be released so that he could hopefully descend safely to the ground.

Undeterred by the extreme danger he faced, Jackson continued. Inside the aircraft, Flight Sergeant Maurice Toft and Flying Officer F L Higgins gathered the parachute together and held on to the rigging lines, paying them out as Jackson squeezed out of the escape hatch and crawled aft. With the Lancaster flying at around 200 mph, the rush of air meant progress was slow.

Desperately hanging on to anything he could, Jackson lowered himself until his feet finally reached the wing. The fire was still raging but, somehow, he managed to spread himself across the wing, his head in line with the leading edge. Grabbing the engine's air intake with his left hand, he removed the fire extinguisher from his battle-dress and discharged it into the fire.

Remarkably, it seemed to work and the fire started to die down, but Jackson's face and hands were severely burned. But as he struggled to make his way back towards the fuselage, the night fighter suddenly returned. Faced with no option, Miffin turned away hard but the sudden movement of the aircraft made it impossible for Jackson to hold on. He was swept through the flames and over the trailing edge of the wing. When last seen his parachute was only partially inflated and burning in several places. Jackson should have been thrown clear of the aircraft but he had come to a sudden halt. He was still attached to the aircraft by his rigging lines and was now left dangling behind the rear turret.

Realizing the fire could not be controlled, Miffin gave the order to abandon the aircraft. Toft and Higgins, who had been frantically feeding out the rigging lines and canopy of Jackson's parachute, both managed to get out of the aircraft and were later taken as prisoners of war. Also taken prisoner were Sandelands and Smith but Fred Miffin and Hugh Johnson died in the aircraft. As for Norman Jackson, he had somehow been thrown clear of the aircraft and despite his horrific injuries survived the descent, even though part of his parachute had been on fire. As daylight broke he managed to crawl to a nearby village where he was taken as a prisoner of war. He was in a pitiful state but after several months in hospital he made a good recovery. It was only after the repatriation of the surviving members of his crew at the end of the war that the full story of Jackson's quite extraordinary bravery in trying to fight the fire was told. Soon after came the announcement of the award of the Victoria Cross to Norman Jackson. Few, if any, VCs could have been more gallantly earned.

The number of aircraft available to Bomber Command was now growing by the month. Although No. 3 Group's Stirlings were being phased out of operational service, they were being replaced by newer Lancasters, while the Halifax squadrons of Nos 4 and 6 Groups were replacing their rather outdated variants with the improved Mark III. There were other reasons to be optimistic too. Losses were starting to fall as the Luftwaffe's fighters became stretched, particularly since the Americans had introduced long-range fighter escort for their daylight raids.

With the exception of a couple of large-scale visits to Duisburg and Dortmund, the rest of May 1944 was all about providing support to the forthcoming Allied landings in northern France, by softening up enemy defensive positions and important lines of communications.

Three-quarters of Bomber Command's operational sorties were now being flown against targets in France and other occupied territory outside of Germany. This was in complete contrast to just a matter of weeks before, during the height of the Berlin offensive, when three-quarters of Bomber Command's effort had been directed at targets in Germany. And by the time the Allies landed in Normandy in June, less than 9 per cent of bombs dropped were against targets in Germany.

In response to the Allied landings Göring deployed more than twenty Jagdgruppen forward from their bases in Germany to northern France. But these additional units were never going to be enough to influence the air battle over Normandy. Besides, moving them to France simply weakened the Luftwaffe's ability to defend the Reich.

The air war over north-west Europe was now entering its final phase. Bomber Command had flown nearly 2,700 night sorties in support of the Allied landings in the first week alone and was now able to resume daylight raids for the first time in over a year. July 1944 was spent supporting the Allied advance in north-west Europe as well as carrying out other top priority operations elsewhere, most notably against the German V-weapon sites in the Pas de Calais. With so much going on in France, Harris would have to wait to resume his full-scale strategic air offensive against Germany.

Chapter Seventeen

Final Defence of the Reich

With fire and the terrific blast and penetrative power of the heavy bombs, the RAF is playing havoc with both the restorations above ground and the cellar and basement homes and factories below. It is vital they should be knocked out.

With the Allies having broken out of Normandy, Harris resumed his offensive against Germany. The war had entered its final phase and the words are taken from a newspaper article following a major Bomber Command raid as a way of reassuring the British public of the need to continue the bombing of German cities.

The first of a number of major raids in the last week of July 1944 was against Kiel. The raid took place on the night of the 23rd/24th and involved more than 600 aircraft. It was Bomber Command's heaviest raid against the city of the war. The following night the target was Stuttgart, again involving more than 600 bombers, and was the first of three heavy raids against the city in just five nights. The second was flown on the night of 28/29 July and coincided with more than 300 bombers going to Hamburg; the first heavy raid on the city since the campaign a year before.

These were massive efforts but the reality was the strategic air offensive against Germany was still considered to be of secondary importance. More priority was given to the railway system and the increasing number of V-weapon and storage sites in France. On the ground the Allied advance had, in places, been swift and decisive. Paris was liberated, so too had half of Belgium, and soon after the Allies swept into Holland. One by one the Nachtjagd's forward airfields were being overrun, forcing the Luftwaffe to withdraw its night fighters east of the Ruhr. Meanwhile, in the East, Russian forces were advancing towards the West bringing hope that the war might be over by Christmas.

Perhaps for the first time during the Second World War, the way ahead for Bomber Command was unclear. In truth there was little the heavy bombers could do to support the advances on the ground and so the two main options were to target either Germany's synthetic oil production or its communications system. But, as far as Harris was concerned, there was a third option too – to resume large-scale attacks against German industrial cities.

A plan for renewing the Battle of Berlin was considered, as was the idea to attack a single big city other than Berlin, but it had not been forgotten that the previous campaign against the Nazi capital had failed to bring the downfall of Germany. In all probability Berlin would withstand another aerial onslaught, even though a renewed campaign might bring about a temporary breakdown in the morale of its civilian population. And so, in the end, it was the oil-versus-transportation debate that was long and, at times, heated. The two were, in fact, interlinked.

The night war raged on and there was to be no let-up in the ferocity of the air battle being fought over Germany. Losses were felt equally hard on both sides. Georg Hermann Greiner of IV./NJG 1, for example, now credited with thirty-seven aircraft shot down, was caught by surprise when his Bf 110 was attacked from behind by a roaming RAF night fighter. Flying with him as usual that night was Feldwebel Rolf Kissing, his long-term *Bordfunker* and personal friend, and a new 18-year-old *Bordschütze* flying only his second operational sortie. In *Hunters of the Reich: Night Fighters* by David P Williams, Greiner later recalled the calamitous outcome:

> ... *a fierce, precise burst of fire set our starboard engine on fire and struck Rolf Kissing in the head. He must have been unconscious immediately as his head had sunk forward to his chest.*

Greiner used all his experience to try and shake off his attacker but his burning engine was like a beacon in the sky. With Kissing badly wounded, he had to make the decision whether to bale out without his colleague or to try and land the crippled fighter. There was no way Greiner could leave his friend. He explained what happened next:

We were quite unable to believe our eyes when the fire in the engine, blown hither and thither by the slipstream of our dive, went out. We were still not out of danger, although most unusually, and quite contrary to the rules, tactics and common sense, the second attack did not materialise. The area below us was dark and I could see no possibility of performing an emergency landing, we were running out of fuel and it was impossible to keep the machine in straight and level flight. There was no chance of reaching our own airfield, so I needed to find an emergency field, but it was dark all around me – no light to guide a late home-comer. In order to make our identity clear to our colleagues I fired off Very cartridges with the colours of the day. Seconds later, and directly beneath us, the airfield lights of Düsseldorf shone out in their full glory. In consideration for Kissing – and for my Messerschmitt – I decided not to try a belly-landing. I lowered my undercarriage by means of compressed air. As a result of the enemy fire I could not place any reliance on my automatic pilot. I saw the ambulance, which we had requested by radio, from some distance away and we landed safely despite the defective landing gear. Feldwebel Kissing died that same night.

Greiner's account of nursing a crippled aircraft to a diversion airfield, with a fatally wounded colleague on board, and to then make an emergency landing, is typical of many stories told on either side. So too was the grief felt by Greiner for the loss of Rolf Kissing after three years of flying together in combat. But there was no time to dwell. Life, and the war for that matter, went on.

While the Nachtjagd was suffering the loss of key men, so too was Bomber Command and one of its most notable losses was Guy Gibson, one of the RAF's most famous pilots of the Second World War. Since leading the Dams raid the year before, Gibson had been rested from operations and his most recent posting was as a staff officer at Coningsby. He had, however, still managed to fly on the occasional op and was given special permission to act as Master Bomber for a raid against Rheydt and Mönchengladbach on the night of 19/20 September.

As there was no Mosquito available at Coningsby for the raid, Gibson travelled to nearby Woodhall Spa with his station navigation officer, Squadron Leader James Warwick, where the crew were allocated an aircraft belonging to 627 Squadron. They took off just before 8 p.m. but the Mosquito did not return.

At first it was not certain that Gibson's aircraft was overdue. With Woodhall Spa and Coningsby being so close together, each airfield thought the Mosquito might have landed at the other. And when that turned out not to be the case, the hope was that the aircraft had landed elsewhere. But after a while it became apparent that the Mosquito was lost. Gibson had last been heard over the target area directing the attack, which had ended shortly before 10 p.m. What time he left the target is unclear but it is assumed that he loitered in the area for a while as about half an hour later the Mosquito came down in flames at Steenbergen in Holland where it exploded on impact. At the time of his death Gibson was aged twenty-six. Of all the RAF's VC winners, few, if any, will be better known than Wing Commander Guy Gibson VC DSO and Bar DFC and Bar.

It was not just the RAF that was losing some of its most highly decorated and well known veterans of the night war over Germany during these latter months of the war. The Luftwaffe, too, was mourning the loss of some of its own and one was Major Helmut Lent whose life came to a tragic end on 7 October 1944, not in combat but during a routine transit flight.

Lent was one of the Luftwaffe's best. He had been the first to shoot down fifty aircraft at night and, in July 1944, had become the first to reach a century of night successes to earn the coveted Diamonds to his Knight's Cross with Oak Leaves and Swords; Germany's highest recognition for gallantry. On 5 October he was carrying out a routine flight to Paderborn to visit Hans-Joachim Jabs, the Kommodore of NJG 1, when his Ju 88 suffered an engine failure while on approach to land. As the aircraft descended it caught a power cable before crashing into the ground. Also on board were Lent's long-term *Bordfunker*, Oberfeldwebel Walter Kubisch, a second *Funker*, Oberleutnant Hermann Klöss, and Leutnant Werner Kark, a wartime correspondent. Although all four were pulled out of the wreckage alive, Kubisch and Klöss died soon after, while Kark died the following day. Then, the gallant Helmut Lent succumbed to his injuries two days after the crash.

At the time of his death Lent was twenty-six years old and was the Luftwaffe's highest-scoring night fighter pilot at the time, having been credited with shooting down a total of 110 aircraft; all but seven at night.

He was given a state funeral in Berlin, with the guard of honour consisting of some of the Luftwaffe's finest night fighter pilots: Jabs; Oberstleutnant Günther Radusch (Kommodore of NJG 5); Major Rudolf Schönert (Kommandeur of NJGr 10); Hauptmann Heinz Strüning (Staffelkapitän of 3./NJG 1); Hauptmann Paul Zorner (Kommandeur of III./NJG 5); and Hauptmann Heinz-Martin Hadeball (Kommandeur of I./NJG 6). Ahead of the coffin and carrying Lent's impressive array of decorations was Oberstleutnant Werner Streib, now *Inspekteur der Nachtjagd*, while Göring took the salute.

Only two Nachtjagdflieger were awarded Germany's highest decoration for gallantry. After Lent the other was Heinz-Wolfgang Schnaufer who passed his century of successes just two nights after Lent's death. Schnaufer had been awarded the Knight's Cross at the end of 1943 for forty night successes and given command of IV./NJG 1. The Oak Leaves followed in June 1944 and, in quick succession, the Swords for his eighty-ninth success. Most had been achieved with his extremely capable *Bordfunker*, 24-year-old Oberfeldwebel Friedrich 'Fritz' Rumpelhardt, and Oberfeldwebel Wilhelm Gänsler, his *Bordschütze*, both holders of the Knight's Cross.

When Schnaufer reached a hundred successes, all at night, he became the second Nachtjagdflieger (and the Luftwaffe's ninth, and last) to receive the Diamonds. The *Wehrmachtbericht* entry for 10 October 1944 reads:

During the night of the 9th to the 10th October Hauptmann Schnaufer, Gruppenkommandeur in a Nachtjagdgeschwader, whom the Führer has decorated with the Oak Leaves with Swords to the Knight's Cross of the Iron Cross, scored his 100th night aerial victory.

Less than a month later, Schnaufer became the Luftwaffe's youngest Kommodore at the age of twenty-two when he was given command of NJG 4.

Meanwhile, control of Bomber Command had reverted back to the Air Ministry. With the Allied armies approaching the Rhine, having overrun the V-weapon sites on the way, there was now little requirement for precision raids. Also, the strategic arguments about the general area bombing of German cities had seemingly been abandoned by the Air Staff as Harris was directed to conduct his campaign against oil production. Other key targets – such as the German rail and waterborne transport systems, tank production and depots, ordnance depots, and vehicle production plants and depots – were all stated to be of equal second priority.

Harris, though, still believed in general area bombing and saw the opportunity to conduct a final, and probably overwhelming, strategic air offensive against Germany. And so in mid-October 1944 Bomber Command returned to Germany with a vengeance after Harris received a revised directive making reference to 'Special Operations', codenamed Operation *Hurricane*, specifying an all-out Allied air offensive against targets in the Ruhr.

The first part of the operation was carried out on the 14th, the day after Harris had received the revised directive, with more than a thousand aircraft dropping over 4,000 tons of high explosives and incendiaries on Duisburg. That night, another huge force of more than a thousand bombers returned to the city in a raid conducted in two parts, separated by a couple of hours.

It had been a long, tiring day and night for many of Harris's crews who flew on both raids against Duisburg, as recorded in the log book of Flying Officer Alan Rowe, a Lancaster pilot serving with No. 3 Group's 115 Squadron based at Witchford in Cambridgeshire. He and his crew flew the first raid in daylight (4 hours 10 minutes) before landing back at base for a few hours rest before taking part in the second raid that night (4 hours 25 minutes).

In the space of just twenty-four hours during 14/15 October, more than 9,000 tons of bombs had been dropped on Duisburg; about the same weight of bombs as the Luftwaffe dropped on London during the entire war. The British newspapers were again quick to report the story with headlines such as '*The Death Throes of a City*' and words such as:

> *Below these mounting banks of smoke lies Duisburg. The city is a mass of flames. In the giant RAF raids of Saturday and Sunday – twin attacks that ended the life of Germany's greatest inland port – 10,000 tons of bombs, including half a million incendiaries, were unloaded: one ton to every forty-five inhabitants.*

The Daily Mail later ran the headline '*Cellar Cities Draw RAF Back to Ruhr*' with an accompanying article that not only described the raid but also explained the need to continue the bombing of German cities. The opening lines read:

> *The second Battle of the Ruhr, which opened with the attacks on Duisburg in early October and has continued with increasing fury, is going well. But many people are asking why it should be necessary. 'Surely the Germans have not been able to restore the bombed cities of 1943 so quickly? Why go back to bomb?' they ask. Well, the Germans have toiled during all this year to rebuild and repair plants. In addition to the fire-swept shells of the former cities, it may well be that they have built up underground communities and factories.*

The article then includes the tonnage of bombs dropped against German cities in recent raids: Duisburg – 10,000 tons; Essen and Cologne – each 9,000 tons; Düsseldorf – 4,500 tons; and Bochum – 3,000 tons.

During October 1944 Bomber Command flew over 17,000 operational sorties with more than three-quarters being directed against targets in Germany and over 50,000 tons of bombs dropped. It was more than double the previous highest tonnage dropped on the Nazi homeland in a single month, but its effectiveness was being questioned beyond the corridors of Bomber Command's headquarters. Despite all the large-scale efforts that month – against targets such as Saarbrucken, Dortmund, Duisburg, Wilhelmshaven, Stuttgart, Essen (twice) and Cologne (three times) – only around 6 per cent of Bomber Command's effort had been targeted against oil targets and there had been no concentration of effort against the enemy's lines of communications at all.

In a new directive Harris was reminded that oil was the main priority and so November started with two attacks, flown on consecutive nights and both relatively small-scale in terms of numbers, against the Meerbeck oil plant at Homberg. Then, on the night of 2/3 November, it was an all-out effort against Düsseldorf. Nearly a thousand aircraft – Lancasters and Halifaxes supported by Mosquitos – took part, resulting in significant damage to a number of industrial premises, as well as housing. It was Bomber Command's last raid against the city of the war.

The end of the war might well have been in sight, but the battle was far from over in the air. Both sides fought relentlessly and great acts of courage continued, including that of Sergeant Derek Allen, a Lancaster mid-upper gunner serving with the Australian 467 (RAAF) Squadron at Waddington. Allen was awarded the CGM after his aircraft had been attacked by an enemy night fighter. His citation includes:

Allen opened fire but the bomber was struck, causing much damage. A second attack followed and the Lancaster was again hit, resulting in the port engine catching fire. All efforts to extinguish the fire were unavailing, the aircraft lost height and began to lose control, and so the captain ordered the crew to bale out. The rear gunner was unable to open the turret doors and was trapped. With complete disregard for his own safety, Allen promptly went to assist his comrade. The aircraft was now on fire and falling rapidly. Nevertheless he hacked away at the turret doors with an axe and finally succeeded in freeing his comrade. Just as Allen was about to jump the aircraft broke in two. However, he fell clear and pulled his ripcord and descended safely. In the face of extreme danger, this airman displayed conduct in keeping with the best traditions of the Royal Air Force.

As the air war raged on over Germany the Luftwaffe struggled to keep pace with the combined onslaught of the American and Bomber Command raids. Not only were the defenders of the Reich significantly outnumbered, they were also suffering from a severe shortage of fuel. The situation is best summed up in a translation of a German document dated 5 November 1944:

Our numerical inferiority can only be countered by confronting the enemy with temporary and local concentrations of power. It should be added that due to the comparative inexperience of many of our pilots, our losses, not only in actual combat, but also during take-off and landing, are much higher than those of the enemy. A mere increase in aircraft production will not provide a solution to our difficulties at the front. As regards our night fighter force, the position is rather more favourable at present. Substantial reinforcements have been received from disbanded bomber and transport units, and striking power has greatly increased. Our total strength of about 1,800 aircraft enabled about 200 fighters to take to the air during each enemy attack. Night fighter crews have achieved considerable success. However, a plan must be devised for the concentration of our forces in Western Germany. Since the present fuel shortage only permits the employment of night fighters for a few days each month, our forces, of which one Gruppe should be concentrated in the Ruhr and one Gruppe in the Reich/Main area, should carry out operations at full strength on certain days and times based on previous experience. A further solution would be to convert some night fighter units to the Me262. This would enable us to attack and inflict heavy losses on the Mosquito squadrons which are operating in ever-increasing strength over north-west Europe.

Although the document appears to be upbeat as far as the night war was concerned, the pendulum of air power had swung fully in favour of Bomber Command. The reference to the ever-increasing presence of the Mosquito squadrons also shows how the Mozzie had become the scourge of the German defences, with its crews achieving results far in excess of what could have been expected from the relatively small number of aircraft involved; and with few losses. The document also suggests converting some of the Luftwaffe's new Messerschmitt Me 262 jet fighters to the night fighter role to take on the Mosquitos. This, in time, would happen but it would be more a move of desperation rather than one that would change the outcome of the war.

Although the pendulum had swung in favour of Bomber Command, Harris's crews were still not having things all their own way, far from it, and another casualty was 24-year-old Squadron Leader Robert Palmer of 109 Squadron who was posthumously awarded the Victoria Cross.

Palmer was an experienced pilot for his tender age and had already completed more than a hundred ops, many with the Pathfinders, for which he had been awarded the DFC and Bar. For his 111th op, a daylight attack against Cologne's Gremburg marshalling yards on 23 December, he was acting as the Master Bomber for the raid. Flying an Oboe-equipped Lancaster of 582 Squadron, he arrived over the target area to find the weather clear of cloud. It was not at all what had been forecast and he knew the bombers following behind would be fully exposed to the enemy defences. But his task was to provide an accurate and easily visible aiming point for the Main Force to bomb and so his attack would be crucial to the success of the raid.

As he began his run–in towards the target Palmer's aircraft was hit by flak. Undaunted, he still pressed on. Even when two of his engines were fully ablaze Palmer held the aircraft steady for just long enough to reach exactly the right point to release his bombs. The blazing Lancaster was last seen spiralling to earth. Only the rear gunner escaped with his life. It was yet another sad reminder that the air war was far from won.

Chapter Eighteen

To the Bitter End

The air war has now turned into a crazy orgy. We are totally defenceless against it. The Reich will be gradually turned into a complete desert.

The words are taken from the diary of the Reich Minister of Propaganda, Joseph Goebbels, during the final weeks of the war. But the Nachtjagd had entered 1945 still boasting eight night fighter wings, totalling more than a thousand aircraft (mostly Bf 110s and Ju 88s), of which around 70 per cent were serviceable at any one time. However, the continued shortage of fuel would effectively half this figure within three months.

Bomber Command, meanwhile, entered the New Year with ninety-five front-line squadrons, forty-four of which were equipped with Lancasters and thirty with Halifaxes, spread across its seven operational groups. Unlike the Luftwaffe, the RAF had no such shortage of resources. There was also no shortage of courage and just as 1944 had ended with a Bomber Command VC, that to Robert Palmer, the opening day of 1945 ended with another.

This time the recipient was 24-year-old Flight Sergeant George Thompson, a wireless operator serving with 9 Squadron at Bardney. Thompson was taking part in an attack on the notorious Dortmund-Ems Canal when his Lancaster was hit by anti-aircraft fire. Shrapnel from one shell crashed into the fuselage just in front of the mid-upper turret while another caught the nose compartment. A fire soon broke out, fuelled by hydraulic oil, and with much of the nose having been blown away, air was rushing through the fuselage to further fan the flames.

Inside the aircraft it was a scene of utter devastation. Dense smoke filled the fuselage but Thompson could see that the gunner in the blazing mid-upper turret was unconscious. Without hesitation, and despite the exploding ammunition, Thompson made his way down the fuselage into the fire, easing his way round a gaping hole in the floor to reach his colleague. He then pulled the gunner from his turret and edging his way back round the hole in the fuselage floor, carried him away from the flames. Then, with his bare hands, he extinguished the gunner's burning clothing.

Thompson had sustained serious burns to his face, hands and legs but he then noticed the rear turret was also on fire. Despite his own severe injuries, Thompson again set off down the fuselage and for a second time he braved the flames. With great difficulty, he extricated the helpless gunner and carried him clear, again using his bare and badly burnt hands to beat out the flames on his comrade's clothing.

It was only after the crew had made it back across friendly lines to make a crash-landing near a Dutch village that the full extent of the carnage in the rear of the fuselage could be seen. The figure of the charred Thompson was barely recognizable but he was still alive. Sadly, though, he later succumbed to his awful injuries, as did one of the gunners, but the other owed his life to George Thompson who was posthumously awarded the Victoria Cross for his remarkable courage and self-sacrifice.

Although the war was now in its final months, it would still be several weeks before the Allies reached the Rhine. Discipline still had to be maintained when identifying targets and bombing from the air. Flying Officer Bill Spence, a bomb aimer serving with 44 Squadron, now based at Spilsby in Lincolnshire, later described the procedure if for any reason the target could not be identified for the crew to release their bombs:

If we were unable to bomb the target then we had to bring the bombs back to base. If we were unable to drop mines then the brief was to jettison the mines 'safe' in deep water. If we had any bombs or mines 'hung-up' then attempts were made to get rid of them over the sea. This would be done manually if all other attempts failed. I remember we had a mine 'hung-up' over the Kattegat east of Denmark. I was using H2S to drop them with the flight engineer operating the bomb-release. When he examined the bomb bay immediately after the drop had been made he reported that one was still in position. A quick assessment on the H2S, and I told the pilot to maintain his course and to re-open the bomb doors. I instructed the flight engineer to keep pressing and releasing the bomb-release tit and judged that the mine may be

*frozen on and that the repeated surge of current may release it. This is what
happened, and the navigator recorded the release time and distance flown
from the designated drop zone. With this information, base assessed that this
mine had dropped between the mainland and an island, and we later learned
that a ferry carrying German troops between the two had gone down due to
a mine!*

Another young airman, 20-year-old Sergeant Frank Cornett, a flight
engineer serving with 115 Squadron at Witchford in Cambridgeshire, also
recalled the early days of 1945. He and his crew were nearing the end of
their tour of operations when they were found by a night fighter, either out
of ammunition or, for whatever reason, had decided not to attack:

*Returning one night from an op, a Ju 88 formated on our port wing tip and
stayed there for a couple of minutes in a position impossible for our guns
to bear on him. He then flashed his navigation and cockpit lights before
scarpering; we never saw him again and assumed that he was out of ammo.
This event, for me, demonstrated a somewhat less than hostile attitude by the
night fighter pilot.*

It had been a let-off for Cornett and his colleagues. The air war was far from
won and there was still time for the Luftwaffe to play another trump card
with the introduction of its new jet fighter, the Me 262, into the night arena.

As the world's first operational jet-powered fighter aircraft, the 262 was
awesome in terms of its performance. But, in truth, it had entered the war
at too late a stage to influence its outcome. Nonetheless, armed with four 30
mm cannons and with its two turbojets giving the aircraft a top speed of 900
km/h (560 mph) and a rate of climb of 1,200 metres per minute (4,000 feet
per minute) up to its operational ceiling of 11,500 metres (35,000 feet), it
was a potent weapon of war.

Initially, there were no radar-equipped 262s and so the Nachtjagd flew
the standard day fighter variant, the Me 262A, at night. Tactics relied on a
mix of close control from the ground and searchlights in the target area to
illuminate the RAF bombers, the old but proven *Wilde Sau* tactics. However,
the conversion of some 262s to a tandem-seat trainer had opened the door

for this high-performance jet to be developed as a night fighter. The second seat (intended for the student pilot) was used for a radar operator, albeit at the expense of a fuel tank, with its range extended by fitting two 300 litre (66 gallons) external tanks under the forward fuselage.

The result was the impressive Me 262B-1a/U1 night fighter, fitted with the FuG 218 *Neptun* radar and *Naxos* radar-homing device. However, only a few of these latest and specialist night fighting variants were in operational service by the final weeks of the war. Although the antlers reduced the 262's top speed slightly, it was still faster than the Mosquito. There were plans to fit the 262 with *Schräge Musik*, as well as to develop a B-2 variant with an improved radar dish in the nose to replace the antlers and to increase its fuel capacity by stretching the fuselage, but it was a case of too little, too late.

The only jet night fighter unit to be formed was 10./NJG 11 based at Burg-Magdeburg under the command of Kurt Welter, tasked with intercepting the RAF Mosquitos operating over and around Berlin. Welter's unit was eventually credited with shooting down more than forty Mosquitos, although this figure is unconfirmed. Nonetheless, it is believed that most of the dozen or more Mosquitos lost in the Berlin area during the opening weeks of 1945 fell victim to the Luftwaffe's new jet night fighters, although it seems that most of the successful night interceptions were a result of the trusted *Wilde Sau* tactics rather than radar.

With no immediate end to the war in sight, Bomber Command began a new phase of large-scale raids. Berlin had again been considered but after the meeting of Allied heads at Yalta in early February, it was to Chemnitz, Dresden and Leipzig that Harris would next send his bombers as part of Operation *Thunderclap*.

These three large cities in Saxony were just behind the German lines on the Eastern Front, and *Thunderclap* should have begun on 13 February with an American daylight raid on Dresden. But bad weather meant the raid had to be cancelled and so *Thunderclap* eventually got underway that night when Bomber Command sent more than 800 aircraft to Dresden.

In two separate raids more than 2,500 tons of explosives and incendiaries were dropped on the city. The first, carried out by No. 5 Group, saw nearly 250 Lancasters drop 800 tons of bombs, but layers of cloud meant the raid was only moderately successful. The second raid, however, carried out three hours later by more than 500 bombers (a combined force from Nos 1, 3, 6 and 8 Groups), and supported by a bedlam of electronic noise generated by RCM aircraft, was far more successful. The cloud had cleared and conditions were perfect. More than 1,800 tons of bombs were dropped with devastating accuracy.

The Main Force had carried out their attacks with little interference from enemy night fighters. Less than thirty had managed to intercept the two raids that night. One frustrated Ju 88 pilot was Feldwebel Hermann Kinder of NJG 100. Operating from Radeberg airfield, 12 miles to the north-east of Dresden, he was twice scrambled during the night but without any communications with divisional headquarters there was little he or the others could do. An excerpt from Kinder's diary for that day is included in Alfred Price's book *The Last Year of the Luftwaffe*:

> *My saddest day as a night fighter…Result: major attack on Dresden, in which the city was smashed to smithereens – and we were standing by and looking on. How can such a thing be possible? One's mind turns more and more to sabotage, or at least a certain irresponsible defeatism among the 'gentlemen' up there. Feeling that things are approaching an end with giant strides. What then? Poor Germany!*

Although successful in its overall aim, Dresden became one of the most controversial and, perhaps, one of the lowest points of Bomber Command's strategic bombing offensive of the Second World War. While it has always been made clear that Dresden was bombed for military purposes and not to cause excessive civilian casualties, as has been suggested in the post-war era, the resulting firestorm across the city caused an excessively high number of casualties on the ground. It will never be known for certain just how many lives were lost in Dresden that night but post-war analyses suggest the figure could be in excess of 50,000. The discussions and arguments about the military relevance of bombing Dresden, when the war was nearly won, will no doubt continue.

Thunderclap continued the following night with a raid on Chemnitz by 500 Lancasters and more than 200 Halifaxes. Again, the raid was carried out in two parts, again three hours apart, but cloud over the target area meant that most of the bombing missed the target. Leipzig had escaped this round of attacks but Chemnitz was bombed again just three weeks later with several important industrial installations destroyed.

In between these raids Bomber Command's last Victoria Cross of the war was awarded to Captain Edwin Swales, a South African serving with 582 Squadron, for his gallantry during a raid against a vital rail junction at Pforzheim on the night of 23/24 February.

Swales was an experienced Pathfinder pilot with a DFC and was acting as the Master Bomber for the raid that night. After successfully locating the target he was providing aiming instructions to the rest of his force when his Lancaster was twice attacked by a Bf 110 night fighter. During the first attack one of his engines was hit, causing it to fail and put the rear turret out of action, and the fuel tanks holed, while the second attack took out a second engine making his crippled bomber vulnerable to further attack. Unperturbed, Swales carried on with his task. Despite being almost defenceless he stayed over the target to continue his clear and precise aiming instructions to the Main Force until he was satisfied that the attack had achieved its aim.

Swales was now in an almost impossible situation. His aircraft was badly damaged and he could barely keep it in the air. Determined not to let it, or his crew, fall into enemy hands, he set course for home. For more than an hour he nursed the Lancaster back towards home, but having then encountered heavy cloud and turbulent conditions, the aircraft was becoming increasingly difficult to control and was steadily losing height. But it was only when the aircraft was safely back over friendly lines, and the situation had become critical, that Swales ordered his crew to bale out. Time was short and it took all of his skill to hold the aircraft steady long enough for the rest of his crew to escape. The last member of his crew had only just left the aircraft when the Lancaster plunged to earth, still with the gallant Swales on board. The citation for his Victoria Cross concludes:

Intrepid in the attack, courageous in the face of danger, he did his duty to the last, giving his life that his comrades might live.

The Allied attacks against Germany were relentless as many of Bomber Command's sorties were now being flown by day as well as by night. But still the defenders refused to throw in the towel. However, with rapidly dwindling fuel supplies the Luftwaffe was in a desperate situation. On 1 March 1945, Goebbels wrote in his diary:

The air war has now turned into a crazy orgy. We are totally defenceless against it. The Reich will be gradually turned into a complete desert.

It was, indeed, a desperate situation for those defending the Reich. The Allies had long held the upper hand and now enjoyed air supremacy on all fronts. In desperation, more than anything else, some of the Luftwaffe's senior commanders supported a return to intruder missions over England to hamper the nightly attacks over Germany. Although others opposed the idea, those in favour of a major intruder effort won and Göring sanctioned the operation.

The argument had been swayed by the reality that these were desperate times and everything that could be done to stop Bomber Command's night offensive over Germany needed to be done. Given the codename *Unternehmen Gisela* (Operation *Gisela*), it would take Bomber Command and the British defences by surprise. The plan was for a large force of up to 600 night fighters, all those that could be made available, to be sent on one simultaneous operation over eastern England. Approaching the Humber Estuary in two waves, and low enough to avoid detection by British radar, the night fighters were to then climb to medium altitude, somewhere around 15,000 feet, to engage the RAF bombers in the vicinity of their own airfields, mostly in Lincolnshire and Yorkshire.

Because of the distance and loiter time required, the Ju 88G, an aerodynamically improved variant of the 88-series, was the only night fighter capable of carrying out the task. These were amongst the Nachtjagd's most up-to-date night fighters with some of the latest G-6 sub-variants in the process of being fitted with the experimental FuG 240 *Berlin* cavity magnetron based radar. With the radar dish in a bulbous solid nose it negated the need for the large multiple dipole-based antenna arrays used on earlier AI radar designs, and so increased the aircraft's performance. But like so many of these latest German technological advances, it had arrived too late in the war and only then in small numbers.

With the night fighter crews briefed it was then a matter of waiting for the right opportunity to mount *Gisela*. The raid was then delayed by the possibility that the plan had been compromised following the capture of a Luftwaffe crew.

Finally, on the night of 3/4 March 1945, *Gisela* took place. It was a night when Bomber Command split its forces to attack two main targets, an aqueduct at Ladbergen on the Dortmund-Ems canal and the synthetic oil refinery at Kamen. In terms of the number of aircraft involved, Bomber Command's effort that night was moderate; 200 Halifaxes of No. 4 Group went to the oil refinery, with a small force of Pathfinders to provide the marking, while No. 5 Group sent over 200 Lancasters and Mosquitos to the canal. Further support, including sixty RCM sorties and diversionary operations, were carried out by nearly a hundred aircraft from other groups.

As things were to turn out, No. 4 Group's attack against the oil refinery went well and with no Halifaxes lost over Germany. Elsewhere, the jamming operations, although effective, had attracted enemy night fighters to the No. 5 Group attack on the canal. Eight Lancasters were claimed by four night fighter pilots in a matter of minutes: Heinz-Wolfgang Schnaufer claimed two; Martin Drewes one; Georg Hermann Greiner claimed three; and Josef Kraft two. Schnaufer would claim three more Lancasters the following week, all during a raid on Dessau, to end the war with a quite staggering total of 121 aircraft, all at night, making Heinz-Wolfgang Schnaufer the highest-scoring night fighter pilot in the history of air warfare. As for the other successful pilots that night over the Dortmund-Ems canal, Georg Hermann Greiner would add the Oak Leaves to his Knight's Cross for shooting down fifty aircraft, more than half of which had come in the final year of the war. Martin Drewes would end the war having shot down forty-three aircraft at night (fifty-two overall), while 24-year-old Josef Kraft would end the war with fifty-six; they would both also receive the Oak Leaves to their Knight's Cross.

The Lancaster crews had been unfortunate to have come across some of the Nachtjagd's best night fighter pilots over the canal and the night of 3/4 March 1945 had been as hard-fought as any during the latter weeks of the Second World War. From Bomber Command records it shows that seven aircraft were lost during the attack on the canal rather than the eight claimed, although it was still a costly night and provided an unwelcome reminder that there was yet more fighting, and death, to come during the final days of the war. Even the aircraft taking part in the diversionary raids did not get away without loss. Lancasters laying mines in the Kattegat and Oslo Fjord had been found by Ju 88s of I./NJG 3. One was flown by the Kommandeur, 25-year-old Major Werner Husemann, another veteran of the night war over Germany and holder of the Knight's Cross. The one Lancaster to be lost while laying mines, an aircraft belonging to No. 1 Group, fell to his guns; it was Husemann's thirty-third victim of the war.

As for the *Gisela* part of that night, the first Ju 88s took off around 11 p.m. but it was not quite the mass force that had originally been hoped. Even so, some 200 night fighters from NJGs 2, 3, 4 and 5 headed towards the Dutch coast from where they would cross the North Sea. To maximize surprise they had been briefed to avoid making contact with the returning bombers until they were over English soil.

As they headed out over the sea the Ju 88 crews came across awful weather, with heavy rain and squally winds, but the frontal system meant the RAF bombers were forced to return home above the cloud, leaving the German night fighters free to fly below.

It was soon after midnight when the leading bombers returned over the English coast and the first engagement took place. One of the Ju 88s intercepted a B-17 Flying Fortress III of 214 Squadron returning from dropping *Window* as part of the supporting operations that night. Although the B-17 crew escaped with their lives and managed to land back at their base at Oulton in Norfolk, this event marks the opening engagement of *Gisela*. However, another B-17 crew were not so lucky. They were shot down over Oulton, one of two successes that night for Leutnant Arnold Döring of 10./NJG 3.

Word of an enemy intruder over eastern England quickly spread far and wide, and with several radar contacts being reported RAF Mosquitos were scrambled to intercept the raiders. But with the Germans using their own form of *Window* (called *Düppel*) to confuse the Mosquitos' radar, the intruders were free to roam at will. Returning bomber crews were instructed to look out for the enemy intruders and told to divert to other airfields in the south or west of the country that were considered far enough away to be out of danger.

For one Mosquito crew of 169 Squadron returning from the Kamen raid to their airfield at Great Massingham, the warning came a little late. They were shot down while trying to get away from the chaos on the east coast. The Mosquito came down at Buxton in Norfolk with Squadron Leader Victor Fenwick and his observer, Flying Officer John Pierce, both killed.

The warning had also come too late for several bomber crews, as for the next two hours the intruders caused havoc over eastern England. Night fighters of NJG 2 and NJG 4 were able to account for eight Halifaxes returning to Yorkshire while two Lancasters came down near Lincoln; both probably falling to Oberleutnant Walter Briegleb of 7./NJG 2. Another to claim a brace was Hauptmann Gerhard Raht, the Kommandeur of I./NJG 3, who shot down his fifty-second and fifty-third victims of the war in a twenty-minute spell soon after 1 a.m.

A further five aircraft from the HCUs – three Lancasters and two Halifaxes – were shot down within the space of just ten minutes but, even then, it was not all over. It was not until after 2 a.m. that the last bomber was shot down; a Halifax III of 346 Squadron, based at Elvington, which came down at Hurworth in Yorkshire. And it would be another thirty minutes before the last intruders had been chased back out to sea.

In all, twenty RAF bombers were shot down over English soil and another dozen or more badly damaged. More than eighty men were dead and many more injured. Several targets of opportunity, such as airfields and railway yards, had also been attacked. Three of the night fighters were lost having hit the ground while flying too low in the dark. One Ju 88 of NJG 5 crashed while taking evasive action during an attack and another from the same unit hit power lines while attacking a Royal Observer Corps vehicle. The driver, 38-year-old Jack Kelway, was killed, as was the German crew. The third German night fighter to come down, that flown by Hauptmann Johann Dreher of 12./NJG 3, hit some trees while attacking a Halifax coming in to land at Elvington in Yorkshire. It was the last Luftwaffe aircraft of the war to come down on English soil; all the crew were killed.

In addition to the three Ju 88s lost over England, six more crews had been forced to bale out on their way home having run out of fuel and eight more crews were missing. From the Luftwaffe's official point of view *Gisela* was a success but the operation would never be repeated again. Despite the achievements of the night fighter crews that had taken part that night, the harsh reality was that *Gisela* had failed to achieve the results that had been hoped and proved to be the Nachtjagd's last major operation of the war.

Despite having been caught unaware by *Gisela*, Bomber Command resumed *Thunderclap* on the night of 5/6 March when 760 aircraft returned to Chemnitz with extensive damage caused to the city, although another twenty-two RAF bombers were lost. The following week, in the space of just twenty-four hours, Bomber Command twice established new records for the number of bombers sent to a target. First, on 11 March, 1,079 aircraft went to Essen and then the following day 1,108 aircraft (748 Lancasters, 292 Halifaxes and 68 Mosquitos) attacked Dortmund. This record would stand for the rest of the war.

These two latest maximum efforts had seen a further 9,500 tons of bombs dropped on German soil. The strategic bombing campaign had now taken its full effect. Goebbels' diary for 12 March 1945 reads:

The morale of the German people, both at home and at the front, is sinking even lower. The air terror which rages uninterruptedly over German home territory makes people thoroughly despondent.

The campaign against oil production had been particularly effective, as detailed in Goebbels' diary entry the following day:

When I call to mind that the amount of petrol available to the Luftwaffe has fallen from 193,000 tons to 8,000 tons, then I realize what can be expected of the Luftwaffe and what cannot. What use is the mass output of new fighters when we have not even the petrol or the crews to put them into action?

March 1945 saw the highest tonnage of bombs dropped in any single month of the war. The Allies soon crossed the Rhine and advanced towards Berlin, but the air war being fought at night over Germany remained as fierce and relentless as ever. Hauptmann Martin Becker, known for his multiple kills and now Kommandeur of IV./NJG 6, set a record on the night of 14/15

March. Flying his Ju 88G he was credited with shooting down nine RAF bombers in one night; eight Lancasters taking part in a raid against a synthetic oil refinery at Lützkendorf, plus a Halifax. Along with his *Bordfunker* that night, 23-year-old Leutnant Karl-Ludwig Johannsen, who was credited with shooting down three of the bombers, this remarkable achievement earned the crew a mention in the *Wehrmachtbericht* on 16 March 1945:

> *Hauptmann Becker, commander in a night fighter wing, and his radio operator, Leutnant Johannsen, brought down to a crash 9 four-engine bombers on the night of 14 to 15 March. When Becker, after the 6th kill could not continue to shoot due to a gun jam, his radio operator, Leutnant Johannsen, destroyed 3 more Anglo-American bombers.*

This feat earned Becker the Oak Leaves and Johannsen the Knight's Cross, and surpassed the eight shot down in one night recorded by Hauptmann Johannes Hager of II./NJG 1 just a few weeks earlier. Two nights later Becker scored his final success of the war to take his total to fifty-eight, all at night, placing him in the top ten of the Luftwaffe's highest-scoring night fighter pilots.

For the Nachtjagdflieger to achieve any success in these final night encounters of the war meant them having to avoid the RAF's marauding Mosquitos. So menacing had they become around their own airfields that one example of improvisation was that of 'Wim' Johnen, now a Hauptmann and the high-scoring Kommandeur of III./NJG 6 who was returning to his base at Leipheim after intercepting a raid. Johnen had just scored his thirty-fourth success of the war, a Lancaster over Würzburg, and was recovering to base desperately short of fuel while being hassled by a Mosquito. With RAF intruders known to be in the area his airfield was subject to a blackout. But Johnen needed to land before his Bf 110's engines packed up altogether, and so he asked the airfield's controller to illuminate two dim lamps, which provided him with just enough of a reference to expertly touch down in the dark.

Others, though, were not so fortunate and at least three of the Nachtjagd's most experienced and highest-scoring night fighter pilots are known to have fallen to Mosquitos in the final weeks of the war. The first was

23-year-old Oberleutnant Hans-Heinz Augenstein (forty-six victories), the Staffelkapitän of 12./NJG 1, whose Bf 110G-4 was shot down to the west of Münster by the RAF ace Flight Lieutenant Edward Hedgecoe DFC of 85 Squadron. Hauptmann Heinz-Strüning (fifty-six), the Kapitän of 9./NJG 1, was flying one of three Bf 110G-4s to fall in one night to another RAF ace, Squadron Leader 'Dolly' Doleman DSO DFC of 157 Squadron. The third ace to fall to a Mosquito was Oberstleutnant Walter Borchers (sixty-three), the Kommodore of NJG 5. His Ju 88G-6 was shot down near Chemnitz by Wing Commander Walter Gibb DSO DFC of 239 Squadron.

The RAF's Mosquito crews were doing all that had been asked of them over Germany and were a constant thorn in the side for the Nachtjagd. So worried had the German night fighter crews become by the roaming Mozzies that they learned to hug the ground after take-off until well clear of their base before climbing away to look for the bombers. Then, when recovering to their airfield at the end of the sortie, they would adopt a similar approach at low level from some distance away. It was extremely hazardous but the risk of hitting the ground, or some other obstacle for that matter, was considered worth taking rather than to fall to the guns of a Mosquito. But one of those who did not get away with it was Oberleutnant Alfons Köster, the Kommandeur of IV./NJG 3, who was killed when he hit a farm building near Varel in northern Germany while recovering to base.

These final days of the war were desperate times for the defenders of the Reich and death continued to come in all sorts of ways. Major Gerhard Friedrich and his crew, for example, were killed on the night of 16/17 March when their Ju 88G-6 caught the full blast of a Lancaster bomb load over Stuttgart. Friedrich had recently been given command of I./NJG 6 and only the day before had been awarded the Knight's Cross after claiming his thirtieth victim. The seven men aboard the Lancaster were also killed.

Friedrich's death that night coincided with the Nachtjagd's last notable success of the war when twenty-four Lancasters, all from No. 1 Group, failed to return from a raid against Nuremburg. It was Bomber Command's last main effort against this notoriously difficult city, and the losses represent more than 10 per cent of the group's effort that night. Most fell to the German night fighters while making their way to the target.

But roaming RAF night fighters, sent out to provide cover for the raiding force, had been hard at it too. One Mosquito XXX of 239 Squadron was flown by the experienced RAF night fighter pilot, Squadron Leader Dennis Hughes DFC. His radar operator, Flight Lieutenant Richard Perks, picked up a contact at 5 miles. Their target was crossing ahead of them and just above. For a while the Mosquito chased down the target. Then, when they were to the north of Nuremberg, it started to descend.

The Mosquito had followed the radar contact down and when they were just 1,000 feet above the ground Hughes and Perks could make out the shape of a Ju 88. Their combat report takes up the story of what happened next:

Closing slowly, fire was opened at 200 yards and strikes were seen all over the enemy aircraft. A second burst set the root of the starboard wing and engine on fire. Enemy aircraft turned to port and slowly lost height in wide orbits. These developed into a vertical dive with explosion in mid-air shortly before hitting the ground in three pieces.

It was Hughes' fourth success and his victim that night was the Ju 88G-6 of Major Werner Hoffmann. Hoffmann had already accounted for three RAF bombers earlier that night, two Lancasters and a Halifax, but they were to be his last successes of the war. After intercepting the raid he had been making his way back to base at low altitude when the Mosquito had jumped him by surprise, and for the second time Hoffmann owed his life to his parachute.

On the ground, the major cities of the Ruhr were falling into Allied hands and, one by one, the Nachtjagd's airfields were overrun. Bomber Command was now flying its final operations of the war. The last major raid against Hamburg was flown on the night of 8/9 April, after which it dispatched 500 Lancasters and a dozen Mosquitos to Potsdam, a suburb to the south-west of Berlin, on the night of the 14th/15th in support of the Russian advance. It was the first heavy attack against Berlin for more than a year and proved to be Bomber Command's last major raid against a German city of the war. But it was not the last of all the major raids. That was a daylight raid against the Berghof (Hitler's 'Eagle's Nest') and the *SS* barracks at Berchtesgaden in the Bavarian Alps on 25 April 1945.

With the war in Europe all but over, it was feared that the Germans were assembling ships to evacuate troops to Norway to continue the war from there, and so on the night of 2/3 May 1945 fifty-three Mosquitos carried out an attack against the dockyards at Kiel. One Mosquito was lost, with its crew killed, as were two Halifaxes of 199 Squadron supporting the raid. It is possible they collided as both aircraft crashed just to the south of Kiel; only three of the sixteen men on board the two aircraft survived. They were the last Bomber Command aircraft to be lost during the war.

And so the night war over Germany had finally ended. It had been fought with great courage and distinction on both sides. In all of its operations Bomber Command had flown nearly 300,000 sorties at night and more than 65,000 by day, for the loss of more than 8,000 aircraft. Its night offensive against Germany had been a constant drain on the enemy's resources. It has since been estimated that one million men were committed for home defence plus countless more valuable assets, such as aircraft and guns. All were required for the defence of the Reich and so could not be used elsewhere. But for 55,573 aircrew of Bomber Command there would be no home coming and for their families the grief would never go away.

Bibliography

Aders, Gebhard, *History of the German Night Fighter Force 1917–45* (Jane's, London, 1979).

Ballantyne, Kenneth, *Another Dawn Another Dusk* (Laundry Cottage Books, Wellington, 2009).

Bekker, Cajus, *The Luftwaffe War Diaries* (Macdonald, London, 1967).

Bennett, Air Vice-Marshal D C T, *Pathfinder* (Frederick Muller Ltd, London, 1958).

Bishop, Patrick, *Bomber Boys: Fighting Back 1940–45* (Harper Press, London, 2007).

Boiten, Theo, *Nachtjagd: The Night Fighters versus Bomber War over the Third Reich, 1939–45* (The Crowood Press Ltd, Marlborough, 1997).

Boiten, Theo & Bowman, Martin, *Battles With the Luftwaffe* (Harper Collins, London, 2001).

Bowyer, Chaz, *For Valour: The Air V.C.s* (William Kimber & Co Ltd, London, 1978).

Charlwood, Don, *No Moon Tonight* (first published by Angus & Robertson, Australia, 1956).

Clarke, R Wallace, *British Aircraft Armament Vol 1* (Patrick Stephens Ltd, Yeovil, 1993).

Currie, Jack DFC, *The Augsburg Raid* (Goodall Publications, London, 1984).

Delve, Ken and Jacobs, Peter, *The Six-Year Offensive* (Arms and Armour Press, London, 1992).

Falconer, Jonathan, *The Dam Busters: Breaking the Great Dams of Western Germany 16–17 May 1943* (Sutton Publishing Ltd, Stroud, 2003).

Forsyth, Robert, *Jagdwaffe: Defending the Reich 1944/45* (Ian Allan, Hersham, 2006).

Franks, Norman, *Claims to Fame: The Lancaster* (Arms and Armour Press, London, 1994).

Halley, James J, *The Squadrons of the Royal Air Force and Commonwealth 1918–1988* (Air-Britain (Historians). Ltd, Tonbridge, 1988).

Jacobs, Peter, *Aces of the Luftwaffe; The Jagdflieger in the Second World War* (Frontline Books, Barnsley, 2014).

— *Bomb Aimer Over Berlin: The Wartime Memoires of Les Bartlett DFM* (Pen & Sword Books Ltd, Barnsley, 2007).

— *The Lancaster Story* (Arms and Armour Press, London, 1996).
Maynard, John, *Bennett and the Pathfinders* (Arms and Armour Press, London, 1996).
McKinstry, Leo, *Lancaster: The Second Word War's Greatest Bomber* (John Murray, London, 2009).
Middlebrook, Martin, *The Battle of Hamburg: The Firestorm Raid* (Cassell & Co, London, 1980).
— *The Berlin Raids* (Viking, the Penguin Group, London, 1988).
Middlebrook, Martin, and Everitt, Chris, *The Bomber Command War Diaries: An Operational Reference Book 1939–1945* (Penguin Books, London, 1990).
Mitcham, Samuel W, *Eagles of the Third Reich* (Stackpole Books PA, 1988).
Murray, Williamson, *Strategy for Defeat, the Luftwaffe 1939–45* (Eagle Editions Ltd, Royston, 2000).
Musgrove, Gordon, *Pathfinder Force: A History of 8 Group* (first published by Macdonald & Jane's, London, 1976).
Parry, Simon W, *Intruders over Britain: Luftwaffe Night Fighter Offensive 1940–45* (Air Research Publications, London, 1992).
Price, Alfred, *Battle Over the Reich* (Ian Allan, London, 1973).
— *The Last Year of the Luftwaffe: May 1944 to May 1945* (Arms and Armour Press, London, 1991).
Rolfe, Mel, *Looking into Hell: Experiences of the Bomber Command War* (Arms and Armour Press, London, 1995).
Searby, John, *The Bomber Battle for Berlin* (Guild Publishing, London, 1991).
Shores, Christopher and Williams, Clive, *Aces High* (Grub Street, London, 1994).
Spick, Mike, *Luftwaffe Fighter Aces* (Greenhill Books, London, 1996).
Sweetman, John, *Bomber Crew: Taking on the Reich* (Abacus, London, 2004).
— *The Dambusters Raid* (Arms and Armour Press, London, 1990).
Tavender, I T, *The Distinguished Flying Medal: A Record of Courage 1918–1982* (Hayward, Polstead, 1990).
Weal, John, *Jagdgeschwader 2 'Richthofen'* (Osprey Publishing Ltd, Oxford, 2000).
Williams, David P, *Night Fighters, Hunters of the Reich* (Spellmount, Stroud, 2011).
Williamson, Gordon, *Knights of the Iron Cross* (Blandford Press, Poole, 1987).
Zaloga, Steven J, *Defense of the Reich 1941–45* (Osprey Publishing Ltd, Oxford, 2012).

Index

206 Night Duel Over Germany